Dandelion

Phonics Instructional Manual

Grade 1

PhonicBooks®

DK Learning

DK | Penguin Random House

Produced for DK by Westchester Education Services

Publisher Sarah Forbes
Managing Editor Katherine Neep
Managing Art Editor Sarah Corcoran
Senior Editor Amelia Jones
Production Controller Isabell Schart
Production Editor Shanker Prasad

First American Edition, 2024
Published in the United States by DK Publishing,
a division of Penguin Random House LLC
1745 Broadway, 20th Floor, New York, NY 10019

24 25 26 27 28 10 9 8 7 6 5 4 3 2 1
001-344992-Oct/2024

Published in Great Britain by
Phonic Books, an imprint of Dorling Kindersley Limited

A catalog record for this book
is available from the Library of Congress.
ISBN 978-0-5938-4853-1

Printed and bound in China

www.dk.com

MIX
Paper | Supporting responsible forestry
FSC www.fsc.org FSC™ C018179

This book was made with Forest Stewardship Council™ certified paper – one small step in DK's commitment to a sustainable future.
Learn more at **www.dk.com/uk/information/sustainability**

CONTENTS

INTRODUCTION

WHAT IS PHONIC BOOKS?

Phonic Books specializes in publishing systematic synthetic phonic books for beginner and catch-up readers.

The company was founded in 2006 by Wendy Tweedie, Tami Reis-Frankfort, and Clair Wilson, three special needs teachers passionate about teaching all children to read. Using their expertise, they set about developing phonic reading books for young children and older readers.

Following demand from customers, the range has extended from the initial 10 titles to over 300 today, and is continuing to grow. Our US range of books caters for students in Pre-K and Kindergarten to older readers in Middle School.

With a growing reputation for quality and effectiveness, our books are now used by schools, tutors, and parents in the US and 40 countries around the world.

HOW TO USE THIS MANUAL ?

The Phonics Instructional Manual Grade 1 is organized into three main parts. The first part introduces foundational concepts and prevalent teaching strategies in phonics instruction.

In the second part, the focus shifts to the practical elements of the Phonic Books program for Grade 1. It provides an overview of the program, complementary teaching methods, a scheme of work, guidelines for lesson planning, and strategies for assessment, providing teachers with the necessary tools for effective teaching.

The third part is the heart of the manual: the lesson plans for the Phonic Books program for Grade 1. The initial set of lesson plans align with the Dandelion Launchers series, a set of stories (readers) designed for beginners which is organized into 20 progressive stages. These lesson plans require the use of both the Dandelion Launchers readers and the corresponding activity books. The readers act as the instructional text, introducing new letters and sounds, while the activity books provide supplementary exercises in reading, writing, spelling, and comprehension. Teachers are guided to specific pages and exercises in these resources.

Each stage in the Dandelion Launchers series is designed to build a gradual understanding of phonics, introducing new letters and sounds while reinforcing previously learned phonics and high-frequency words. It begins with sounds of the alphabet in Stages 1–7, progressing to consonant blends and digraphs in Stages 8–15, then on to two-syllable words and more complex spelling patterns, tch, ve, le, and the suffixes -ed and -ing, in Stages 16–20.

The second and third sets of lesson plans extend to more advanced spelling patterns. These encompass vowel teams in the Dandelion Readers Level 1 series and VCe or silent 'e' spellings in the Dandelion Readers VCe Spellings set.

The lesson plans are adaptable and can be taught in any order. For example: in Phonic Books, the VCe spelling is introduced after students are comfortable with vowel digraphs that are not split, although some curricula introduce them earlier.

Teachers can integrate these lesson plans with different US phonics curricula. Curriculum mapping grids are available on the Phonic Books website to align these lesson plans with their specific curriculum requirements.

ADVICE FOR TEACHERS

Decodable books, such as the Phonic Books series, are important for teaching foundational skills. These controlled texts allow the student to practice their phonetic knowledge and read successfully at each developmental stage. They also encourage students to use the most effective and reliable reading strategies for life (sounding out words).

Many teachers find they need additional resources to support students who are beginner and older readers. For example: students may face challenges with letter sounds, phonemic awareness, retaining phonics lessons, or have gaps in their vocabulary. The Phonic Books series, encompassing both decodable readers and activity books, can be used as a classroom resource in various ways: with a whole class, in reading groups, or in 1:1 reading support.

The Phonic Books website also contains many free teaching resources as well as advice for teachers. The resources include phonics infographics, teaching strategies, word lists, word chains, dictation exercises, phonic code tables, high-frequency word charts, game templates, and progress trackers. The website also includes assessment tools such as reading assessments and assessment cards, alongside advice on how to use the Phonic Books series in different educational settings.

SUPPLEMENTARY RESOURCES

This instructional manual primarily focuses on the Dandelion Launchers series of decodable books and the corresponding activity books. However, Phonic Books has a wealth of parallel books and supplementary materials to help teachers with their phonics instruction. More details are provided in the program overview section on page 19.

FOUNDATIONS OF PHONICS

WHAT IS PHONICS?

Phonics is a method of teaching reading and writing that focuses on the relationship between sounds (**phonemes**) and their spellings (**graphemes**). It involves teaching students to connect sounds in words with letters or groups of letters and to blend these sounds to form recognizable words.

English has a complex writing system. It has 26 letters but roughly 44 sounds (this depends on pronunciation), leading to roughly 160+ different spellings for these 44 sounds. In order to teach them in a methodical way, they have been organized according to the 44 sounds they spell. This organization is called the **Alphabetic Code** or **Phonic Code**. Research has shown that students who are taught these sound–letter correspondences will learn to decode words more successfully. Decoding underpins fluency, and fluency underpins reading comprehension.

Unlike languages with "transparent" writing systems like Italian and Spanish, where letters spell sounds in a simple and consistent way, English has an "opaque" writing system. Its complexity is a result of layers of adopted words from different languages and shifts in pronunciation over many years. Consequently, learning to read in English is more time-consuming, often taking years compared to the few months it might take in more phonetically consistent languages.

Where to start in phonics instruction

All phonics programs start with the sounds of the letters of the alphabet. The Phonic Books program starts with the simple principle of one letter corresponding to one sound. Students initially learn a few letters at a time, building simple words as they progress.

THE ALPHABETIC CODE abc

The **Alphabetic Code** is the framework that shows how the 44 sounds of English are represented by letters and letter combinations.

Key aspects include:

1. 26 letters are used and reused in many different combinations to represent the 44 sounds of speech.
2. A sound can be represented by 1–4 letters.
3. A sound can be spelled in numerous ways.
4. A spelling (or grapheme) can represent different sounds.

Students need to recognize these letter–sound relationships automatically to become fluent readers. Due to the complexity of the code, many phonics programs will first introduce a simple part of it and later the more complex letter–sound correspondences.

CHALLENGES IN THE ALPHABETIC CODE

Navigating the complexities of the Alphabetic Code can be a daunting task, especially for students learning English. The Alphabetic Code is marked by a notable disparity between the sounds (phonemes) and the letters (graphemes) used to represent them. This mismatch leads to various challenges.

English uses the same letters to represent different sounds because of the mismatch between the number of letters and sounds. Because of this disparity, letters are reused to spell the extra sounds. For example, the letters 's' and 'h' together spell a completely new sound: /sh/ as in the word "**sh**ip." This is a **consonant digraph**. That wouldn't be such a problem if our Alphabetic Code were simple and straightforward—but it isn't!

Sounds spelled by 1–4 letters

Sounds in English can be spelled by 1–4 letters. In the word "cat," each letter spells one sound. In the word "chip," the consonant digraph 'ch' spells the sound /ch/. Here two letters spell one sound. In the word "night," the vowel team 'igh' spells one sound /ie/. Finally, in the word "dough," the four-letter spelling 'ough' spells just one sound, /oe/.

Multiple spellings for one sound

A further complication is that a sound can be spelled in different ways. For example, the sound /ae/ can be spelled in numerous ways: r**ai**n, m**ay**, c**a**m**e**, th**ey**, w**eigh**, v**ei**l, gr**ea**t, etc. Students need to learn these alternatives so that when they see them within words, they know how to sound them out. And when they learn to encode (spell), students will need to remember which alternative fits in which word. Multiple spellings for one sound are not covered in this manual.

One spelling, multiple sounds

Not only are there different ways to spell these sounds, but once learned, students find that some spellings can be pronounced in different ways. For example, the spelling 'ea' spells the sound /e/ in "h**ea**d," /ee/ in "m**ea**t," and /ae/ in "gr**ea**t."

These are difficult concepts to teach, and students need a structured system to learn them. This is why it is so important that reading instruction is taught in a systematic and structured way. When taught well, the Alphabetic Code is unlocked and students learn to decode and encode any word.

UNLOCKING THE ALPHABETIC CODE

Demonstrating the mechanics

We begin by illustrating the basic mechanics of the English language: reading from left to right, and understanding how individual letters and their combinations represent distinct sounds in speech.

Teaching the code

We then teach the Alphabetic Code, focusing on specific letter–sound correspondences in the English language.

Neglecting to teach the Alphabetic Code risks depriving students of the key to learning to read and the vast opportunities for learning and exploration it offers.

THE ALPHABETIC CODE

Consonant sound spellings

/j/	
j	**j**et
g	**g**entle
ge	bar**ge**
dge	ju**dge**

/n/	
n	**n**o
nn	pla**nn**ing
kn	**kn**ow
gn	**gn**at
pn	**pn**eumonia

/z/	
z	**z**ip
zz	bu**zz**
s	i**s**
se	choo**se**
ze	snoo**ze**
x	**x**ylophone

/r/	
r	**r**at
wr	**wr**ite
rr	ca**rr**y
rh	**rh**ino

/h/	
h	**h**ot
wh	**wh**ole

/qu/ (/k/ + /w/)	
qu	**qu**een

/t/	
t	**t**in
tt	ge**tt**ing
ed	jump**ed**
bt	de**bt**
pt	**pt**erodactyl
te	grani**te**

/x/ (/k/ + /s/)	
x	fo**x**
cc	a**cc**ept

/y/	
y	**y**es

/ng/	
ng	si**ng**
n	pi**n**k

/s/	
s	**s**ip
ss	gra**ss**
se	hou**se**
c	**c**ent
ce	voi**ce**
st	ca**st**le

/v/	
v	**v**ery
ve	ha**ve**

/ch/	
ch	**ch**ip
tch	ma**tch**

/b/	
b	**b**ig
bb	ra**bb**it

/th/ (voiced)	
th	**th**at

/th/ (unvoiced)	
th	**th**in

/f/	
f	**f**at
ff	sta**ff**
ph	**ph**one
gh	lau**gh**
ffe	gira**ffe**

/w/	
w	**w**ig
wh	**wh**en

/g/	
g	ra**g**
gg	ju**gg**le
gh	**gh**ost
gu	**gu**est

/d/	
d	**d**i**d**
ed	grabb**ed**
dd	mu**dd**le

/l/	
l	**l**ip
ll	fu**ll**
le	app**le**
el	trav**el**
il	pup**il**
al	fin**al**

/sh/	
sh	**sh**op
ch	ma**ch**ine
s	**s**ugar

/p/	
p	ho**p**
pp	ha**pp**y

/m/	
m	**m**an
mm	su**mm**er
mb	la**mb**
mn	Autu**mn**

/k/	
k	**k**ite
c	**c**at
ck	du**ck**
ch	**ch**ord

/zh/	
s	lei**s**ure
ge	presti**ge**
z	sei**z**ure

THE ALPHABETIC CODE

Vowel sound spellings

/oe/

o	m**o**st
o–e	n**o**t**e**
oe	t**oe**
oa	b**oa**t
ow	gr**ow**
ough	th**ough**
ou	s**ou**l
ew	s**ew**

/ae/

a	t**a**ble
ai	r**ai**n
a–e	g**a**m**e**
ea	gr**ea**t
ay	s**ay**
ey	th**ey**
ei	v**ei**n
aigh	str**aigh**t
eigh	**eigh**t

/er/

er	p**er**k
ur	t**ur**n
ir	g**ir**l
or	w**or**ld
ear	l**ear**n
ar	coll**ar**
yr	zeph**yr**

/ow/

ow	c**ow**
ou	**ou**t
ough	dr**ough**t

/oi/

oi	j**oi**n
oy	b**oy**

/i/

i	**i**n
y	m**y**th

/o/

o	n**o**t
a	w**a**s

/ie/

i	w**i**ld
ie	p**ie**
i–e	l**i**k**e**
igh	n**igh**t
y	dr**y**
eigh	h**eigh**t

/ee/

e	m**e**
ee	m**ee**t
ea	s**ea**t
e–e	**e**v**e**
ie	ch**ie**f
y	funn**y**
ey	k**ey**
ei	rec**ei**ve
i	var**i**ation
eo	p**eo**ple

/or/

or	f**or**
our	y**our**
ore	m**ore**
oor	d**oor**
oar	b**oar**d
ar	w**ar**m

'aw'

aw	l**aw**n
awe	**awe**some
a	b**a**ll
al	w**al**k
au	**Au**gust
ough	f**ough**t
augh	d**augh**ter

/e/

e	b**e**d
ea	br**ea**d
ai	s**ai**d
ie	fr**ie**nd
eo	l**eo**pard

/oo/

oo	c**oo**k
oul	c**oul**d
u	p**u**t
o	w**o**man

/a/

a	c**a**t

/ear/

ear	n**ear**
eer	d**eer**
ere	h**ere**

/u/

u	t**u**b
ou	t**ou**ch
o–e	s**o**m**e**
a	**a**bout
o	M**o**nday
oo	bl**oo**d

/ar/

ar	c**ar**

/ue/

u–e	m**u**l**e**
u	p**u**pil
ew	f**ew**
ue	c**ue**

/air/

air	ch**air**
are	d**are**
ear	b**ear**
eir	th**eir**
ere	wh**ere**
ayor	m**ayor**
ayer	pr**ayer**
ae	**ae**rosol

/oo/

oo	b**oo**t
ue	bl**ue**
ew	gr**ew**
u	s**u**per
ui	s**ui**t
u–e	fl**u**t**e**
ou	s**ou**p
oe	sh**oe**
o	d**o**
ough	thr**ough**

PHONICS CONCEPTS

What is a phoneme?

A **phoneme** is the smallest unit of sound in a word. For example: the word "cat" has three phonemes: /k /a/ /t/.

Why do we need phonemes?

Phonemes are essential in learning to read and write because they are the building blocks of words, enabling us to segment and blend sounds to form words. Understanding phonemes helps in the development of literacy skills.

The English Alphabetic Code is based on the 44 phonemes in the English language. The letters of the alphabet represent those sounds with 160+ letter combinations.

When we teach reading, we need to show how the Alphabetic Code works: that the *letters* on the page *spell sounds in words.*

What is a grapheme?

A **grapheme** is a written representation or *spelling* of a sound (phoneme) in a word. A grapheme can be spelled by 1–4 letters.

In a **1-letter grapheme**, each sound is spelled by one letter:

c	a	t
⬇	⬇	⬇
/k/	/a/	/t/

In a **2-letter grapheme**, a sound is spelled by two letters:

sh	o	p
⬇	⬇	⬇
/sh/	/o/	/p/

In a **3-letter grapheme**, a sound is spelled by three letters:

n	igh	t
⬇	⬇	⬇
/n/	/ie/	/t/

In a **4-letter grapheme**, a sound is spelled by four letters:

d	ough
⬇	⬇
/d/	/oe/

What is a digraph?

A **digraph** is when two letters represent one sound in a word (phoneme).

di	graph
⬇	⬇
two (from Greek)	to write letters (from Greek)

Therefore, a digraph means two written letters.

A **consonant digraph** is when two letters represent a consonant sound. For example: the letters 's' and 'h' spell the sound /sh/ in the word "ship."

A **vowel team** is when two or more letters represent a vowel sound. For example: the letters 'a' and 'i' spell the sound /ae/ in the word "rain."

What are consonant blends?

Consonant blends are also called **consonant clusters**. These are two or more adjacent consonants in a word that spell two separate sounds. For example, in the word "stop" the letters 's' and 't' spell the sounds /s/ and /t/.

stop

What are Vowel–Consonant–e (VCe) spellings?

A **Vowel–Consonant–e (VCe) spelling** is when the spelling for the vowel sounds /ae/, /ee/, /ie/, /oe/, and /ue/ is split by a consonant:

/ae/ a–e → gate
/ee/ e–e → eve
/ie/ i–e → fine
/oe/ o–e → hope
/ue/ u–e → cute

What is a schwa?

A schwa is a weak vowel sound in an unstressed syllable.

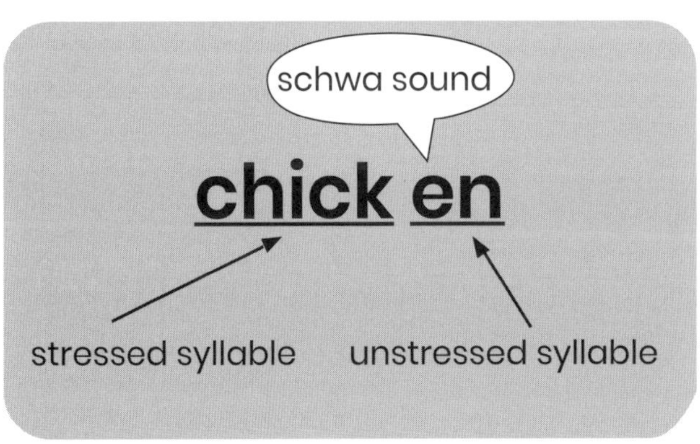

An example of a schwa is 'e' because it is a weak vowel sound in an unstressed syllable. It gets swallowed up when we pronounce the word "chicken," becoming "chickin" or "chick'n." We need to teach students to use their "spelling voice" in order to spell the word correctly and not as they hear it.

LANGUAGE UNITS AND PRINCIPLES

Words to morphemes

There are different ways of looking at a word.

A **word** is a distinct meaningful unit of speech or writing.

Letters are characters used for representing sounds in speech.

Syllables are mouthfuls of words.

Phonemes are speech sounds in words.

Graphemes are spellings of sounds in words.

Morphemes are units of meaning in words.

Distinguishing phonology, phonological awareness, and phonics

Phonology is an area of linguistics that deals with speech sound systems and sound patterns of spoken language.

Phonological awareness is the ability to break down words into smaller parts: syllables (mag net), alliteration (Bobby beetle bounced), onset and rime (m at), and phonemic awareness (m a t).

Phonemic awareness is the ability to identify and manipulate individual sounds in words (to blend, segment, and manipulate sounds).

Phonics is the teaching of:

- letter/sound correspondences for reading and spelling: c a t = /k/ /a/ /t/
- blending of individual letters/sounds for reading: m a t
- segmenting of individual sounds/letters for spelling: m a t

The Alphabetic Principle

The **Alphabetic Principle** is a fundamental concept in phonics instruction.

According to this principle, written letters or graphemes correspond to specific sounds (phonemes) of a spoken language. These sounds come together to form words.

This is crucial for learning to read, as it allows students to decode written text into spoken language.

Mapping words vs learning words by sight

There are two key word recognition strategies in reading: **mapping words** and **learning words by sight**.

Learning a word by shape (sight) is inefficient and clogs up precious memory.

house memorize one word by shape

Learning to map words helps readers to generalize and continue to "self-teach" new words.

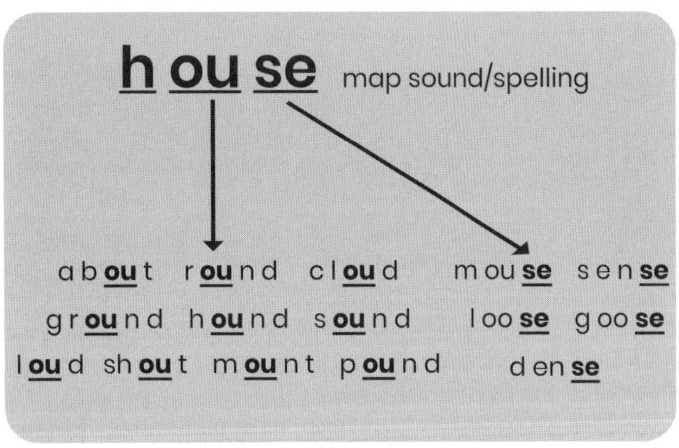

HIGH-FREQUENCY WORDS

High-frequency words are words that appear very frequently in stories and other written texts, such as "or" and "the." It is important for students to learn how to recognize these words quickly and effortlessly.

Many high-frequency words do not follow regular phonetic patterns or are not decodable until students have learned more advanced phonics patterns. This irregularity can make them challenging for students to decode them using phonics rules alone. Therefore, it is important for students to learn these words using different recognition strategies. In some other phonics programs, these words might be referred to as "tricky words," "sight words," or "heart words."

Teaching high-frequency words helps students read more smoothly and focus their decoding efforts on less common and more complex words. Mastery of high-frequency words significantly enhances reading fluency and comprehension, allowing students to become more confident readers.

High-frequency words: teaching by sound, not shape

Teaching high-frequency words by sound rather than shape offers a more effective approach to phonics instruction.

When learning high-frequency words through this method, students not only memorize these words more efficiently, but they also gain skills that are transferable to new, unfamiliar words.

This approach enhances the ability of students to decode and understand a wider range of vocabulary, supporting their overall reading fluency and comprehension.

How to teach students to spell high-frequency words

When we teach high-frequency words as whole words, we are encouraging students to remember them by shape. This method contradicts the phonics approach that explains that all words can be decoded—but some have complex spellings! Unfortunately, many of the common words beginner readers encounter are such words.

So how do we combine phonics with teaching difficult high-frequency words? Build on the knowledge the reader already has and explicitly teach the tricky part.

Here is an example of how to teach the word "car," which contains the phoneme /ar/ that is introduced in Dandelion Readers Level 1 Book 12 in the Phonic Books program.

1. Segment the word into its phonemes (sounds).

car

/c/ /ar/

2. Map the word showing its grapheme (spellings of the phonemes).

ç ar

3. Identify the tricky spellings in the word and show familiar words with these spellings.

ç ar

4. Ask the student to say the words as they write the word.

'c' 'ar' → car

DECODING AND ENCODING

It is important for teachers to distinguish between the concepts of **decoding** and **encoding**. Decoding involves translating symbols or letters into sounds and words. Encoding, on the other hand, is the reverse process, where words and sounds are translated into symbols or letters.

For students to understand this reversible code, it's important that decoding and encoding are taught together. This approach helps students understand that "mat" can be segmented into the sounds /m/ /a/ /t/ and spelled out, just as these sounds can be blended together to form the word "mat." By teaching reading and spelling together in the same lesson, teachers can provide a more comprehensive and effective lesson.

The following figure overleaf illustrates how the two essential skills of decoding and encoding work in tandem to form a complete understanding of reading and spelling.

Decoding

(translating symbols/letters to sounds and words)

is the reverse of ⟷

Encoding

For students to understand this reversible code, decoding and encoding should be taught together!

mat /m/ /a/ /t/ "mat" →

Sound out the words and blend them together into a word.

mat /m/ /a/ /t/ *"mat"* →

Sound out the words and blend them together into a word.

Teach reading and spelling in the same lesson!

SYNTHETIC PHONICS VS ANALYTIC PHONICS

In **synthetic phonics** instruction, the reader is taught to sound out individual sounds in a word and blend these sounds together to form the word. This method emphasizes the *synthesis* (blending) of individual sounds into a word. For example, the word "frog" is learned by sounding out each phoneme, /f/ /r/ /o/ /g/, and then blending these sounds to say "frog."

Conversely, **analytic phonics** focuses on teaching readers to break the word up into parts. This begins with an *analysis* of the whole word, which is broken into onset and rime, e.g. 'fr' + ' ' → "frog."

The conclusion based on research, notably Watson and Johnson (2004) and the Rose Report (2006), is that synthetic phonics is the most effective way to teach all children to read.

Analytic phonics often includes using known words as analogies. For example: if you know that "cat" ends with 'at' then you know that "mat" must also end with 'at.'

Systematic Synthetic Phonics

Systematic Synthetic Phonics (SSP) is a method that focuses on the systematic instruction of phonics. In this approach, students are taught to recognize graphemes and their corresponding phonemes. SSP involves a sequenced order of teaching where children first learn simple letter–sound correspondences (like 's' for /s/) and then progress to more complex sound patterns (like 'igh' for /ie/). The method emphasizes the blending or synthesizing of these sounds to read words.

SSP is a highly structured approach that ensures that no phonics elements are left out and each new skill builds upon previously learned skills. This approach is widely considered effective for phonics instruction and is used in many educational systems.

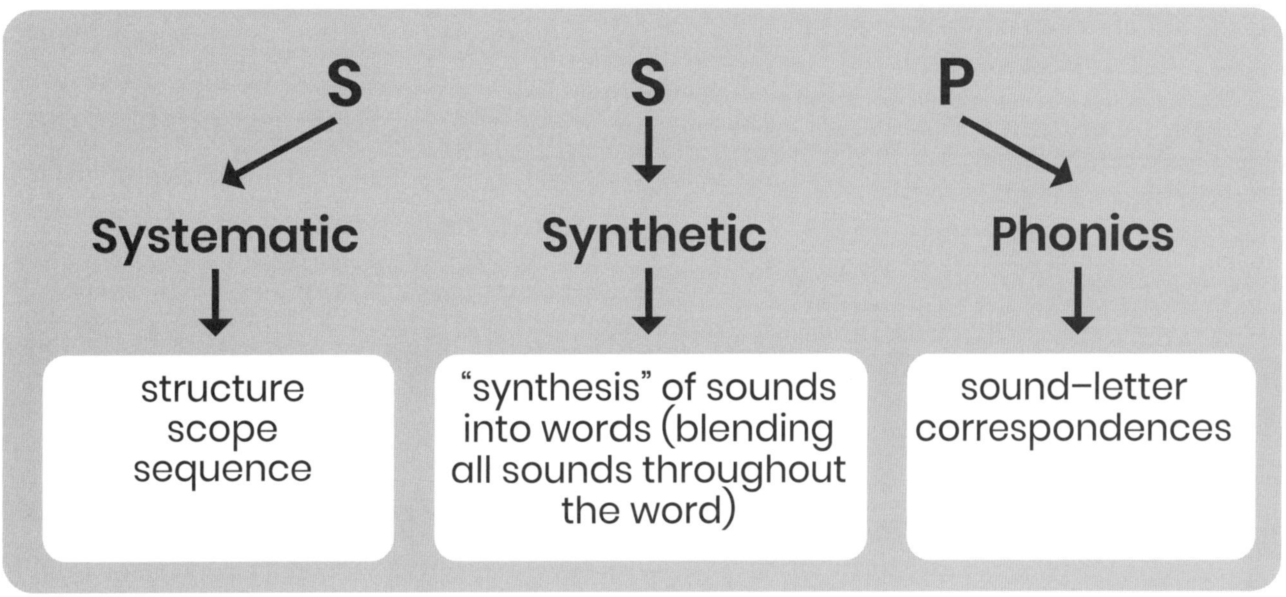

Systematic phonics in reading instruction

Teaching reading through systematic phonics is important because of the complexity of the English Alphabetic Code. To navigate this complexity, teachers should employ a scaffolded pedagogical framework:

- simple to complex: starting with the most basic elements and gradually introducing more challenging concepts
- stair-step progression
- systematic scope and sequence
- practice and consolidation along the way
- cumulative teaching

This methodical approach ensures that learners have a solid foundation, enabling them to confidently tackle the complexities of reading.

PHONEMIC AWARENESS AND READING STRATEGIES

Phonemic awareness: why it matters

Phonemic awareness is a pivotal skill for beginner readers that will play an important role in their journey towards literacy. Research has shown that phonics and phonemic awareness grow in tandem, and the most effective reading instruction teaches phonemic awareness with phonics.

The Simple View of Reading

The Simple View of Reading is a model that demonstrates the view that reading has two basic components: word recognition and language comprehension. This model offers a clear and effective framework for reading instruction.

The use of decodable books, the interaction between teachers, parents, and students, and the transition from learning to read to reading to learn are crucial elements of the Simple View of Reading approach. They shape how students progress towards independent reading across various texts and subjects.

Oral language × decoding = reading comprehension

Oral language

1a What to teach
Language and knowledge enrichment through reading fiction and nonfiction texts to beginner readers

Decoding

1b What to teach
The Alphabetic Code, phonemic awareness, decoding (blending), and encoding (segmenting)

Learn to read

2a Who reads what
Teachers and parents read "authentic texts" to students to enrich oral language, background knowledge, and story grammar.

2b Who reads what?
Beginner readers apply the phonics they have learned in decodable books until they can read any grade text and "authentic texts."

Read to learn

3 Who reads what?
Learners can read all books across the curriculum.

3-cueing vs decoding

The benefits of **3-cueing** versus **decoding strategies** is the subject of ongoing debate in literacy education. While 3-cueing focuses on using context and visual cues to identify words, decoding emphasizes the systematic breaking down of words into their phonetic components.

Decoding is increasingly recognized for its effectiveness in developing strong, foundational reading skills. This approach is grounded in systematic phonics and equips learners with the tools to tackle new and complex words independently. Conversely, 3-cueing relies on guessing that can lead the reader away from the text.

INSTRUCTIONAL MATERIALS

The role of decodable books in reading instruction

Practical application

Decodable books serve as practical tools where students apply their phonics knowledge in a controlled text. They offer students an opportunity to practice the phonic knowledge and skills they have learned. When students are taught mathematics, they are given exercises to practice what they have been taught, in order to internalize the new learning and to develop automaticity. Decodable texts perform a similar role in reading instruction.

Strategy and success

Based on the Science of Reading, decodable books focus on the decoding of graphemes and blending them into words, which steers students away from guessing. The controlled vocabulary is tailored to the phonic skills of the students, providing immediate reading success and boosting their confidence.

Focusing on a target phoneme (sound) or grapheme (spelling)

Decodable books target specific phoneme–grapheme correspondences, allowing students to practice reading with a focus on newly taught sounds and spellings. As students progress, the complexity of words in these books increases, and they start to look similar to more traditional reading books.

Motivation and independence

The sense of achievement students gain from successfully reading these books increases their motivation to continue learning to read, embodying the sentiment, "I can do this!"

Detractors of decodable books confuse the purpose of these books. They are not created to compete with wonderful children's literature, but are used for only a short time, as "training wheels" to help children develop good decoding skills. As students' proficiency in decoding grows, these supports can be removed, enabling them to take off and explore more complex reading materials. This means they can move on to and enjoy independent reading of rich and varied children's literature.

3-cueing approach
a guessing strategy that leads the reader away from the text

Guess the word.
1. Look at the picture.
2. What could it be? (letters? mail?)
3. What is the first sound in the word?

Pip has mail in his hand.
"I must get the mail to
my pals," he says.

Decoding approach
a strategy that focuses on letter–sound correspondences in words

Read the word.
1. Sound out the letters and blend the sounds into a word.
/m/ /ai/ /l/ → "mail"

Pip has mail in his hand.
"I must get the mail to
my pals," he says.

THE PHONIC BOOKS PROGRAM

METHODOLOGY

The principles underlying our books are based on current thinking in the **Science of Reading**. We believe that all students can learn to read, and the best way to achieve this is by teaching them how the English writing system works by following a systematic approach. Written English is based on an alphabetic code that students need to unlock. Teaching students to recognize these graphemes and how to sound them and blend them into words is the route to reading success.

Our books and resources develop the five pillars of learning to read:

1. phonemic awareness
2. phonics
3. vocabulary
4. fluency
5. comprehension

At a later stage, students need to learn about morphemes (units of meaning) to enhance their vocabulary and comprehension.

Our books follow a systematic phonics approach. Starting by introducing only a few letters and sounds at a time, the reader can experience success from the very beginning. Our program teaches the following reading skills using explicit systematic phonics.

BLENDING AND SEGMENTING

Students learning to read with explicit systematic phonics are encouraged to sound out letters in words and push the sounds together into words. This is called **blending**. Each letter is sounded out separately and blended from left to right, throughout the word. This is the most reliable strategy to read a new word.

It's helpful for beginner readers to blend using "continuant" consonant sounds (e.g. /m/, /n/, /l/, /r/, and /s/) because these sounds are easier to prolong and blend together smoothly.

Students learn that spelling is the reverse activity of blending. When spelling, they learn to isolate each sound in the word and represent it with a spelling. This is called **segmenting**.

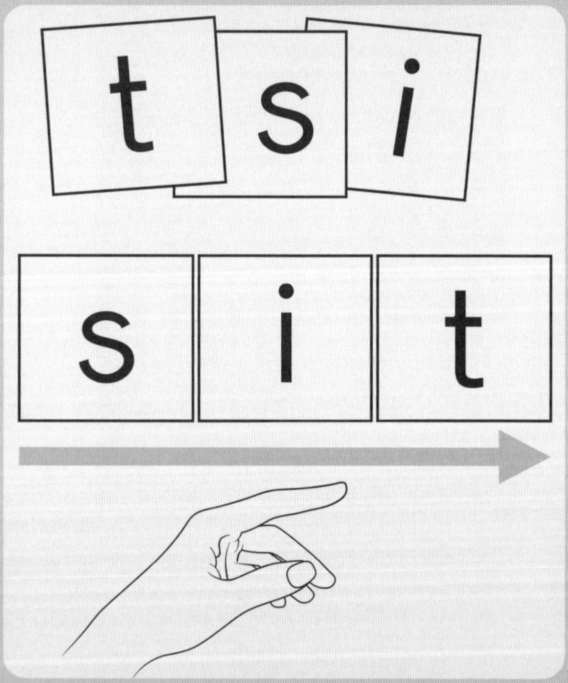

PHONEME MANIPULATION

Students learn to identify and isolate phonemes in words and to manipulate them by deleting, adding or swapping sounds in the words. This skill helps the reader to self-correct when making errors in reading.

Once students have been taught letter–sound correspondences, they can practice this new knowledge within controlled **decodable texts**. This means that students can sound out words that they can't yet read. Decodable texts encourage students to use "blending" sounds into words as the first strategy when reading, using the phonics they have been taught.

Learning a new skill takes a lot of practice so our books for beginner readers include games to practice reading words in the book. Our Dandelion Readers offer a **reading practice page** to ensure a successful reading experience of the text in the book.

All our books have cumulative progression which allows for previous learning to be included as the reader progresses. This ensures what has been learned is included and practiced along the way.

Students learn new **vocabulary** through reading and our books offer an opportunity for this. As they learn to decode a growing number of words, new words are introduced which will help them develop their language skills.

The **activity books** are a supplementary resource to support students who need extra practice at each level. Although our books can be used independently, we recommend using the activity books alongside to enhance and consolidate learning. Some activities, such as blending, segmenting, and phoneme manipulation precede the books, whereas others are directly linked to the books in the corresponding series and are designed to develop reading fluency, spelling, writing, and comprehension skills.

PROGRAM OVERVIEW

In line with explicit systematic phonics and the Science of Reading, our books offer stair-step phonics progression for Grade 1, starting from the simple to the more complex parts of the Alphabetic Code.

There are three distinct series of Dandelion decodable books that cover the sounds of the alphabet and double consonants: Dandelion Launchers, Dandelion Launchers Extras, and Dandelion World. Consistent in their scope and sequence, these series start by introducing only a few sounds and letters at a time (Stage 1 introduces only five sounds: s, a, t, i, m), ensuring students can experience success from the outset. Additionally, the Dandelion Readers Sets 1–3 readers follow a similar progression but with more text per page, catering to more advanced beginner learners.

For extended learning for Grade 1, the Dandelion Readers Level 1 (Vowel Spelling) series is designed to address common challenges students face with vowel teams. Vowel teams are introduced explicitly and gradually, providing reading practice for children learning increasingly complex spellings in the Alphabetic Code. Additionally, our Dandelion Readers VCe series, provides coverage of the silent 'e' patterns a–e, e–e, i–e, o–e, and u–e.

Dandelion Launchers

This series is a fully decodable phonic series for beginner readers. Each pair of books in the series introduces only a few letters/sounds at a time, which allows for independent reading from the beginning. The series provides practice while offering different stories, with each stage introducing new letters/sounds and reviewing previously taught letters/sounds and high-frequency words. A game is included at the back of each book, offering a fun way to practice the new phonic skills and knowledge introduced at each stage.

Dandelion Launchers Extras

These books are designed to complement the Dandelion Launchers series, providing additional practice for the sounds of the alphabet at CVC (Consonant-Vowel-Consonant) level. They follow the same cumulative scope and sequence as the original Dandelion Launchers series, meaning they progress in the same way and cover the same content. The Extras series includes 30 different readers that aim to reinforce the learning by introducing only a few letters/sounds at a time, similar to the original series, but with different stories.

Dandelion World

Dandelion World is the parallel series to Dandelion Launchers and covers a range of engaging nonfiction topics. Each book includes a nonfiction knowledge builder feature for children and adults to read together. This is a fun way to enhance vocabulary and deepen comprehension of the book's content.

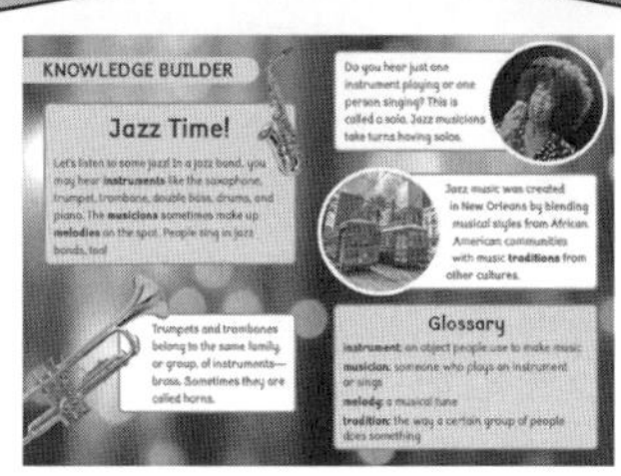

Dandelion Readers Sets 1–3

The Dandelion Readers Sets 1–3 are three series of books that follow a similar progression found in Dandelion Launchers. These series feature a greater amount of text on each page, with the text volume progressively increasing throughout each series. While this manual does not include specific lesson plans for these series, they can be used as supplementary materials for your lessons.

Dandelion Readers Vowel Spellings Series

Dandelion Readers is a series of books for beginner readers that introduces different spellings for vowel sounds. More text is included on each page to build reading stamina. A helpful Reading Practice section allows further practice of each new spelling taught. The Level 1 set is suitable for Grade 1 level and comprises 12 readers.

Dandelion Readers VCe Series / Dandelion World VCe Series

The Dandelion Readers VCe Series is a series of decodable books that specifically targets the silent 'e' spellings in the English language. Aimed at advancing beginner readers, this series introduces the key VCe (Vowel-Consonant-e) spellings, a–e, e–e, i–e, o–e, and u–e, through various engaging and illustrated stories. Each book in the series focuses on one VCe spelling pattern at a time, ensuring that students can gradually master these spelling conventions. There is also a corresponding Dandelion World VCe series of nonfiction readers, which follows the same scope and sequence.

Activity books

Each series has accompanying activity books. These books are integral to the reading program, as they include teaching and practice activities to support the learner.

PROGRAM FEATURES

The Phonic Books program for Grade 1 is designed to engage beginner readers by offering a range of features tailored to support reading success and build confidence in students.

- **Engaging content:** the program includes engaging nonfiction texts and imaginative stories featuring appealing characters that captivate young readers. The text is designed to be engaging, ensuring that readers remain engaged and motivated.
- **Accessible design:** the books use a dyslexia-friendly font and present text on suitable backgrounds, making them more accessible and easier to read.
- **Structured progression:** a highly structured sequence carefully guides the student from simple to more complex phonics concepts.
- **Cumulative learning:** the books follow a cumulative progression, ensuring that previously learned phonics skills are revisited and reinforced.
- **High-frequency words:** the program gradually introduces high-frequency words.
- **Decodable texts:** the program uses controlled decodable texts that allow students to apply their phonic knowledge to reading texts.
- **Vocabulary development:** as students' decoding skills improve, new words are introduced to help develop their language skills.
- **Interactive games and activities:** the program also offers a variety of games and activities, such as fishing games, snap cards, and dice games, to make learning more interactive and enjoyable, while helping to consolidate learning.
- **Activity books:** accompanying activity books are available to reinforce the skills learned in the books. These books are designed to support reading fluency, spelling, writing, and comprehension skills.
- **Free printable resources:** a range of free printable reading and spelling sources are available on the Phonic Books website.

CURRICULUM ALIGNMENT

Our books can be used to complement any phonics program once the students have been taught the letters/sounds in the books. However, they follow the progression of the **Sounds-Write® Reading and Spelling Program**. Curriculum mapping grids for Grade 1 can be found on our website.

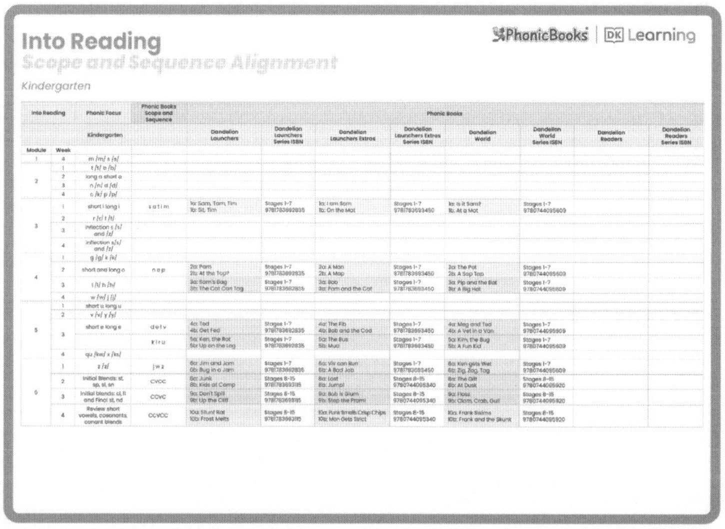
Into Reading
Scope and Sequence Alignment
Kindergarten

SCOPE AND SEQUENCE

The scope and sequence provided below offers a detailed overview of our Phonic Books program for Grade 1 level readers. It outlines each stage of the curriculum, detailing the specific book titles that cover each stage. It also highlights the corresponding parallel series that focus on the same phonic skills, which can be used for additional practice. These parallel series present varied contexts, ranging from diverse storylines to informative nonfiction texts, as exemplified by the Dandelion World series. The tables also specify the word structures covered at each stage, such as CVC words for the first seven stages. This structured approach is designed to present teachers with a clear roadmap of the program's progression.

Stages 1–7

Dandelion Launchers	**Dandelion Launchers Extras**	**Dandelion World**	**Stage**	**Phonic focus**	**Word structure**
Book 1a: Sam, Tam, Tim Book 1b: Is it Sam?	Book 1a: I am Sam Book 1b: On the Mat	Book 1a: Sit, Tim Book 1b: At a Mat	1	s a t i m	CVC
Book 2a: Pam Book 2b: The Pot	Book 2a: A Man Book 2b: A Map	Book 2a: At the Top? Book 2b: A Sap Tap	2	n o p	
Book 3a: Sam's Bag Book 3b: Pip and the Bat	Book 3a: Bob Book 3b: Pam and the Cat	Book 3a: The Cat Can Tag Book 3b: A Big Hat	3	b c g h	
Book 4a: Ted Book 4b: Meg and Ted	Book 4a: The Fib Book 4b: Bob and the Cod	Book 4a: Get Fed Book 4b: A Vet in a Van	4	d e f v	
Book 5a: Ken, the Rat Book 5b: Kim, the Bug	Book 5a: The Bus Book 5b: Mud	Book 5a: Up on the Log Book 5b: A Fun Kid	5	k l r u	
Book 6a: Jim and Jam Book 6b: Ken Gets Wet	Book 6a: Viv Can Run Book 6b: A Bad Job	Book 6a: Bug in a Jam Book 6b: Zig, Zag, Tag	6	j w z	
Book 7a: Rex Yells Book 7b: Rex Will Not Sit	Book 7a: Bob on the Sill Book 7b: The Hill	Book 7a: The Jazz Gig Book 7b: In the Dell	7	x y ff ll ss zz	

Stages 8–15

Dandelion Launchers	Dandelion Launchers Extras	Dandelion World	Stage	Phonic focus and skill focus
Book 8a: Junk Book 8b: The Gift	Book 8a: Lost Book 8b: Jump!	Book 8a: Kids at Camp Book 8b: At Dusk	8	CVCC
Book 9a: Don't Spill Book 9b: Floss	Book 9a: Bob is Glum Book 9b: Stop the Pram!	Book 9a: Up the Cliff Book 9b: Clam, Crab, Gull	9	CCVC
Book 10a: Stunt Rat Book 10b: Frank Swims	Book 10a: Punk Smells Crisp Chips Book 10b: Mom Gets Strict	Book 10a: Frost Melts Book 10b: Frank and the Skunk	10	CCVCC
Book 11a: Nuts for Lunch Book 11b: The Champ	Book 11a: The Big Chip Book 11b: Chit Chat	Book 11a: Crunch, Munch! Book 11b: Chimp Chums	11	ch
Book 12a: Shep and Tosh Book 12b: Fresh Fish	Book 12a: The Shop Book 12b: The Fish Pond	Book 12a: Trash in the Trench Book 12b: Sled Dogs Dash	12	sh
Book 13a: This and That Book 13b: Will This Fit?	Book 13a: Thud! Crash! Book 13b: That's It!	Book 13a: Sloths Book 13b: The Thrill of a Run	13	th
Book 14a: The Back Pack Book 14b: Which Shall I Pick?	Book 14a: The Clock Book 14b: When Can I Get On?	Book 14a: Shells and Rocks Book 14b: Flick the Puck	14	ck, wh
Book 15a: Ding Dong! Book 15b: The Strong Wind	Book 15a: Spring Book 15b: Ting-a-ling	Book 15a: Spring Has Sprung Book 15b: Long Bat Wings	15	ng, qu

Stages 16–20

Dandelion Launchers	Dandelion World	Stage	Phonic focus and skill focus
Book 16a: The Itch Book 16b: The Ditch	Book 16a: Catch the Fun! Book 16b: A Clutch in the Hutch	16	tch and ve
Book 17a: The Sandpit Book 17b: The Muffin Shop	Book 17a: Selling Crops Book 17b: The Bandit Kittens	17	two-syllable words
Book 18a: Stranded Book 18b: Stan is Shocked	Book 18a: Planted in Space Book 18b: The Bobcat Hunted	18	two-syllable words, -ed
Book 19a: Thinking of a Gift Book 19b: Swimming	Book 19a: Sharks Swimming Book 19b: At the Fun Park	19	two-syllable words, -ing
Book 20a: Cuddles Book 20b: Muddle in the Middle	Book 20a: Apple Fest Fun! Book 20b: Cuddle Pup	20	two-syllable words, le

Dandelion Readers Sets 1–3

Set 1 Units 1–10	Set 2 Units 1–10	Set 3 Units 1–10	Phonic focus and skill level
Book 1: Sam	Book 1: Sam and Tim	Book 1: Sit on It	s a t i m
Book 2: Pip	Book 2: The Nap	Book 2: Pip, Sam, and Tam	n o p
Book 3: In the Bag	Book 3: In the Can	Book 3: A Hot Cab	b c g h
Book 4: Bad Cat	Book 4: At the Vet	Book 4: In the Van	d e f v
Book 5: Bun in the Sun	Book 5: Red Gum	Book 5: The Hut	k l r u
Book 6: Zip and Zap	Book 6: Meg and the Bun	Book 6: Top Dog	j w z
Book 7: Bob Is Not Well	Book 7: Up a Big Hill	Book 7: I Will Sell	x y ff ll ss zz
Book 8: The Lost Box	Book 8: Lost in the Pond	Book 8: The Best Gift	VCC CVCC
Book 9: Flip and Flop Slip	Book 9: The Trap	Book 9: Fred Has a Plan	CCVC
Book 10: The Stink	Book 10: Punk and the Plums	Book 10: The Stilts	CCVCC

Set 1 Units 11–20	Set 2 Units 11–20	Phonic focus and skill level
Book 11: Pip Gets Rich	Book 11: Twin Chimps	ch
Book 12: “Hush!”	Book 12: The Cash	sh
Book 13: The Path Up the Hill	Book 13: Thump, Thump	th
Book 14: The Trick	Book 14: Raj Gets a Shock	ck
Book 15: The Ring	Book 15: The Sting	ng
Book 16: The Quest	Book 16: The Quilt	qu ve
Book 17: When Meg was a Pup	Book 17: What a Bad Dog!	two-syllable words, wh
Book 18: A Wicked Snack	Book 18: Dan is Trapped	two-syllable words, -ed
Book 19: Sinking Sand	Book 19: A Red Jacket	two-syllable words, -ing
Book 20: The Paddle	Book 20: Apple Crumble	two-syllable words, le

Dandelion Readers Level 1

Level 1	Sound	Phonic focus and/or skill level
Book 1: The Mail	/ae/	ai
Book 2: The Tree	/ee/	ee
Book 3: Raj Gets a Soak	/oe/	oa
Book 4: My Turn	/er/	ur
Book 5: Bread and Jam	/e/	ea
Book 6: Mr Brown	/ow/	ow
Book 7: The Cocoon	b/oo/t	oo
Book 8: A Fright in the Night	/ie/	igh
Book 9: In the Wood	l/oo/k	oo
Book 10: Paw Prints	/aw/	aw
Book 11: Oil	/oi/	oi
Book 12: Trip to the Farm	/ar/	ar

Dandelion Readers VCe Spellings

VCe Spellings Books 1–6	Phonic focus and/or skill level
Book 1: Late	a–e
Book 2: Pete	e–e
Book 3: A Fine Life	i–e
Book 4: The Note	o–e
Book 5: Club Rules	u–e
Book 6: Show Time	a–e, e–e, i–e, o–e, u–e

GETTING STARTED

Start by reviewing the scheme of work charts outlined in the next section. These are designed to provide an easy-to-navigate and in-depth understanding of the entire Phonic Books program for Grade 1. They will guide you through the program's progression, detailing the sequence in which phonemes and graphemes are introduced in each lesson plan. Each lesson plan specifies which phonic skills are being developed to ensure a systematic approach to learning. The charts are organized by series and include several key components: the phonic focus for each lesson plan, lesson objectives, order of lessons, high-frequency words, vocabulary lists, and lesson resources. Recommendations are given for when to conduct reading assessments to track students' progress. Whether planning lessons, tracking a student's progress, or understanding the journey ahead, the scheme of work charts are a useful reference.

Next, move on to the lesson structure and teaching methods section. The lesson structure section explains the program's lesson framework, including the pattern of activities and methods used for effective teaching. Each lesson plan is divided into five distinct lessons. Explanations are provided on how the lessons are structured and the purpose of the different lesson elements are explained. The teaching methods section that follows explains how to teach the core lesson activities and uses examples from the activity books to illustrate how the resources can be integrated into the lessons.

The differentiation section on page 55 provides guidance on how to tailor lessons to meet diverse student needs. It provides strategies for using the activity book resources to create customizable lessons, including support for the lowest attaining 20% of students, those with special educational needs, and students for whom English is a second language.

Lastly, regular student assessment is important for enhancing both learning and teaching. The lesson plans incorporate formative assessments through various activities and games. However, periodic summative assessments are also an important tool for gauging student progress. Refer to the section on reading assessments (page 58) for guidance on when and how to conduct these assessments.

After reviewing these sections, you are now ready to proceed with the main lesson plans of the program, which begin on page 120.

SCHEMES OF WORK

Stages 1–7: Sounds of the alphabet

Lesson plan	Objectives	High-frequency words	Resources
Stage 1: s, a, t, i, m	In this first lesson plan, students will learn to accurately read new words by applying the phonic sounds /s/, /a/, /t/, /i/, and /m/. They will focus on blending these sounds to form and recognize simple CVC words.	n/a	Dandelion Launchers Stages 1–7: Book 1a: Sam, Tam, Tim Dandelion Launchers Stages 1–7 Activities
Stage 2: n, o, p	In subsequent lesson plans, students will consolidate previously learned sounds and learn new sounds. In this lesson plan, students will: • review /s/, /a/, /t/, /i/, and /m/ • read new words using the sounds /n/, /o/, and /p/	I, is, a	Dandelion Launchers Stages 1–7: Book 2a: Pam Dandelion Launchers Stages 1–7 Activities
Stage 3: b, c, g, h	Students will: • review /s/, /a/, /t/, /i/, /m/, /n/, /o/, and /p/ • read new words using the sounds /b/, /c/, /g/, and /h/	Sam's, has, a, get, the, is, Tam's	Dandelion Launchers Stages 1–7: Book 3a: Sam's Bag Dandelion Launchers Stages 1–7 Activities
Stage 4: d, e, f, v	Students will: • review /s/, /a/, /t/, /i/, /m/, /n/, /o/, /p/, /b/, /c/, /g/, and /h/ • read new words using the sounds /d/, /e/, /f/, and /v/	the, up, off, into, is, a	Dandelion Launchers Stages 1–7: Book 4a: Ted Dandelion Launchers Stages 1–7 Activities
Stage 5: k, l, r, u	Students will: • review /s/, /a/, /t/, /i/, /m/, /n/, /o/, /p/, /b/, /c/, /g/, /h/, /d/, /e/, /f/, and /v/ • read new words using the sounds /k/, /l/, /r/, and /u/	the, a, it's	Dandelion Launchers Stages 1–7: Book 5a: Ken, the Rat Dandelion Launchers Stages 1–7 Activities
Stage 6: j, w, z	Students will: • review /s/, /a/, /t/, /i/, /m/, /n/, /o/, /p/, /b/, /c/, /g/, /h/, /d/, /e/, /f/, /v/, /k/, /l/, /r/, and /u/ • read new words using the sounds /j/, /w/, and /z/	and, was, his, I, have, a, of, to, the, legs, into	Dandelion Launchers Stages 1–7: Book 6a: Jim and Jam Dandelion Launchers Stages 1–7 Activities
Stage 7: x, y, ff, ll, ss, zz	Students will: • review /s/, /a/, /t/, /i/, /m/, /n/, /o/, /p/, /b/, /c/, /g/, /h/, /d/, /e/, /f/, /v/, /k/, /l/, /r/, /u/, /w/, and /z/ • read new words using the sounds /x/, /y/, /ff/, /ll/, /ss/, and /zz/	yells, I, the, and, was, no, be, a, said	Dandelion Launchers Stages 1–7: Book 7a: Rex Yells Dandelion Launchers Stages 1–7 Activities

Stages 8–15: Consonant blends and digraphs

Lesson plan	Objectives	High-frequency words	Resources
Stage 8: CVCC	Students will learn to blend and segment consonants and vowels to read and write CVCC words, focusing on the incorporation of previously learned sounds.	I, of, this, old, said, to, the, that	Dandelion Launchers Stages 8–15: Book 8a: Junk Dandelion Launchers Stages 8–15 Activities
Stage 9: CCVC	Using their knowledge of previously learned sounds, students will focus on creating and decoding words with initial consonant blends such as 'bl,' 'cr,' 'st,' and 'fl.'	we, have, a, of, don't, says, the, to, is	Dandelion Launchers Stages 8–15: Book 9a: Don't Spill Dandelion Launchers Stages 8–15 Activities
Stage 10: CCVCC	Students will build on their skills by learning and practicing words with CCVCC word structures, such as "print."	is, he, as, I, be, a, says, the	Dandelion Launchers Stages 8–15: Book 10a: Stunt Rat Dandelion Launchers Stages 8–15 Activities
Stage 11: ch	Students are introduced to the consonant digraph /ch/ and will learn how to read and write it in various words.	a, was, to, the, for, his, I, have, said, plant, of	Dandelion Launchers Stages 8–15: Book 11a: Nuts for Lunch Dandelion Launchers Stages 8–15 Activities
Stage 12: sh	Students are introduced to the consonant digraph /sh/ and will learn how to read and write it in various words.	I, a, was, you, be, my, to, no, yelled, said	Dandelion Launchers Stages 8–15: Book 12a: Shep and Tosh Dandelion Launchers Stages 8–15 Activities
Stage 13: th	Students are introduced to the consonant digraph /th/ and will learn how to read and write it in various words.	to, I, have, a, of, the	Dandelion Launchers Stages 8–15: Book 13a: This and That Dandelion Launchers Stages 8–15 Activities
Stage 14: ck, wh	Students will expand their phonic skills by learning new digraphs /ck/ and /wh/.	the, for, says, you, a, is, have	Dandelion Launchers Stages 8–15: Book 14a: The Back Pack Dandelion Launchers Stages 8–15 Activities
Stage 15: ng, qu	Students will expand their phonic skills by learning new digraphs /ng/ and /qu/.	is, the, I, have, a, of, happy birthday, to, you	Dandelion Launchers Stages 8–15: Book 15a: Ding Dong! Dandelion Launchers Stages 8–15 Activities

Stages 16–20: Simple two-syllable words and suffixes

Lesson plan	Objectives	High-frequency words	Resources
Stage 16: tch and ve	Students will continue to develop their understanding of phonics concepts to learn the spelling 'tch' for the sound /ch/ and 've' for the sound /v/. Students will practice segmenting and blending these consonant blends in words.	of, the, to, you, I'll, says, has, begins, too, I, for	Dandelion Launchers Stages 16–20: Book 16a: The Itch Dandelion Launchers Stages 16–20 Activities
Stage 17: two-syllable words	Students will progress to reading and writing two-syllable words, integrating their knowledge of phonemes, digraphs, and consonant blends.	are, the, pretend, is, island, says, has, her, I'll, you, for	Dandelion Launchers Stages 16–20: Book 17a: The Sandpit Dandelion Launchers Stages 16–20 Activities
Stage 18: two-syllable words, -ed	Students will refine their skills with two-syllable words and learn about the suffix -ed, focusing on its three sounds: /d/, /t/, and /id/. They will practice distinguishing these variations and explore how -ed changes the sound and syllable structure based on the preceding sound in a word.	the, his, he, I, to, onto, tree, began, all, of	Dandelion Launchers Stages 16–20: Book 18a: Stranded Dandelion Launchers Stages 16–20 Activities
Stage 19: two-syllable words, -ing	Students will learn to incorporate the -ing suffix into words and in two-syllable words.	his, are, of, for, I, says, into, surprise, to, the, is, coming, fingers, my	Dandelion Launchers Stages 16–20: Book 19a: Thinking of a Gift Dandelion Launchers Stages 16–20 Activities
Stage 20: two-syllable words, le	Students will continue practicing two-syllable words and learn and practice words ending in 'le.'	has, was, the, adopted, her, is, to, she, into	Dandelion Launchers Stages 16–20: Book 20a: Cuddles Dandelion Launchers Stages 16–20 Activities

Dandelion Readers Level 1

One vowel spelling for each vowel sound

Lesson plan	High-frequency words	New vocabulary	Resources
/ae/: 'ai' spelling	has, his, is, begins, to, the, I, this, my, he, says, open, we, they, say	mail, pal, wails	Dandelion Readers, Level 1: Book 1: The Mail Dandelion Readers, Level 1 Activities
/ee/: 'ee' spelling	is, buzzes, we, as, to, the, says, be, are	screen, plant, seed, pit	Dandelion Readers, Level 1: Book 2: The Tree Dandelion Readers, Level 1 Activities
/oe/: 'oa' spelling	is, he, the, no, has, of, his, says, your, she, day	soak, loads, foam, moan and groan	Dandelion Readers, Level 1: Book 3: Raj Gets a Soak Dandelion Readers, Level 1 Activities
/er/: 'ur' spelling	is, my, says, me, have, give, you're, hurled, his, to	have a turn, hurl	Dandelion Readers, Level 1: Book 4: My Turn Dandelion Readers, Level 1 Activities
/e/: 'ea' spelling	of, the, said, I, don't, you'll, his, he, was, began, to, me, yanked, my	spread, tread, leaped	Dandelion Readers, Level 1: Book 5: Bread and Jam Dandelion Readers, Level 1 Activities
/ow/: 'ow' spelling	Mr, was, the, mailman, growled, mopped, his, frowned, I, to, he, asked	growl, brow, frown	Dandelion Readers, Level 1: Book 6: Mr Brown Dandelion Readers, Level 1 Activities
b/oo/t : 'oo' spelling	night, swooped, the, hatched, out, popped, he, began, to, look, there, was, no, open, into	moonlit, swooped, cocoon, snooze	Dandelion Readers, Level 1: Book 7: The Cocoon Dandelion Readers, Level 1 Activities
/ie/: 'igh' spelling	we, the, tonight, asked, settled, switched, was, flashed, to, stretched	den, drifted, tight fit	Dandelion Readers, Level 1: Book 8: A Fright in the Night Dandelion Readers, Level 1 Activities
l/oo/k: 'oo' spelling	his, to, the, said, was, into, looked, he, vanished, limped, you, jumped	wood, brook, chipmunk	Dandelion Readers, Level 1: Book 9: In the Wood Dandelion Readers, Level 1 Activities
/aw/: 'aw' spelling	home, she, the, ripped, sofa, gnawed, controls, is, I, to, crawled, drawer, said, tickled	paw prints, clawed, gnawed	Dandelion Readers, Level 1: Book 10: Paw Prints Dandelion Readers, Level 1 Activities
/oi/: 'oi' spelling	picked, I'm, puffed, noise, came, the, was, we, have, no, said, is, spoiled, little, joined, he, his, my, voice, I, gave, some	boiling hot, soil	Dandelion Readers, Level 1: Book 11: Oil Dandelion Readers, Level 1 Activities
/ar/: 'ar' spelling	we're, to, the, said, parked, gasped, marched, into, pecked, large, began, arched, his, purred	rather fast, jolt, gasped, pecked	Dandelion Readers, Level 1: Book 12: Trip to the Farm Dandelion Readers, Level 1 Activities

Dandelion Readers VCe Spellings

VCe (Vowel–Consonant–e) spellings

Lesson plan	Objectives	High-frequency words	New vocabulary	Resources
a–e	Students will learn and practice the 'a–e' spelling for the sound /ae/ (e.g. "l**ate**"). In this and subsequent lesson plans, reading practice pages and games help to consolidate learning, reading practice pages and games help to consolidate learning.	was, he, for, school, birthday, no, said, the, his, they, she, goal, day	shame, blame	Dandelion Readers, VCe Spellings Book 1: Late VCe Spellings Activities
e–e	Students will learn and practice the 'e–e' spelling for the sound /ee/ (e.g. "th**eme**").	is, I'll, make, to, said, his, he, the, began, boots, no, do	complete, completed, concrete, extremely	Dandelion Readers, VCe Spellings Book 2: Pete VCe Spellings Activities
i–e	Students will learn and practice the 'i–e' spelling for the sound /ie/ (e.g. "f**ine**").	his, were, little, they, lived, of, leaves, he, to, the, we, my, said, politely, be, baby	fine, hive, politely, stack	Dandelion Readers, VCe Spellings Book 3: A Fine Life VCe Spellings Activities
o–e	Students will learn and practice the 'o–e' spelling for the sound /o e/ (e.g. "r**ope**").	the, Toad, he, saw, said, follow, to, onto, was, into, my, hello, you, have, me	task, cope	Dandelion Readers, VCe Spellings Book 4: The Note VCe Spellings Activities
u–e	Students will learn and practice that the VCe spelling 'u–e' can represent two sounds: /oo/ as in "r**ude**" and /ue/ as in "c**ute**".	play, said, we, the, they, to, began, cheat, you, are, by, I, again	accuse, refuse, brute, include	Dandelion Readers, VCe Spellings Book 5: Club Rules VCe Spellings Activities
a–e, e–e, i–e, o–e, u–e	Students will consolidate their understanding of VCe patterns by practicing these previously learned patterns in different words.	show, said, the, robot, say, who, of, began, play, he, put, his, I, they, as, was, to, all, were, give	compete, throne, graceful, advice	Dandelion Readers, VCe Spellings Book 6: Show Time VCe Spellings Activities

LESSON PLAN STRUCTURE

Each lesson plan is divided into five distinct steps, focusing on:

1. Preparation
2. Application for reading
3. Application for writing
4. Comprehension and consolidation
5. Tracking progress

A typical lesson plan follows the structured format below, though not every lesson will follow this exact structure. Lessons or activities should be offered daily, when possible, and last not more than 15 minutes for younger students.

Step 1: Preparation

In this first step, the teacher begins by outlining the goal of the lesson plan: learning the new sounds and reinforcing previously learned ones. Spend a couple of minutes introducing these new sounds and the story that will be central to teaching the upcoming lessons. Then demonstrate the correct pronunciation of these sounds. **Sound cards** or **Word-building cards** from the activity books can be effective in modeling the new sounds, making the lesson more engaging and interactive.

Following the introduction, move on to a word-building activity. The students listen to the sounds in each word and then build the words using sound cards or magnetic letters, and with the aid of picture cards. The objective is for students to construct words corresponding to the pictures by employing the sounds they have learned. It's important that students focus on the sounds first, then find the letters that represent these sounds. This reinforces the link between phonemic awareness and written language.

The next phase of the lesson focuses on segmenting and blending sounds in words. A multisensory approach is effective for teaching. Use gestures to aid learning like pointing to the letters as they are sounded out and using a swishing motion with your finger for blending. This helps for transitioning to spelling activities, which link phonic skills with reading and writing.

This first step typically concludes with a word chain activity, incorporating both real and nonsense words. This activity is designed to reinforce the concepts taught in the lesson, while also being fun and interactive.

Step 2: Application for reading

In the second step, students apply their phonic skills by reading a decodable text. They are encouraged to sound out the words and blend them together. When the reading is laborious, the teacher can reread the sentence after the students to help them comprehend the text. Ensure that any new vocabulary is discussed and explained.

The Phonic Books lesson plans in this instructional manual suggest that reading the story should take the form of a directed reading by the teacher. However, a number of options for teachers reading the book are also recommended:

- The teacher reads the book and students follow.
- Students engage in choral reading.
- Students engage in individual whisper reading while the teacher circulates and listens to each student.
- Students participate in paired reading, taking turns reading to one another—either by reading and rereading the books or by taking turns to read alternate pages.

It is important to emphasize that students must have an opportunity to read to the teacher individually so that they engage actively with the text and the teacher can offer error correction. This is also the time when the teacher can assess their decoding skills and their phonic knowledge.

For extension, as students progress through the program and learn to read more fluently, the teachers can support students to read with expression and prosody. For example, adjusting their pitch, pace, and emphasis. This helps students to improve their reading fluency, improve their understanding of texts, and make reading more enjoyable. In Stages 16–20 of the program, the activity book introduces a **Reading fluency** exercise. Here, students are presented with an extract from the story and are instructed to read it twice. The first reading emphasizes fluency and accuracy.

The second reading focuses on expressive reading, helping to bring the text to life.

Step 3: Application for spelling

To strengthen letter formation skills, it is important to integrate multisensory activities early on. Before progressing to writing complete words like "sit," ensure students have practiced forming individual letters such as 's,' 'a,' 't,' 'i,' and 'm.' This can include activities like skywriting, where students trace the letters in the air while saying the corresponding sounds, and practicing writing each letter multiple times before attempting to write words.

Letter formation activities are not provided in the lesson plans in this manual. Students should have regular opportunities throughout the weeks to practice forming letters correctly, ensuring they are adequately prepared for writing tasks involving complete words.

In this step, students practice writing the graphemes they have learned in the previous lessons. The teacher should encourage the students to say the sounds as they write them and to blend the sounds in each word together.

Following this, the students can progress to writing entire words. Students can engage in various activities designed to reinforce this skill. For instance, they might participate in exercises like **Fill in all the missing sounds** activity, which challenges students to identify and write the missing sounds in words.

Additionally, the activity books include **Sentence dictation** activities. During these activities, students should be encouraged to sound out each word as they spell it. This practice not only enhances their spelling skills but also reinforces their understanding of how individual sounds come together to form words within the context of a sentence.

Step 4: Comprehension and consolidation

In this step, the teacher revisits the story, reading it aloud to help students consolidate their understanding.

Following the reading, students engage in a variety of comprehension activities. For example, the **Retelling the story** activity found in the activity books contains pictures and words on a photocopiable page. Students retell the story or create their own story using the pictures and word cards provided. Additional comprehension exercises are also available in the activity books, offering a range of options for further reading practice or support.

Step 5: Tracking progress

In this final step, the focus shifts to monitoring and assessing the progress students have made with the new phonic skills and sounds they have learned. To facilitate this, teachers can draw from a range of activities designed for formative assessments.

For example, the **Bookmark** in the activity books contains lists of words that can be used for practicing reading and spelling. Teachers can use these bookmarks to conduct quick, formative assessments of each student's progress.

Additionally, the Dandelion Launchers series of activity books include **Reading certificates**. These can be used to track each student's progress through the reading stages, and they also help to encourage and motivate the students.

Stages 8–15 introduces a **Spelling assessment** activity at the end of each stage. Use these to assess students' ability to spell the sounds they have learned.

Additional activities to supplement lessons

Additional activities can be found in the activity books and online teaching resources. These can be used to widen literacy development, but they also offer the flexibility to create differentiated lessons to meet the diverse needs of students. They can be used to address gaps in understanding, enhance punctuation and comprehension skills, or provide extension for more advanced students. Here are some examples.

Matching upper to lower case/Fishing game: These activities can be used for teaching and practicing recognition of lower case and upper case letters.

Punctuation: Introduced in the VCe Spellings Activities, this activity involves giving students an extract from a story with missing capital letters and periods. Students identify the correct placement and quantity of these punctuation marks. This exercise is useful for reinforcing punctuation rules and writing skills.

Word trail cards: This activity features pictures and words to offer an interactive reading activity. Students find and read the corresponding word to each picture, thereby promoting word recognition and reading fluency. It also helps to build sequencing skills as students follow the trail from one card to the next.

Timed reading: This activity involves students reading a series of words as quickly as they can, recording their times in three attempts. This repetitive practice can help to improve a student's reading pace and fluency.

Reading practice cards: In Stages 16–20, word cards are introduced for reading practice. These cards provide examples of words containing sounds the students have just learned. These pages can be photocopied for use in a matching game format or to introduce new vocabulary, offering a more structured approach to reading practice.

Stepping stones or **Reading game:** Using counters and dice, players read aloud words or letter sounds they land on during each turn. These games not only make learning fun but also provide practice in reading and phonic skills.

Four-in-a-row game: In this fun and interactive game, players read a word and place a counter on it, aiming to get four counters in a row (horizontally, vertically, or diagonally).

Splitting two-syllable words: Later in the program, students are introduced to two-syllable words. In this activity, students practice splitting words into syllables, writing each syllable, then reassembling them while vocalizing each syllable. This improves phonemic awareness and students' understanding of word structure.

Parallel books

Lesson plans for Stages 1–20 use the Dandelion Launchers series as the lesson resources; however, Phonic Books has parallel books in the same series and in the Dandelion Launchers Extras, Dandelion World, and Dandelion Readers Sets 1–3 that can be used to teach the same lessons. These alternative or supplementary resources are clearly indicated in the lesson plans, specifying which parallel books align with each lesson. This provides teachers with the flexibility to vary their teaching materials and cater to different preferences.

In the subsequent section on teaching methods, there is a more in-depth exploration of how to effectively implement these techniques. It includes specific references to the activity books and offers practical guidance on how to integrate these resources into a multisensory teaching approach.

TEACHING METHODS

This section expands on the teaching methods mentioned in the preceding section on lesson plan structure, connecting them to the program's activity books. It provides practical tips for integrating these methods and resources into your lessons. The figure below shows an example of an activity from one of the activity books.

The top of each page clearly indicates the specific stage and the phonic skills being targeted.

Teacher instructions at the bottom of the page offer step-by-step directions for teaching the activities.

Activities can be photocopied, allowing for widespread use for multiple students.

Introducing new letter sounds

In the Phonic Books program, multiple letter sounds are introduced in each lesson. This provides students with an immediate foundation for word creation. In the second and subsequent lesson plans, previously learned sounds should be reviewed in short bursts of revision.

An important part of this process is demonstrating the correct pronunciation of each sound, e.g. modeling the consonant sounds without the 'uh' sound: /m/ and not /muh/. Learning to pronounce the sounds precisely will help beginner readers to blend them into recognizable words.

After modeling the sound, encourage students to carefully watch and replicate the sound.

Employing a multisensory approach in teaching new letter sounds can improve the effectiveness of the learning process. Using **Sound cards** or **Word-building cards** from the activity books can be useful for modeling these new sounds.

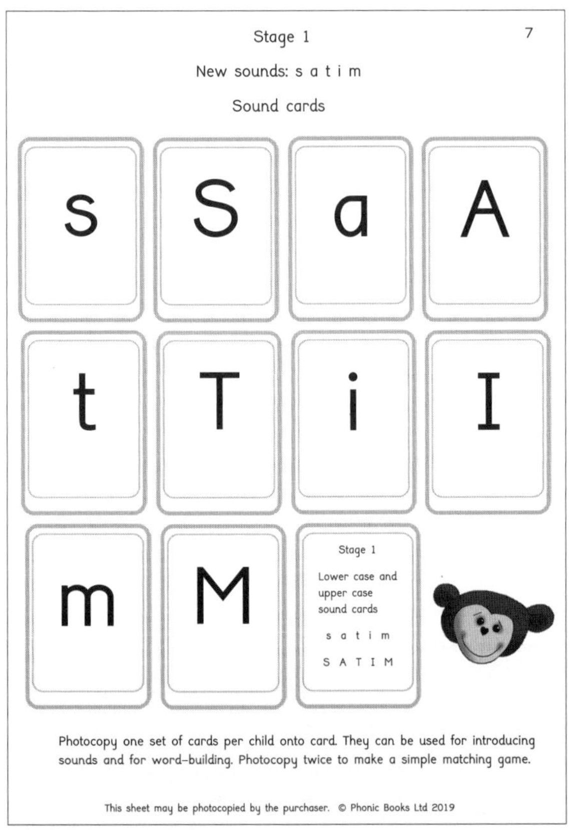

How to teach word building

Word building is the most effective activity to teach segmenting, blending, and spelling. Word building teaches segmenting with letters. **Segmenting** is the ability to separate sounds in words. The smallest sounds are called phonemes. We use segmenting when we sound out a new word, for example /k/ /a/ /t/ → "cat." We say the sounds separately and then we push them together to make a word.

We also use segmenting when we spell. When spelling the word "cat," we need to segment the word into the sounds /k/ /a/ /t/ and then spell those sounds with letters. Many programs introduce segmenting as an oral activity. For example, students listen to the sounds in words and then count them or place counters to represent the sounds.

While these activities may develop segmenting, they are not the most effective way to learn this skill. It is important to recognize that when we speak, we don't say all the sounds precisely. Many sounds get gobbled up, or clipped, and others change depending on where they are in the word.

Research has shown that teaching segmenting is more effective when introduced with letters. Oral segmenting is only a stepping stone that has no benefit on its own.

How to teach segmenting with letters

The most effective way of teaching segmenting is through a word-building activity. The teacher asks the student to build a word. This entails listening to the sounds in the word, placing the letters into the correct sequence, then sounding out the word and reading it. This should also be combined with writing the word as this links reading and spelling.

Step 1: Lines scaffold the word

Draw the number of lines on a whiteboard that correspond to the number of sounds in the word. In this example, draw three lines for the word "mat." Place the cards needed to build the word jumbled up above the lines.

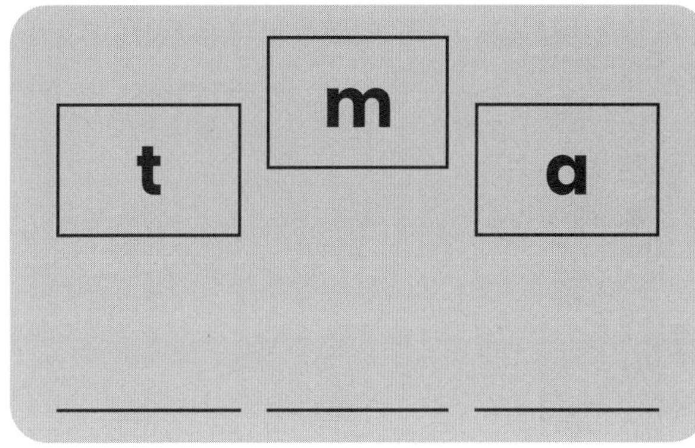

Step 2: Build the word

Tell the student that you are going to build the word "mat." Point to the first line and ask the student to listen to the first sound as you say the word slowly. Move your finger along the lines in sync with the sounds in the word.

When the student says /m/, ask them to bring down the letter for /m/ onto the first line. Repeat this process with the remaining letters/sounds in the word.

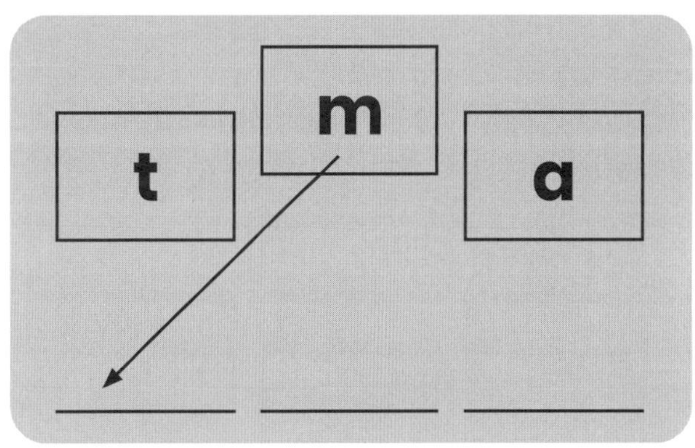

Step 3: Sound out and blend into the word

Now that the student has built the word, ask them to sound out the word and blend the sounds together into a word: /m/ /a/ /t/ → "mat."

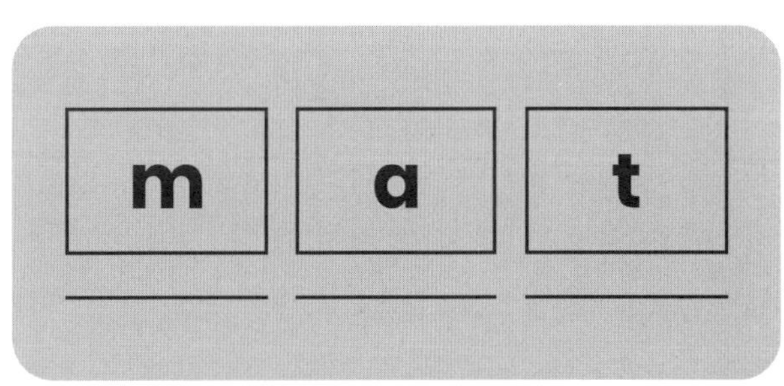

Step 4: Spell the word

Ask the student to spell the word under the lines and to say the sounds as they write each letter.

Finally, the student sounds out the word they have written and reads it.

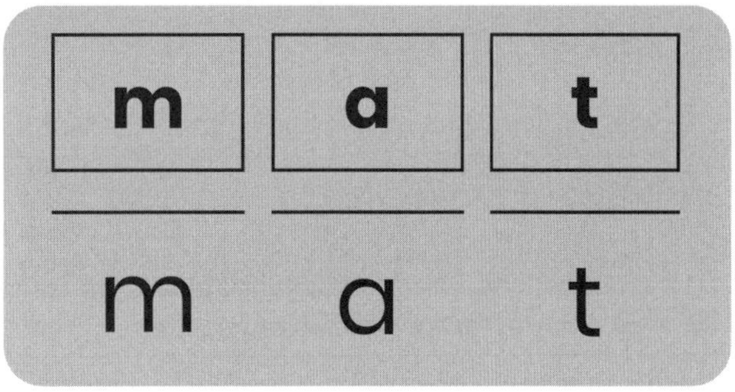

As you can see, word-building activities that use letters give the student a visual representation for the sounds in words. We show them the sequence of the sounds and how they are represented by letters. This is a direct and effective way of teaching segmenting and blending. It also demonstrates the link between reading and spelling in a clear way.

Word-building activities are a core feature of the activity books in the program. In the early stages, this activity takes the form of letters and picture cards, like in this example from Dandelion Launchers, Stage 1.

28

Stage 2

New sounds: n o p

Word-building cards

P p m

p t P

i o a

Photocopy this page onto card. Cut out the letters and pictures. Encourage the child to build the words for the pictures using sounds. It is important to focus on sounds first, and then find the letters that represent these sounds.
Picture cards: Pip pot Pam

This sheet may be photocopied by the purchaser. © Phonic Books Ltd 2019

As the program progresses, a more advanced word-building activity is introduced, as demonstrated in the example from Dandelion Launchers, Stage 8.

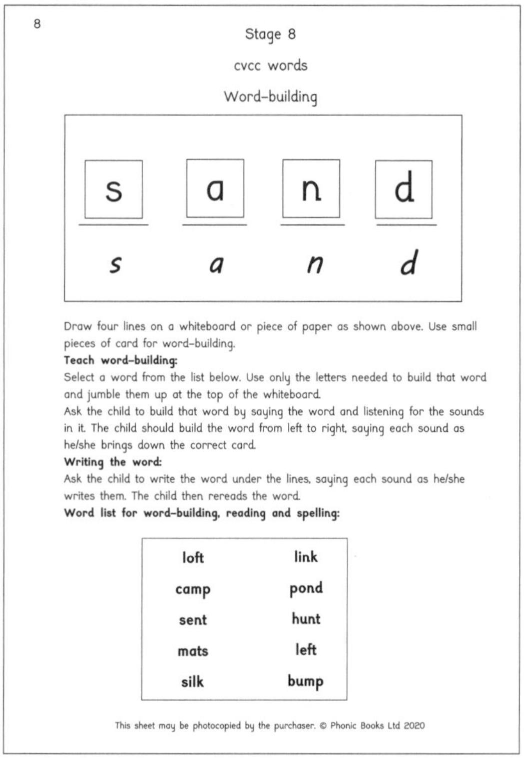

8

Stage 8

cvcc words

Word-building

s a n d

s a n d

Draw four lines on a whiteboard or piece of paper as shown above. Use small pieces of card for word-building.

Teach word-building:
Select a word from the list below. Use only the letters needed to build that word and jumble them up at the top of the whiteboard.
Ask the child to build that word by saying the word and listening for the sounds in it. The child should build the word from left to right, saying each sound as he/she brings down the correct card.

Writing the word:
Ask the child to write the word under the lines, saying each sound as he/she writes them. The child then rereads the word.

Word list for word-building, reading and spelling:

loft	link
camp	pond
sent	hunt
mats	left
silk	bump

This sheet may be photocopied by the purchaser. © Phonic Books Ltd 2020

This activity involves using a whiteboard or paper with lines drawn underneath each sound. Small card pieces are used to construct words. The activity starts by the teacher selecting a word from a specified list, then jumbling its letters at the top of the whiteboard. The student then builds the word by articulating and identifying the sounds, arranging the cards from left to right. Each sound is emphasized as the corresponding card is placed. Afterwards, the student writes the word below the lines, saying each sound during the writing process.

Three blending methods

Blending is a pivotal skill in learning to read, where students combine individual sounds (phonemes) to form whole words. Here are three distinct methods designed to enhance a student's ability to decode and blend words. Each method offers a unique approach to breaking down words into sounds and merging them to form complete words.

Method 1: Decode and blend

"Say the sounds and read the word."

/m/ /a/ /t/ ➡ "mat"

m a t

The student points to and says the sounds in the word one at a time, pointing to each sound. Then they move their finger under the whole word, blending all the sounds into the word. This first method has a greater load on working memory relative to the next two methods.

Method 2: Stretch and blend

"Stretch the sounds and push them together to read the word."

/m/ /a/ /t/ ➡ "mat"

m a t

The teacher points to the first letter/sound, asking the student to say the sound and stretch it until their finger reaches the next sound in the word. The teacher moves their finger under the whole word, as the student blends all the sounds in the word.

Method 3: Blend and add

"Blend the first two sounds, then add the next sound."

m a

'm a'

m a t

'ma' + t ⟶ m a t

The teacher conceals the third letter/sound. Next, the teacher moves their finger under the first two sounds and asks the learner to blend just two sounds, e.g. 'm' + 'a' = 'ma.' Then the teacher repeats 'ma.' The teacher reveals the last letter/sound and asks the student to add 't.' Finally, the teacher points under the whole word as the student reads "mat."

Methods 2 and 3 have a lesser load on working memory relative to the first method.

How to write a word chain

A **word chain** is a list of words used to develop phonemic awareness skills: blending, segmenting, and phoneme manipulation. These are the underlying skills needed for reading. Word-chain activities are the most effective way to develop these skills.

In a word-chain activity, the teacher will ask the student to build a word (with letter cards or letters) and read it. The student is then asked to make a change to the word; for example, "Change the word 'pot' to 'pit'." The student will need to identify where the change in the word has occurred and then change, remove, or add the letter needed to read the new word.

What does a word chain look like?

This is an example of a word chain:

Letters: s, a, t, i, m, n, o, p

Word chain: nip—nap—tap—top—mop—map—sap—sip—tip

Many programs include word-chain activities, but it is useful to know how to write one. This skill allows the teacher to design a word-chain activity that can address a specific difficulty a student may have. For example, the student may confuse the sound and spelling of /ch/ and /sh/. A word chain to address this difficulty would look like this:

Letters: m, u, sh, ch, n, b, f, i, p, a, r, c
Word chain: mush—much—munch—bunch—bun—shun—shin—fin—finch—inch—pinch—pin—bin—ban—bash—brash—brush—crush—crash

The two examples above use real words, and this is suitable for young students. For older students, you can also use nonsense word chains. A typical example would look like this:

Letters: b, l, i, n, a, o, t, u
Word chain: blin—blan—lan—lon—lont—lunt—lut—blut

Here are some guidelines for creating a word chain:

1. Use one syllable words.
2. Use spellings from the simple code. It can get very confusing if vowel teams are included as many of them can be pronounced in different ways.
3. The word chain can include changing sounds, removing sounds, and adding sounds.
4. Make only one change at a time.

How to teach reading

One of the primary goals in teaching phonics is to equip students with the skills necessary to decode and comprehend text effectively. When students are reading, encourage them to sound out each word phonetically and then blend these sounds to form words. This lays the groundwork for developing fluent reading skills, as it enables students to approach unfamiliar words with confidence. Slow, laboured reading can interfere with comprehension. When a student reads very slowly, reread each sentence after them to maintain comprehension of the text.

Once students are comfortable with sounding out and blending words, a next step could be to read a book from a previous lesson for a second time or multiple times to enhance fluency. This repetition helps to consolidate students' decoding skills. As students revisit the text, they begin to transition from mechanical decoding to reading with greater fluency.

This can be progressed to teaching them to vary their pitch, pace, and emphasis according to the words and punctuation in the text. Reading with expression not only makes the reading experience more fun but also aids in comprehension, as it brings the text to life and highlights its meaning.

How to correct reading errors

One of the most important elements of learning is receiving error feedback. With every error feedback, the student can adjust their knowledge or skill and can fine-tune them and make their reading increasingly accurate. Making and correcting errors is a great learning opportunity!

Reading with our students is a fantastic opportunity for error feedback. But before we can address the error, we need to know what kind of error the reader is making. Here are a few tips:

1. Error feedback should be a positive experience in which the student can succeed. So, after the feedback has taken place, the student should be able

to use the new information and read a word or sentence successfully.

2. It is very helpful to use a pointer or a pencil to show the student where the error occurred in the word. The error can even occur between letters on the page, so accurate pointing is essential.
3. When the student has read the word correctly, it is helpful to reread the whole sentence so that they can reread the correct word in the context of the text.

What kinds of reading errors do students make?

Lack of Alphabetic Code knowledge

Many students make reading errors because they have insufficient knowledge of the Alphabetic Code. For example, when a student reads the word "goat" as /g/ /o/ /a/ /t/, we can see that they don't know that the grapheme 'oa' spells the sound /oe/.

So, how can feedback be given? Point to both letters and say: "These two letters represent one sound: /oe/. Sound out the word with /oe/ here (pointing to the letters 'oa')." The student then blends the sounds together: /g/ /oe/ /t/ → "goat."

Not matching sounds to graphemes (letter/s)

Students may add or omit sounds when they read. To develop reading accuracy, they will need to match the graphemes to the sounds in the word. Here are typical examples of reading errors.

Adding sounds: When a student reads the word "back" as "black," we can see that they are adding the sound /l/. To give feedback, point to the word and say: "You read "black" but there is no /l/ here (pointing to the place the 'l' would be in the word "black"). Sound out the word." The student should then sound the word correctly: /b/ /a/ /k/ → "back."

Omitting sounds: When a student reads the word "frog" as "fog," we can see that they are omitting a sound in the word. To give feedback, point to the letter 'r' and say: "There is a /r/ here. Sound out the word with the /r/ here (pointing to the letter 'r')." The student then sounds out the word pointing to the letters /f/ /r/ /o/ /g/ → "frog."

Reversing a word

When a student reads "was" for "saw," we can see that they have flipped the word. So, how can feedback be given? Ask the student to sound out the word. /s/ /aw/. Remind the student that 'aw' spells /aw/. Ask the student to blend the sounds into a word: /s/ /aw/ → "saw."

Developing vocabulary

Systematic synthetic phonics focuses on the mechanics of learning to read: developing the skills to sound out, blend to read, and segment to spell. It is a structured, progressive program towards reading fluency. However, alongside that process, it's critical to develop the broader reading skills: prosody, pace, comprehension, and vocabulary. Phonics success is based on careful, steady progression, so that students are only exposed to words in their books which contain the sounds and high-frequency words they know. Yet, every reading experience is an opportunity to develop a student's wider vocabulary, through questioning and discussion. For example: books within the Dandelion World Series include nonfiction Knowledge Builder pages intended for children and adults to read together, which help to reinforce vocabulary and enhance comprehension skills, by encouraging the student to think about what they have read.

Talking about the words students decode: exploring meaning, looking at patterns, and discussing synonyms and antonyms will not only help secure comprehension and reading for meaning, but will also grow and develop a student's more general language knowledge. For example, while reading the word "swift," students can explore synonyms like "quick" and "fast," and antonyms such as "slow." Discussing these words not only enhances vocabulary but also clarifies the concept of speed as it applies to different contexts, thereby enhancing students' understanding of linguistic relationships.

Oracy is one of the key elements of vocabulary development; therefore, alongside the phonics skills, high-quality discussion around texts furthers the learning opportunities and outcomes.

There are lots of different ways to structure the discussion and get the most out of every page in a reading book—at any level.

For instance, in Book 3a: Sam's Bag (Dandelion Launchers), the following prompts could be used around pages 3 and 4 in order to extend the language around the book.

- What words rhyme with "bag"? (tag, sag, rag, nag)
- Where is Tam? (at the bus stop)
- Who else is in the picture? (Sam)
- What might you put in a bag? (pens and pencils, books, water bottle, lunchbox)

- What can you see on the bag? (a name tag)
- Whose name is on the tag? (Tam)
- How do you think Tam feels? (happy, excited, pleased)

Likewise, at a phonetically more challenging level there are still plenty of discursive opportunities, for example in Book 20: Cuddles (Dandelion Launchers) the following prompts could be used around the content on pages 3–4:

- What is another word for "gobble"? (guzzle, gulp, swallow)
- What is another word for "snuggle"? (hug, huddle, cuddle, snuggle)
- What is the opposite of tidbit? (a large plate of food)
- What words on the pages rhyme, and can you think of any others that rhyme with them? (gobbles, guzzles, cuddles, snuggles, nuzzles)
- How do you think Floss will feel after eating the food? (happy, full, content, or still hungry)

How to teach reading comprehension

For students to become fluent readers, they need to be able to understand what they are reading. Students should be encouraged to discuss what happens in the stories and to give spoken answers to comprehension questions. This improves student's understanding of language, develops their wider vocabulary and increases their interest in learning to read.

The activity books contain various types of activities to enable students to put their comprehension skills into practice. For example, Dandelion Launchers Stages 1–7 Activities includes **Retelling the story** activities where students retell the story or create their own story using the pictures and word cards provided on the page.

Other comprehension activities include matching words to the correct pictures from the story, or this **Make a book** activity where students read the text and then draw a picture to match the text on each page.

As the program progresses, more activities are introduced, with increasing emphasis on reading comprehension. For instance, in the VCe Spellings Activities and Dandelion Readers Level 1 Activities, the **What happens next?** activity is introduced.

16

Stage 1

Book 1a: Sam, Tam, Tim

Retelling the story

Tim | Tam | Sam

sit | sat

This page can be photocopied onto card. Cut out these pictures for retelling the story or for children to make their own story. Picture cards are arranged in story order. Choose whether to number them on the back. Word cards can also be used to reinforce vocabulary.

This sheet may be photocopied by the purchaser. © Phonic Books Ltd 2019

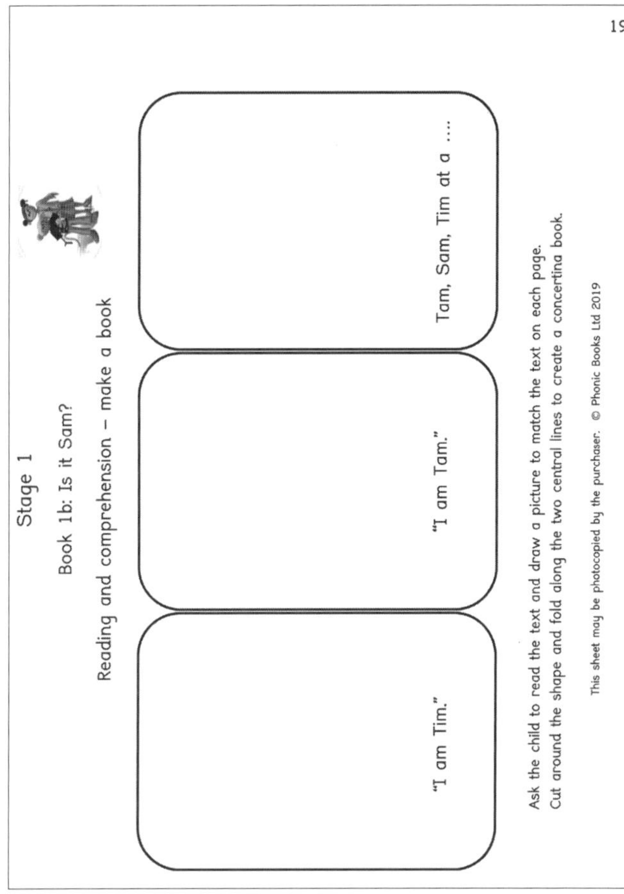

19

Stage 1

Book 1b: Is it Sam?

Reading and comprehension – make a book

Tam, Sam, Tim at a ....

"I am Tam."

"I am Tim."

Ask the child to read the text and draw a picture to match the text on each page.

Cut around the shape and fold along the two central lines to create a concertina book.

This sheet may be photocopied by the purchaser. © Phonic Books Ltd 2019

Here, students are presented with a passage from a story and are invited to underline their favorite part, followed by creating a drawing that corresponds to the narrative. Additionally, the **Find the untruths** activity challenges students with a story passage containing deliberate errors. Their task is to identify these mistakes, helping to develop their attention to detail and comprehension skills.

How to change bad guessing habits?

Many students will have been encouraged to use guessing strategies, such as guessing clues from the picture or the context, and/or skipping the word and reading to the end of the sentence to guess what a word might be. Despite research indicating the limited effectiveness of these strategies, they continue to be widely adopted in educational settings.

Guessing strategies may seem to help students reading a very simple, repetitive text; however, they let students down once the pictures fall away. Guessing leads to inaccurate reading, which affects comprehension. The clues for decoding a word are in the letters on the page and that is where students need to focus their attention.

Many older readers have bad guessing habits that are difficult to undo. One of the ways we can try and change these deeply ingrained habits is to reward the student when they demonstrate decoding. This can be in the shape of counters that the student accumulates as they work out the words by sounding them out.

A popular game is the "chest of gold." The game involves students earning yellow counters as they decode their way through a text. If the student resorts to guessing, the teacher gets the gold from the chest. This game can help the student to focus on the task at hand.

How to teach letter formation

Following reading and comprehension activities, the next step is to teach students how to practice writing the graphemes they have learned.

First, learning how to grip a pencil correctly is an important step for developing neat handwriting. The pencil should rest comfortably between the thumb and index finger, supported by the middle finger, with the other two fingers curled inwards. With their hands resting on the table, students should learn to move the pencil forward using their hand muscles. Regular practice in letter formation and careful monitoring of each student's technique during dictation exercises are key to cultivating long-term neat handwriting and preventing the development of poor habits.

When teaching letter formation, it is recommended to use lined paper that will demonstrate the proportions of ascender and descender letters. This way the students can practice forming letters correctly from the get go.

Teachers play a vital role in this learning process. They can demonstrate letter formation effectively by writing on the whiteboard or visually tracing the letters' movements in the air.

Book 2: Pete 37

Find the untruths

Reading comprehension

The kitchen was a mess. Dad made Steve, the robot. The robot dropped the trash on Mom's bed. The glass smashed. He cracked the sink in the kitchen. Mom had to press 'delete' to stop him. Mom had to do the dishes.

There are **5** untruths in this story. Can you spot them?

Ask the student to read the text carefully and underline any 'untruth' that has been planted in the story.

This sheet may be photocopied by the purchaser. © Phonic Books Ltd 2021

How to teach spelling

The activity books offer a variety of exercises to practice spelling, such as **Fill in the missing sounds**, where students are given incomplete words for them to fill in with the correct letter for the missing sound. To reinforce their learning, students should be encouraged to vocalize the sounds as they write, and then blend these sounds together while forming each word.

They also include activities, such as **Fill in all the missing sounds**, where students fill in every letter for all the missing sounds in the words they've just practiced in the preceding activity.

Finally, as students to progress towards more autonomous writing, the activity books also include **Sentence dictation** activities. These activities are accompanied by illustrative pictures, offering visual context to aid in comprehension. Students are encouraged to phonetically sound out the words as they spell them, reinforcing their understanding of the relationship between sounds and spelling.

Stage 2 29

New sounds: n o p

Fill in the missing sounds

P _ m _ a n m a _

c _ p p _ n P _ p

Fill in the missing sounds to complete the words. Encourage the child to say the sounds as they write them and then blend the three sounds in each word together to read the word.

This sheet may be photocopied by the purchaser. © Phonic Books Ltd 2019

How to do a dictation activity

Dictation is a great way to consolidate the bonds between reading and spelling. It is a controlled exercise where students can succeed because the teacher includes words with spellings the students have already learned. Unlike a story writing activity where the students will attempt to spell words they may not be able to encode yet, dictation provides a "safe" activity where all students can succeed.

Dictation can be done at word level or sentence level. Writing and spelling words is hugely taxing on working memory. The student must hear and understand the word or sentence. Then, they must hold it in working memory while retrieving a letter/s (grapheme) for each sound in each word. Some students may forget the word or part of the sentence. For this reason, it is important to follow a clear routine for dictation.

Dictation activities can serve as useful records of learning and identifying difficulties that students are experiencing. It can be done on small individual whiteboards or in notebooks. The teacher can photograph or keep these and identify any students who need further support.

Many students will still have difficulties forming letters correctly. The purpose of a dictation activity is to see how students use their phonics knowledge to encode words. If the words are illegible, letter formation should be addressed. If not, find another opportunity to work on letter formation.

14

Stage 1

Book 1a: Sam, Tam, Tim

Sentence dictation

"I __ ___."

___ ___.

Cut or fold the sheet along the dotted line above before offering to the child. Offer the sentences below as dictation. Encourage the child to sound out the words as they spell them.

1. "I am Sam." 2. Sam sat.

This sheet may be photocopied by the purchaser. © Phonic Books Ltd 2019

Single word dictation

Choose a list of words that the students have been learning. Make sure they have had sufficient practice reading and spelling these words. Say the word first; next, put it within the context of a sentence; and then repeat the word. This way the students can understand the word before they write it down. Pause after each word to check that all the students have finished writing.

The teacher can say, for example:

> "I am going to dictate some words and I would like you to write them down.
> dog. The dog barked. dog.
> bag. Gran has a bag. bag.
> gap. There is a gap in the road. gap."
> etc.

Sentence dictation

Writing a sentence is more taxing on working memory than remembering one word at a time and spelling it. Some students will find it difficult to hold the complete sentence in working memory. It is good practice to break any long sentences into parts to enable all students to keep up. After all, we are not checking working memory but how students represent the words with graphemes they have learned.

The teacher will need to decide if they provide their students with high-frequency words that have more complex spellings, for example "the." These words can be written on the board to remind the students how to spell them.

The teacher will also need to decide whether they will include capital letters and periods in this activity. This depends on whether this has been taught previously.

Dictated sentences will need to be decodable—this means that all the words, except a few necessary high-frequency words, will be within the knowledge of the students. The teacher can write these sentences or take them from a decodable book the students have read. For beginner readers, just one or two sentences will be sufficient for this activity.

The teacher can say:
"I am going to dictate a sentence.
I would like you to listen to it and then say it.
Then, write it down.
'Bob got on the top.'"

The teacher repeats:
"'Bob got on the top.' Now you say it."
Students repeat:
"'Bob got on the top.'"
Students write the sentence.

How to teach high-frequency words

High-frequency words are frequently used words that can potentially present a challenge to students: they cannot easily read or write them through decoding, such as blending and listening for sounds. This difficulty arises because these words often contain letter–sound combinations that the students have not yet learned.

The program gradually introduces high-frequency words to expand the students' vocabulary. The scheme of work charts, found on page 28, list all the high-frequency words introduced in each book covered by the lesson plans in this manual. Furthermore, each Reader conveniently lists the high-frequency words featured in its story at the beginning of the book, providing an easy reference for both students and teachers.

The chart on pages 47–48 provides the first 300 high-frequency words taught in the program.

Simple spellings

vc
am
an
at
if
in
it
on
up
us

/ck/
ba**ck**
bla**ck**
du**ck**

v
a

vcc
and
end
its

cvc /a/
b**a**t
c**a**n
c**a**t
r**a**n
d**a**d
h**a**d
m**a**n
s**a**t

cvcc
best
fast
help
just
jump
land
left
last
list
milk
must
nest
next
went

cvc /e/
b**e**d
g**e**t
l**e**t
m**e**n
b**e**ll
r**e**d
s**e**t
t**e**n
w**e**ll
y**e**s

ccvc
from
still
spot
stop
gran
step

cvc /i/
b**i**g
d**i**d
h**i**m
s**i**t
s**i**x
m**i**ss

/th/ (voiced)
that
the
them
then
this
wi**th**

/th/ (unvoiced)
think

cvc /o/
b**o**x
d**o**g
g**o**t
h**o**t
m**o**m
n**o**t

/w/
when
which

/sh/
fi**sh**
wi**sh**

/ch/
mu**ch**
su**ch**

cvc /u/
b**u**t
c**u**t
f**u**n
r**u**n

/z/
a**s**
is
ha**s**
hi**s**

/ng/
alo**ng**
bri**ng**
ki**ng**
lo**ng**
so**ng**
thi**ng**

/v/
gi**ve**
ha**ve**
li**ve**
o**f**

Complex spellings

/ae/

cake, came, gave, late, made, make, name, take, day, may, play, say, way, always, away, great, eight, they

/e/

again, said, head, read, bread, any, many, friends

/oe/

go, going, no, so, both, cold, don't, old, hold, told, most, only, open, boat, coat, home, those, grow, know, own, show, though

/ie/

I, child, find, kind, five, like, line, time, white, write, by, my, fly, try, why, high, night, right

/i/

been

/ee/

be, he, me, she, we, even, these, feel, feet, green, keep, need, see, sleep, tree, three, each, eat, leave, tea, please, read, baby, carry, every, really, very, key

/or/

or, door, floor, corn, for, horse, morning, before, more, short

/oi/

boy, toy

/ow/

about, around, found, house, mouse, out, our, round, ground, down, cow, how, now, town

Uncommon spellings

one, once, two, people, everyone

/er/

her, after, better, ever, father, letter, never, over, paper, river, under, water, were, birds, first, girl, picture, work

/oo/

moon, do, to, into, who, together, cool, food, school, soon, too, group, new

Multisyllable words

American, children, different, little, magic, rabbit, suddenly

/aw/

all, fall, ball, call, small, walk, talk, saw

/ar/

are, car, dark, far, farm, hard, garden, park, start

/air/

air, bear, their, there, where

/u/

mother, does, come, some, was

/o/

what, want, watch

/oo/

look, book, good, look, took, wood, put, could, would

/ue/

use

How to teach multi-syllabic words

From Stage 17 onwards, two-syllable words are introduced. This is an important step in learning to read. We often assume that students can transfer their decoding and encoding skills from one-syllable words to words with more than one syllable, but many students struggle with this transition.

To read and spell words with more than one syllable, students need to be able to segment (chunk) longer words into syllables. At this point we begin to work on two levels of phonological processing—the larger, syllable level and at the same time the smaller phoneme level. Some students may find this confusing.

A good place to start is to get students attuned to syllables. It is helpful to explain that a syllable is a mouthful of a word, and that the chin drops between syllables. Children can practice listening to syllables by playing fun clapping games, e.g. clapping the syllables in their names, or the names of animals (elephant, hippopotamus). Once students are attuned into hearing syllables in words, we can begin with building words with more than one syllable.

How to build words with more than one syllable

Preparation: use a whiteboard and the sound cards needed to build the word. Place the sound cards jumbled up on the board.

1. Start with a compound word e.g. “laptop.”
2. Draw two lines on the board (one for each syllable) and ask the students to chunk the word “laptop” into syllables. Make sure that the students pronounce the syllables clearly: “lap” “top.”

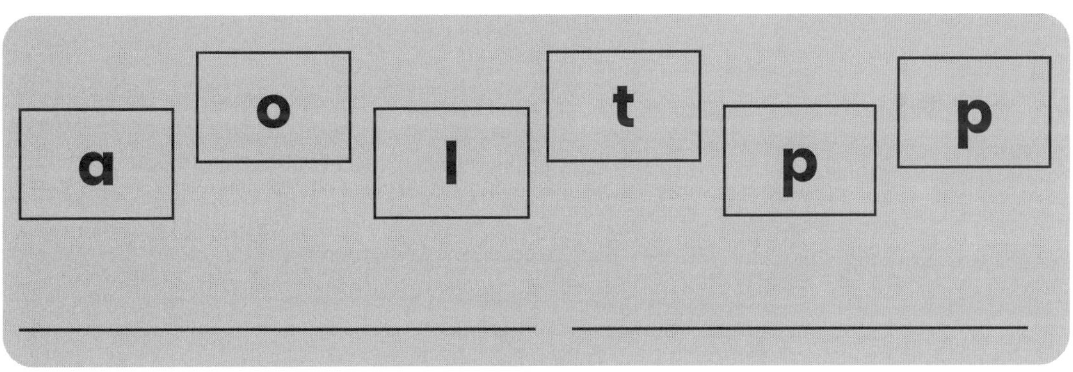

3. Ask the students to tell you the first syllable in the word “laptop” and point to the first line, moving your finger under the whole word as you say it.
4. Students reply “lap.”
5. Ask a student to build the syllable “lap” on the first line, pointing to the first line.

6. Ask the students what the second syllable in the word "laptop," moving your finger under the whole word as you do.
7. Students reply "top." Ask the students to build the syllable "top" on the second line.

l	a	p		t	o	p

8. Now ask all the students to read the word moving your finger as they read each syllable: "lap" "top."
9. Ask the students if they can read the word faster: "laptop."
10. Finally, ask the students to spell the word "laptop" and say each syllable as they spell the word.

laptop

Once the students are confident building, reading, and spelling compound words, the teacher can repeat this word-building activity with two-syllable words, using graphemes the students have learned.

Syllable chunking

Once the students have learned how to build and spell two-syllable words, it is important for them to practice chunking two-syllable words.

Once students have learned how to build and spell two-syllable words, it is important for them to practice chunking multisyllabic words into syllables. This will help them read longer words. When reading a two-syllable word, ask the student where the end of a "mouthful" of the syllable is. A syllable will often have a vowel. Ask the students to note how the jaw drops with every syllable. Students should mark the syllable split with a vertical line. The activities books and Phonic Books website offer many opportunities to do this.

The Activities books and Phonic Books website offer many opportunities to do this.

How to teach alternative spellings for vowel and consonant sounds

One of the difficult aspects of the Alphabetic Code is that sounds can be spelled in different ways. For example, the sound /ae/ can be spelled 'ai' (rain), 'ay' (day), 'a–e' (came), 'ea' (great), and 'a' (baby), and these are only the common spellings! As students learn more and more of the code, we want them to build a mental framework that incorporates this concept of multiple spellings. We want our students to understand that sounds can be represented in different ways and to recognize these spelling patterns when they read. Later, they will need to learn which spelling fits in which word. How can we teach this?

Word sorting

The best way to demonstrate how a sound can be spelled in different ways is through sorting activities. After teaching the students about the graphemes 'ai' and 'ay' for example (ideally through word building), the students should be given words to sort according to spelling. This activity enables the students to compare and contrast words. It will often reveal typical spelling patterns, for example, that the spelling 'ay' comes at the end of a base word while 'ai' will usually appear in the middle of the word.

How many alternatives?

The teacher must decide how many alternatives to include when the students carry out this sorting activity. This will depend on the program being followed. It is important not to present these spellings in an isolated way as the students will not make the connection between them. If this activity is part of an intervention program, it is helpful to introduce the different spellings in a gradual way. Always include previous learning so that the concept of "one sound—different spellings" is built on what the students already know.

Word wall in the classroom

A great way to reinforce the different spellings for a sound is to display them in the classroom. This display will remind students of the different ways to spell a sound. New words can be added to the display as they are encountered. This display will then become a useful spelling tool. For example, if a student spells the word "came" as "cam," the teacher can direct them to the display and say, "Use the a–e spelling in this word."

The language we use

We can reinforce the concept that a sound can be spelled in different ways by the language we use. When a student encounters an additional way to spell the sound, we say, "Yes, this is another way to spell the sound /ae/." This dispels the notion that there is only one way to spell the sound /ae/ and develops a flexible approach to a complex code. Students learn that when they spell a sound there are a number of options, and they will need to choose the correct option when they spell a word.

How (and why) we need to teach the schwa sound

Did you know that the schwa is the most common sound in the English language? This is because there is a schwa sound in most multisyllabic words. Additionally, did you know that the schwa can be pronounced in more than one way?

What is a schwa sound?

In most English accents, multisyllabic words are pronounced with at least one stressed syllable. A schwa sound is a "weak" or "lazy" vowel sound in an unstressed syllable. For example, take the word "mountain." The stress is on the first syllable: "<u>moun</u>-tain." The sound of the vowel in the second (unstressed) syllable is a schwa sound: "<u>moun</u>-t**ai**n." This schwa sound is gobbled up and can sound like a clipped /u/ or /i/. A schwa sound is never present in a stressed syllable.

Why do we need to teach the schwa sound?

Once students can decode two-syllable words, they can read them with the stress patterns they know from their speech. For example, when a student has learned to decode the word "mountain," they will instinctively pronounce the word with the stress on the first syllable. They will do this because they already have the word in their lexicon. If the word is new to the student, it is important to teach them how to pronounce it with the correct syllable stress.

The schwa is a spelling issue—not a reading issue. When students spell a multisyllabic word, they will listen to the sounds in the word and all too often they will spell the "lazy" schwa sound incorrectly because they hear the clipped /u/ or /i/ sound. They may even omit the sound altogether. For example, students may spell the word "mount**ai**n" as "mount**u**n," "mount**i**n," "mount**e**n," or even "mountn."

How do we teach students to spell the schwa sound correctly?

Step 1

Model the word and ask the student to say the word with the correct syllable stress.

Step 2

Ask the students to split the word into syllables and identify the stressed syllable.

moun-tain

Step 3

Ask the students to find the schwa sound in the "weak" syllable.

moun-t**ai**n

Step 4

At this point the teacher can introduce the "spelling voice." Students are encouraged to sound out the schwa as it is spelled. For example: when spelling the word "mountain," the teacher will show the students how to say an exaggerated /ai/ sound as they spell the second syllable. They say the sounds /m/ /ou/ /n/–/t/ /**ae**/ /n/. The /ae/ sound is exaggerated to remind the student how to spell the word. Now the student can underline the spelling of the schwa sound. Other words with the same spelling pattern and stress can be tackled at the same time, for example "fountain," "captain," and "certain."

mountain

How to teach vocabulary when reading a decodable book

Decodable books often include target words that students may not know. There are many reasons why students may not know words in a text:

- The word may be unusual.
- The students may have limited language as English language learners.
- The students may have a language disability.
- The students may have had limited opportunities to read books at home.

Learning new vocabulary is beneficial for all students. It helps them develop their expressive and receptive language. This will also develop their comprehension as they become readers.

When we teach new vocabulary, we want our students to learn how a word sounds and how it is spelled. We want them to make connections to words they already know, so the new vocabulary is stored securely in long-term memory and can be retrieved when needed.

Here is how we recommend teaching students new words encountered in a decodable book. The example here is the word "growl" from Book 6: Mr Brown from the Dandelion Readers, Level 1 series.

1. Demonstrate how letters map onto the sounds in the word.

gr**ow**l or g | r | **ow** | l

2. Say the word clearly. Ask the students to repeat the word. All too often students are not confident in pronouncing new words. /g/ /r /ow/ /l/ → "growl." This is particularly important when the word has more than one syllable as students need to know which syllable to stress.
3. Define the word. For example, "The word 'growl' means to make a deep, rough sound." (A simple definition can often be found in the decodable book.)

4. Give an example from the decodable book. Ask questions, such as, "Why does Meg growl in the story?" Students can answer in their own words. ("Meg growls because of the postman, Mr Brown.")

5. Ask the students to give another example of when a dog might "growl."
6. Ask the students to compare with synonyms. "Is 'roar' a stronger word than 'growl'?"
7. Have the students act out or describe a scenario where an animal might growl. This could be a dog guarding its territory or a cat feeling threatened. This helps them understand the context in which "growl" is used.
8. Keep both words on the board and revisit throughout the week.

How to read a nonfiction decodable book

While the main lesson plans in this teacher guide predominantly focus on Dandelion Launchers, which is centred around fiction, this section delves into nonfiction decoding. This is particularly relevant for teachers who would like to incorporate resources from the Dandelion World series, a nonfiction parallel series to the Dandelion Launchers.

Nonfiction decodable books are wonderful reading resources. They combine two essential parts of reading: word recognition (decoding) and world knowledge (language comprehension and subject vocabulary).

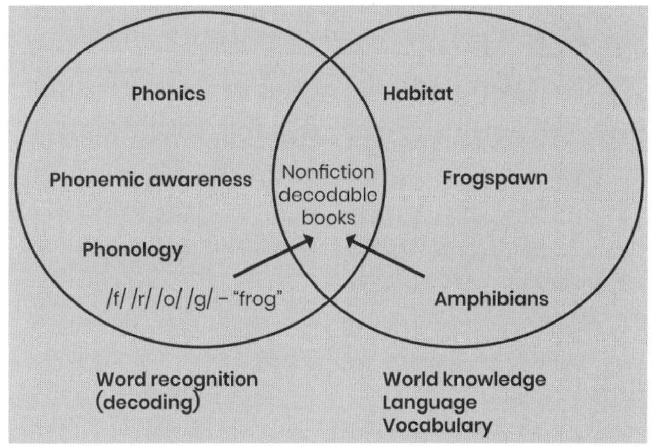

Educators now recognize that world knowledge has an important part to play in reading comprehension. Students who lack world knowledge can't make sense of a text that presumes they have general knowledge. For example, a sentence that describes a character as a "fossil" will have little meaning to a student who has not learned about what fossils are and how they are created.

The Dandelion World series features "Knowledge Builder" pages that include pictures and text about the subject of the book. The series also includes a glossary so that students can learn new words that are beyond their decoding skills. By including knowledge-building pages, which are intended for student to read with an adult, the students can develop their world knowledge orally without being limited only to a text they can read. As learning about a subject supports reading comprehension, it is advisable to immerse the students in the knowledge first and only then read the decodable book.

Before reading the decodable text, teachers can start by asking the students what they know about the topic. This way new learning is built on what the students already understand and know. Then teachers can read the "Knowledge Builder" pages to the students and teach the vocabulary. Next, they can then ask questions to ensure that the students have understood the subject and vocabulary. They then read the decodable books and facilitate a discussion. Finally, teachers can link the text the students have decoded to the subject knowledge already learned.

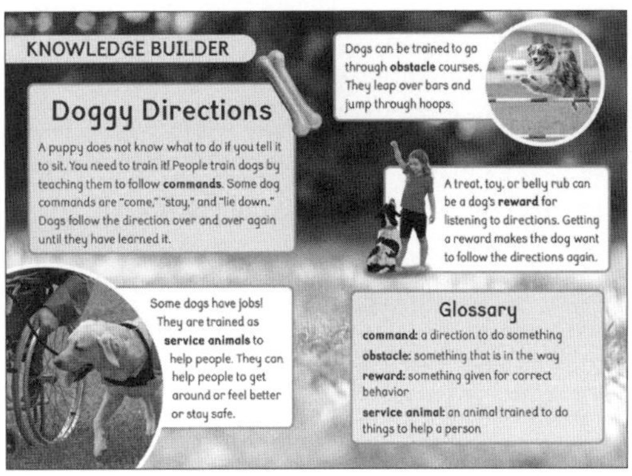

KNOWLEDGE BUILDER

Doggy Directions

A puppy does not know what to do if you tell it to sit. You need to train it! People train dogs by teaching them to follow **commands**. Some dog commands are "come," "stay," and "lie down." Dogs follow the direction over and over again until they have learned it.

Dogs can be trained to go through **obstacle** courses. They leap over bars and jump through hoops.

A treat, toy, or belly rub can be a dog's **reward** for listening to directions. Getting a reward makes the dog want to follow the directions again.

Some dogs have jobs! They are trained as **service animals** to help people. They can help people to get around or feel better or stay safe.

Glossary

command: a direction to do something
obstacle: something that is in the way
reward: something given for correct behavior
service animal: an animal trained to do things to help a person

FLUENCY AND PROSODY

Fluency in reading encompasses the ability to read text accurately and quickly but also with proper expression, known as prosody. Each of these elements are integral for constructing meaning. Fluency and comprehension are interlinked; disfluent reading can significantly hinder comprehension, while difficulty with comprehension can in turn impede fluency. Therefore, the development of a reading pace that supports comprehension, alongside accurate and expressive reading of all words—including high-frequency words—is a fundamental aspect of learning to read.

If students are not able to read fluently, it is a useful indicator of where revision and consolidation are required. Specific grapheme–phoneme correspondences or high-frequency words can be targeted and upskilled to increase a student's confidence. Once students are reading evenly and quickly, with no overt blending, and correctly differentiating between the individual words, it is useful to re-read the text with prosody in mind (reading rhythmically, with intonation and expression).

The basics of sound grapheme–phoneme correspondence knowledge and secure blending skills need to be in place before fluency and prosody can be achieved, but working on these simultaneously, with each text read multiple times, will ensure a more rounded, successful reading experience with much better comprehension outcomes. When students are focusing on the mechanics of decoding, they are far less likely to grasp meaning from the text than when they read quicker, with no audible blending and with a tone that reflects the content. Reading success and enjoyment is dependent on decoding competence *and* fluent, expressive pace, but it's easy for the latter to get forgotten in the race to achieve decoding proficiency.

A large part of reading accurately and with expression is about understanding punctuation and what impact it has on the text. Encouraging students from the very start of their reading journey to "read" commas and full stops, to change their tone at the beginning and end of a sentence, for parentheses, for speech, and to draw breath at the right points is critical for effective prosody.

In texts as early as Book 1a: Sam, Tam, Tim (Dandelion Launchers), the language features signify the tone. For example: the repetition of "Sam sat." and "Tim sat." influences the intonation and encourages a particular rhythm. In Book 2a: Pam (Dandelion Launchers), "Pam is on the pot" might be read slightly louder, with more emphasis and enthusiasm, perhaps with a smile to mirror the humorous illustration and help convey meaning.

It can be useful to model reading the text in different ways, with and without expression, in order to highlight the contrast and demonstrate how much meaning can be grasped by the *way* words are read, not just by the words themselves. Understanding how to interpret literary techniques, such as repetition (for example, as an indication of emphasis) will enhance what students get out of text, but it will also help develop what they put into their own texts, with meaningful, sophisticated writing skills.

As the text complexity develops, so does the opportunity for prosody, for example, in Book 16a: The Itch (Dandelion Launchers):

There is a significant amount of direct speech, where the expression is provided, such as on page 3: "'Can I have a sandwich?' says Alf. 'I'll give you the chips too,' says Hank." Students should practice reading this in a polite, inquisitive tone for Alf and a generous, casual tone for Hank.

On page 4, the sudden change in action: "Munch, munch. Just then, Alf gets a nip. Itch and scratch!" allows for a shift in tone, suggesting a sudden, startled reaction from Alf. The exclamation "Itch and scratch!" should be read in a surprised and sharp tone to convey Alf's discomfort.

As the emotional descriptions change, so too should the tone and expression of the reader. When characters move from being relaxed (page 1) to being startled and in discomfort (page 4), the use of direct speech and exclamations requires a different voice. For example, on page 5: "'It's an ant's nest! A bunch of ants live in it!'" should be read in a surprised and slightly alarmed tone to convey Alf's discovery. On page 6, "'Thanks for the chips!' says the ant. 'I'll have them for my lunch!'" suggests a cheeky, triumphant tone from the ant, contrasting with the earlier tension. This variation in tone and expression helps bring the story to life and engages the reader emotionally.

Alf checks the patch of grass. "It's an ant's nest! A bunch of ants live in it!" 5

"Thanks for the chips!" says the ant. "I'll have them for my lunch!" 6

As the text reveals more of the emotion—through a greater array of punctuation, direct speech, and more sophisticated description, there is less reliance on the illustrations. However, as with earlier texts, they can be used to build into the prosody and to further enhance the meaning that children make.

The objective of reading with prosody (in addition to accuracy) is that children move away from the mechanical, unnatural pattern of decoding, developed in the early stages of phonics learning, to a rhythmic, expressive style that shows an understanding of what the writer intended them to think and feel about a text.

DIFFERENTIATION

Because of the nature of phonics teaching (the fast, systematic pace), the ideal is to keep the class or cohort together, progressing together. However, this relies on the pace of students' learning needs being similar, which isn't always the case, and there are many reasons why some students will struggle with different aspects of phonics learning. Maintaining a clear picture of how individuals are coping with the new skills as they are taught means that needs can be identified the moment they become apparent, ensuring that no student gets left behind. Those needs can then be met through a range of activities (delivered in a variety of formats) to bolster and fill any skill gaps, so that students can keep up with their peers and continue their learning with the rest of the group.

It is important to recognize the level of need in terms of whether students are some way off expectations, or just below them, so that the right support can be provided. In the most part, those not meeting expectations would benefit from small-group work to target and consolidate shared skill challenges before they become significant issues. However, the students who are significantly behind expectations (e.g. within the lowest-achieving 20%) are likely to benefit from more specialized, bespoke, individual intervention delivered one-to-one.

The Phonic Books program has a huge volume of resources to accompany every reading book to practice and consolidate learning at each point in the journey. Therefore, when a couple or small group of students are identified as struggling with the same concept, such as a specific grapheme–phoneme correspondence or particular high-frequency words, small-group work using or adapting the activities provided enables a useful, collaborative environment to reinforce learning and upskill the area of challenge.

For example, if students are struggling with any of the grapheme–phoneme correspondences or with blending specifics, during their reading of Dandelion Launchers Book 2a: Pam, there is a wealth of material to support them:

- Depending on which grapheme–phoneme correspondences are proving a struggle, the **Sound cards** and **Word-building cards** from Book 1a: Sam, Tam, Tim, Book 1b: Is it Sam?, and Book 2a: Pam (all in the accompanying activity book), could be revisited. To avoid these being used in the same way as the main lesson and feeling repetitive or predictable, there are lots of creative ways that they can be manipulated (see the next section).
- Re-playing some of the games, e.g. the (bingo **Game** from the readers, or the **Dice game** from the accompanying activity book) provides the opportunity for repeated practice.

It is also possible that students will be secure in the sounds but have trouble making meaning from the text. This is often due to the cognitive load of decoding. For these obstacles, a different focus would be beneficial, again using the material provided. For example: students could work one-to-one, in pairs, or in small groups to retell or recap the story, using the pictures, words, and sentence matching (in the activity book). The ability to accurately and coherently sequence events is critical in early reading comprehension.

As students progress through the program, and the phonics becomes more complex, the volume, range, and variety of accompanying activities increases, providing plenty of differentiation opportunities. For example, in Dandelion Readers Set 1: The Paddle, if students find the sound for the 'le' spelling challenging, the following material could be utilised in various different formats:

- The grapheme cards from the accompanying activity books, and the Reading practice pages within the readers, would provide an opportunity for revision and reinforcement. Again, the next section provides some creative ideas for differentiation at this level.
- Revisiting the games, for example the **4-in-a-row**, **Stepping stones**, and memory games, also provides useful and fun opportunities for consolidation.

If the stumbling block is around comprehension at a higher level, some vocabulary work would be useful to ensure students understand the words they're decoding. Activities that support this include:

- Looking at real and nonsense 'le' words (from the activity book) is beneficial particularly if students are asked for definitions as they go.

- Matching sentences to pictures (from the activity book) supports sequencing and plot recapping; these activities can all be executed orally, in writing or in a more dynamic, physical capacity such as through role play or mime.
- Using these resources, as well as any of the images from the readers can also help drill down further into the text depth, if discussion is promoted; supporting students to explore how characters feel and think enables much more robust comprehension to be reached.

It is useful to have a flexible approach to differentiation, and to be aware that students are likely to move in and out of different small groups and sometimes not need additional support at all. The idea is that the groups flex and change according to the needs of the class, to ensure continual, steady progress for all students.

English as an additional or foreign language

For students joining the cohort late, and those with English as an additional language, the key is on-entry assessment to see how much phonic knowledge has already been acquired. This means that students start at the right point in the program, whatever their prior experience. Because of the methodical, rigorous nature of systematic synthetic phonics teaching, the pedagogy is very inclusive. However, it's important to be aware of existing concepts of language for those with English as an additional language, which may make grasping the fundamentals (specifically the grapheme–phoneme correspondences) more challenging than for native English-speaking kindergarten students. Having said that, students with English as an additional language are likely to catch up quickly with their peers, and so need fast-paced, short-term differentiated tuition, and then not need ongoing additional support, at least not on a phonic level. It's more likely that the stumbling blocks for students with English as an additional language will be around comprehension, for which any of the strategies identified here can be applied. Additionally, it's worth considering extra pronunciation support (to also be available at home for parental use).

Strategies for phonics differentiation

Any of these creative ideas can be adapted according to specific grapheme–phoneme correspondences and/or high-frequency words. They all work to practice and consolidate the key phonic skills, as well as build confidence and familiarity more generally.

Grapheme–phoneme correspondence recognition

- Hold the sound cards behind your back and draw them out one at a time for students to practice sounding out. You can do this quicker and quicker as they become more confident, mixing up the order and increasing the pace. This works with high-frequency words, too.
- Stick the sound cards around the classroom (or playground) and ask students to hop to one sound, skip to one and jump to another as you call them out.
- Find a selection of items in the classroom that start with the sounds on the grapheme cards, and ask students to sort the items into different groups according to what sound they start with.
- Choose a sound from the cards and encourage students to go on a treasure hunt around the classroom to find as many things as they can that begin with that sound.

High-frequency words

- Play a card-matching game. Can the student find the matching card, for example, for the word "is"?

Blending

- Stick the sound cards on individual building blocks and encourage students to put the blocks together to "build" simple words. Say each sound together and then help students to blend them together to read the words out loud. Next, try separating the blocks again to segment the word back into its individual sounds.
- See the recommendations for how to teach blending (pages 38–39). Methods 2 and 3 can be particularly effective for students who are struggling. For Method 2 (Stretch and Blend), for example the word "mat," use a toy car or moving toy to stretch the sounds until the car moves to the next sound: /mmmmmaaaaat/. For Method 3 (Add and Blend), hide the last letter in the word. Using a toy car, ask the student to blend the first two sounds and move the car underneath the two first letters: 'ma.' Then add the third letter, and move the toy car under the three letters: 'ma' + 't' = "mat."
- Place all the sound cards on the table, and see how many different words students can build. They need to write the words they have built down.

ASSESSMENT

Continuous assessment

To ensure students are confident with the new sounds they have learned in each lesson plan, it's important to track their progress using quick, formative assessments.

For example, the Dandelion Launchers activity books contain **Bookmarks**, which feature words printed on them that incorporate the phonic skills covered in the lessons. Teachers can check students are comfortable using these words before moving on to the next stage in the books.

Additionally, **Reading certificates** are found at the back of the activity books.

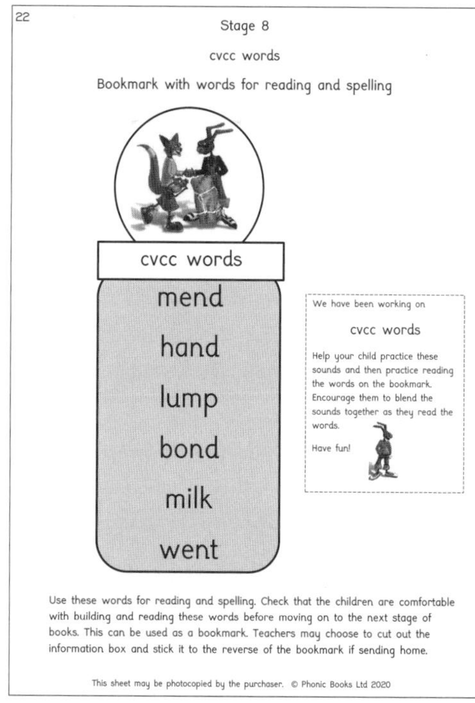
22

Stage 8

cvcc words

Bookmark with words for reading and spelling

cvcc words

mend

hand

lump

bond

milk

went

We have been working on

cvcc words

Help your child practice these sounds and then practice reading the words on the bookmark. Encourage them to blend the sounds together as they read the words.

Have fun!

Use these words for reading and spelling. Check that the children are comfortable with building and reading these words before moving on to the next stage of books. This can be used as a bookmark. Teachers may choose to cut out the information box and stick it to the reverse of the bookmark if sending home.

This sheet may be photocopied by the purchaser. © Phonic Books Ltd 2020

24

Congratulations!

You have read the book **Junk**

Signed by

Date achieved

PhonicBooks

This sheet may be photocopied by the purchaser. © Phonic Books Ltd 2020

Spelling assessments are introduced from Stage 8. These assessments involve dictation exercises where a word is first said in isolation, then used within a sentence, and finally repeated. This method ensures clarity in hearing and understanding the word. For example, the word "tent" might be presented as, "Tent. It was fun to sleep in the tent. Tent."

This approach also encourages phonetic spelling, helping to develop writing skills.

26

Stage 8

cvcc words

Spelling assessment

1. gift
2. mend
3. sank
4. pond
5. bump
6. milk
7. sent
8. honk
9. must
10. limp
11. band
12. went

This list can be used as a spelling assessment at the end of Stage 8. When dictating a word, first say the word on its own. Next, say a sentence with the word in it (to put the word in the context of a sentence) and then repeat the word. This ensures that the child has heard the word correctly, e.g. "Tent. It was fun to sleep in the tent. Tent." Encourage the children to sound out the words while writing them.

Games within the activity books can also serve as a useful assessment tool. They provide immediate feedback, which is crucial for learning. Students understand quickly what they did right or wrong and learn from it, promoting faster and more effective learning.

Reading assessments

The following assessments can be used to work alongside the lesson plans in this manual. They can be used to evaluate reading progress over time and to identify where further help or consolidation is needed.

The assessments will identify the following:

- knowledge of grapheme–phoneme correspondences
- ability to blend sounds together accurately to decode single words
- ability to decode a sequential text at the reader's decoding level
- ability to comprehend a sequential text at the reader's decoding level

When to assess?

The teacher will decide when to assess and at what level. We suggest there should be at least a week after new learning and reading the relevant book, before delivering an assessment at that level. The results will then show which areas need revisiting for further instruction and practice.

We recommend that a teacher assess readers after a stage or unit of work, for example:

- at the end of Stage 7 Dandelion Launchers
- at CVCC, CCVC, and CCVCC level at the end of Stage 10 Dandelion Launchers
- after consonant digraphs th, ch, sh, ck, and ng at the end of Stage 15 Dandelion Launchers.
- at the end of Vowel Spellings Level 1
- at the end of VCe Spellings

High-frequency words

Our Dandelion Launchers series list the high-frequency words which appear in our stories at the beginning of each book.

Words stop being high-frequency words once the relevant sound spellings have been taught, but these words are initially necessary to construct proper sentences even in the earliest books. There are high-frequency words in the assessments: words which appear in the text to be read. Provide the reader with help if needed before the reader reads the text. Point to the grapheme(s), the sound(s) of which the reader has not yet been taught and give the reader the sound(s). Then ask the reader to blend the sounds together and read the word.

Delivering the assessment

Print the reading sheets on cream paper. This will prevent the black print on white paper "glare" which affects some children when reading.

- We recommend you laminate the diagnostic reading sheets for multiple use.

- The teacher will determine how often the reader needs re-assessment. We have provided for two re-assessments on the scoring sheet.
- Three errors in the single words or the text are enough to warrant a re-test at a later date.
- Encourage the reader to have a positive attitude towards being tested, with an understanding that it is to demonstrate their progress with reading. The tester could say something positive to the reader such as:
  "Today we are going to see how well you are doing!"
- Make sure, during testing, that the reader cannot see what is being written.
- Sit opposite rather than next to the reader.
- Use the same notation for each assessment. This will save time and make it easier to compare test results.
- Use a different colored pen for each re-test. This will enable quick comparison of results with an earlier test.
- It is suggested that errors with high frequency-words should not be part of the three-error re-test.

Comprehension questions

Reading accuracy is important, with comprehension as the goal. Increased fluency speed helps with comprehension, but knowledge of vocabulary is also key.

Two to four comprehension questions have been provided with each test. Let the reader re-read the text, if required, to find the answer, as these assessments are not memory tests.

Writing

Reading and writing should always be taught hand in hand at these early stages, enabling students' writing and spelling to progress at the same pace as their reading.

Ensure students practice spelling alongside reading at each new level of learning.

Phonic Books' photocopiable activity books provide many activities for this purpose at each level for all our sets and book series.

Responses recommended on the teacher's record sheet as the reader reads

Reading response	**Explanation of response** (When the reader has made an error, always put a line through the word and write above what the reader has said.)	**Symbol on record sheet**	**Example**	**Scoring**
Correct word	If the reader says the sound accurately (with no /uh/ sound after a consonant sound) or reads the word accurately by sight, write a ✓ above the letter/word.	✓	✓ ✓ ✓ ✓ u k m b ✓ ✓ ✓ pat mat sat	The reader scores 1 point for each correct sound/ word
Don't know	If the reader's response is "I don't know" or there is no response, put a line through the word and write **DK** above it.	**DK**	**DK** ~~stamp~~	No score
Self-corrects	If the reader self-corrects, write a ✓ and **SC** above.	✓ **SC**	✓ **SC** catch	The reader scores 1 point as the word is correct.
Sounds out the word	If the reader sounds out and reads the word accurately, write a ✓ and **SO** above.	**SO**	✓ **SO** stamp	The reader scores 1 point as the word is correct.
Misses a word in the text	If the reader misses out a word in the text, put a line through the word and write **MW** above it.	**MW**	**MW** ~~drink~~	No score
Adds an /uh/ after a sound	If the reader adds an /uh/ after a consonant sound, either in the letter sounds test or when sounding a word out, write ✓ **UH** above.	**UH**	✓**UH** m ✓**UH** fan	1 point

Analysis of errors to be done after the assessment

Reading response	**Explanation of response** (When the reader has made an error, always put a line through the word and write above what the reader has said.)	**Symbol on record sheet**	**Example**	**Scoring**
Adds a sound	The reader added a sound: "pond" for "pod."	**AD**	**AD** pond ~~pod~~	No score
Omits a sound	The reader omitted a sound: "back" for "black."	**OM**	**OM** back ~~black~~	No score
Visual error	The reader made a visual error: "bat" for "pat."	**VE**	**VE** bat ~~pat~~	No score
Guesses the word	The reader guessed the word. Put a line through the word and write what was said above. Later decide why the error was made.	**GU**	**GU** house ~~home~~	No score
Blending error	The reader sounded out the phonemes correctly but blended incorrectly: /s/ /e/ /n/ /d/ "said."	**BL**	**BL** said ~~send~~	No score

Marking the assessment and adding up the scores

Letter sounds:

- After the assessment, write tally marks 'I' in the first column each time one of the special symbols (e.g. DK, SC, VE) is used on the record sheet. This will give you a profile of the reader's approach to saying the sounds.
- If a reader says /em/ for /m/ they do not score a point. Readers cannot blend sounds with letter names. Examples that show the problem are: 'eff' begins with /e/, 'c' begins with /s/, 'g' begins with /j/, 'h' with /ae/, 'w' with /d/. . .
- If a reader says /muh/ for /m/ they score a point, but the reader needs to be taught clipped sounds. By putting a 'UH' above the word, it will remind the assessor that clipped sounds need to be taught to that reader going forward, as this will help increase fluency and eventually, when automaticity sets in, speed of reading.

- If the reader says the wrong sound, put a line through the sound, and write what was said above. Do not correct the reader.
- If the reader does not recognize the capital letters, carry on with the test, putting a line through the letter, and DK above.
- If the reader does not know the lower-case sounds, or makes at least one error, stop the test after finishing saying the sounds, as further work on phoneme–grapheme correspondence at this level is needed.
- Add up the points and write the score in the second column.

Single words

- After the assessment, write tally marks 'I' in the first column each time one of the special symbols (e.g. DK, SC, VE) is used on the record sheet. This will give you a profile of the reader's approach to reading single words.
- These words provide practice for the new sounds in the Stage being assessed as well as incorporating sounds from previous Stages. Score one point for each word read accurately, whether or not the word was sounded out or self-corrected.
- If the word was sounded out, put SO above the word. If there was self-correction, put SC above the word. These are not errors. By using these notations, the assessor will gain an understanding of the level of fluency the reader is operating at.
- BL indicates a blending difficulty. The reader will need more practice with this.
- OM and AD (omitting and adding sounds) point to poor blending skills. VE, which is a visual error, could be due to a specific developmental visual delay which could rectify itself over time. It might be a good idea to have the reader's vision checked. The same would apply if a reader misses a line when reading text, or MW, misses a word whilst reading the text. Notes about this can be put in the "Comments" box.
- Add up the points and write the score in the second column.

High-frequency words

Each school will have its own high-frequency word policy. Our books use a variety of these, listed at the front of each reading book. We are not testing high-frequency words in this test, so we do not score them in the overall score.

A minimum number of high-frequency words have been used in the reading texts and they are listed for practice before reading the text. (Stage 1 Assessment has only single words.)

Sequential text

- Write tally marks 'I' in the first column every time a special symbol is used on the record sheet. This will give you a profile of the reader's approach to reading text.
- Put any comments you may have in the "Comments" box below, for example, "Reader was put off by the amount of text," or "Reader needed a ruler under the line to help keep eyes on the lines of the text."
- To evaluate their decoding skills on the text, you may use the following formula for a percentage score:

  Score achieved ÷ Total score of test × 100 = Percentage score

Comprehension

Comprehension is a very important part of the reading process. Early readers often concentrate hard on the decoding process, and do not take on board the sense of what they are reading. As automaticity sets in and reading becomes more fluent, they will start reading for meaning. For this reason, we recommend you allow them to re-read the text if necessary to answer the questions. The reading assessments are not a memory test.

Two to four comprehension questions are included for diagnostic purposes based on the reading text. Give one point for each question answered correctly. The assessor is to use their discretion as to the accuracy of the answer. Record your comments in the "Comments" box.

Final score

Add up the scores from the column on the right-hand side:

Sound score + Single word score + Text score + Comprehension score = Total score

Write the result in the Total score box at the bottom of the teacher's assessment record. If you wish to find a percentage score for the whole test, use the example formula below:

Score achieved ÷ Total score of test × 100 = Percentage score

32 ÷ 39 × 100 = 82%

Reading Assessment

Dandelion Series

ASSESSMENT FOR DANDELION LAUNCHERS: STAGES 1–7

1. Letter sounds (except q)
2. CVC words
3. Text at CVC, Stages 1–7

Response to reading: (For "record" write the appropriate code whilst testing; add the other codes later.)

Choose which codes are appropriate for you.

- ✓: If correct put a check mark above correct sound/word **(score 1)**
- **abc:** If incorrect put a line through the sound/word and write above what was said. **(no score)**
- **DK:** I don't know/no response **("record" and no score)**
- **SC:** Reader self-corrected **("record" and give 1 point)**
- **SO:** Sounded out and read correctly **("record" and give 1 point)**
- **MW:** Missed out a word **("record" and no score)**
- **UH:** Added sound /uh/ after consonant sound **("record" and give 1 point)**
- **AD:** Added a sound: "pond" for "pod" **(no score)**
- **OM:** Omitted a sound: "wet" for "went" **(no score)**
- **VE:** Visual error: "bat" for "pat" **(no score)**
- **GU:** Guessed the word **(no score)**
- **BL:** Sounds out but blends incorrectly **(no score)**

Name: **Date:**

1. Single sounds

Stage 1	S m t M i A T a s I
Stage 2	P n O p N o
Stage 3	g B h H c G b C
Stage 4	f V d E v F D e
Stage 5	K r L u k R l U
Stage 6	j Z w J z W
Stage 7	ff y ss ll x zz

Comments:	1. Single sounds	1. Single sounds
	DK:	1st attempt /52
	SC:	2nd attempt /52
	VE:	3rd attempt /52
	UH:	

Name: **Date:**

2. Single words

Stage 1	sat	Sam	sit	mat
Stage 2	not	pat	nip	pot
Stage 3	hob	big	hat	cat
Stage 4	van	fig	man	bed
Stage 5	kid	run	let	bug
Stage 6	win	jug	zap	jet
Stage 7	off	yell	buzz	tax
	lass	mix	yes	will

Comments:	2. Single words	2. Single words
	DK: OM:	1st attempt /32
	SC: VE:	2nd attempt /32
	SO: BL:	3rd attempt /32
	AD:	

Name:	**Date:**

High-frequency words:

and the to a said into of

(We are not testing high-frequency words. They are here for you to note whether or not they are recognized by the reader.)

3. Text

Kim and Jess sat in the hot sun.

"Let us run to the hut to get a hat!" said Jess.

Kim had a cap in a bag and Jess had a hat in a box.

Jess got the hat but it fell on the mat.

Cal, the pup, ran into the hut and got the hat.

The pup ran off in a zig zag and hid in the van.

Yes, the pup had a lot of fun.

Will Jess get mad at Cal?

Comments:	3. Text		3. Text	
	DK:	OM:	1st attempt	/83
	SC:	VE:	2nd attempt	/83
	SO:	GU:	3rd attempt	/83
	MW:	BL:		
	AD:			

Name: **Date:**

4. Comprehension questions

1. Why did Kim and Jess need a hat?
2. Where did the hat fall?
3. Who ran off with the hat?
4. Why did Cal hide in a van?

Scores	1st attempt	2nd attempt	3rd attempt
1. Single sounds			
2. Single words			
3. Text			
4. Comprehension			
Total Score / 167			

% score reading text:

% score whole test:

Letter sounds

S	m	t	M	i	A
T	a	s	I	P	n
O	p	N	o	g	B
h	H	c	G	b	C
f	V	d	E	v	F
D	e	K	r	L	u
k	R	l	U	j	Z
w	J	z	W	ff	y

ss	ll	x	zz

Single words

sat	Sam	sit	mat
not	pat	nip	pot
hob	big	hat	cat
van	fig	man	bed
kid	run	let	bug
win	jug	zap	jet
off	yell	buzz	tax
lass	mix	yes	will

High-frequency words

and	the	to	a	said	into	of

Text

Kim and Jess sat in the hot sun.

"Let us run to the hut to get a hat!" said Jess.

Kim had a cap in a bag and Jess had a hat in a box.

Jess got the hat but it fell on the mat.

Cal, the pup, ran into the hut and got the hat.

The pup ran off in a zig zag and hid in the van.

Yes, the pup had a lot of fun.

Will Jess get mad at Cal?

Reading Assessment

Dandelion Series

ASSESSMENT FOR DANDELION LAUNCHERS: STAGES 8–10

1. CVCC, CCVC, CCVCC, CVCCC, and CCCVC words
2. Text with the spellings listed above

Response to reading: (For "record" write the appropriate code whilst testing; add the other codes later.)

Choose which codes are appropriate for you.

- ✓: If correct put a check mark above correct sound/word **(score 1)**
- ~~**abc**~~**:** If incorrect put a line through the sound/word and write above what was said. **(no score)**
- **DK:** I don't know/no response **("record" and no score)**
- **SC:** Reader self-corrected **("record" and give 1 point)**
- **SO:** Sounded out and read correctly **("record" and give 1 point)**
- **MW:** Missed out a word **("record" and no score)**
- **UH:** Added sound /uh/ after consonant sound **("record" and give 1 point)**
- **AD:** Added a sound: "pond" for "pod" **(no score)**
- **OM:** Omitted a sound: "wet" for "went" **(no score)**
- **VE:** Visual error: "bat" for "pat" **(no score)**
- **GU:** Guessed the word **(no score)**
- **BL:** Sounds out but blends incorrectly **(no score)**

Name: **Date:**

1. Stage 8: Single VCC and CVCC words

dust	zinc	ink	belt
just	desk	bulb	and
hump	vest	soft	wept
yelp	hulk	band	cups

Comments:	1. Single VCC and CVCC words	1. Single VCC and CVCC words
	DK:	1st attempt /16
	SC:	2nd attempt /16
	SO:	3rd attempt /16
	AD:	
	OM:	
	VE:	
	BL:	

Name: **Date:**

1. Stage 9: Single CCVC words

blot	twig	slug	grim
cliff	swum	spot	flag
smell	plot	skid	dwell
frog	glad	dress	snug

Comments:	1. Single CCVC words DK: SC: SO: AD: OM: VE: BL:	1. Single CCVC words 1st attempt /16 2nd attempt /16 3rd attempt /16

Name: **Date:**

1. Stage 10: Single CCVCC words

bland	stomp	glint	skunk
swift	spend	clamp	stops
scamp	frost	crept	plump
drink	trend	grunt	swept
claps	slept	skimp	crust

Comments:	1. Single CCVCC words	1. Single CCVCC words
	DK:	1st attempt /20
	SC:	2nd attempt /20
	SO:	3rd attempt /20
	AD:	
	OM:	
	VE:	
	BL:	

Name: **Date:**

1. Stage 10: Single CVCCC words

hands	limps	jumps	melts
ramps	sinks	costs	tilts

Comments:	1. Single CVCCC words		1. Single CVCCC words	
	DK:	OM:	1st attempt	/8
	SC:	VE:	2nd attempt	/8
	SO:	BL:	3rd attempt	/8
	AD:			

1. Stage 10: Single CCCVC words

scram	strip	scrub	scrap

Comments:	1. Single CCCVC words		1. Single CCCVC words	
	DK:	OM:	1st attempt	/4
	SC:	VE:	2nd attempt	/4
	SO:	BL:	3rd attempt	/4
	AD:			

Name: **Date:**

High-frequency words:

for to the out of

(We are not testing high-frequency words. They are here for you to note whether or not they are recognized by the reader.)

2. Text

Dad set up a tent for Gwen next to the hut.

The tent had a camp bed. Gwen sat on it.

Jed, the pet dog, crept up to the tent and went in to jump on Gwen.

Gwen held a hand up to stop him and fell off the camp bed.

In a blink, a brisk wind swept the camp bed on top of Gwen and Jed.

Jed slunk off out of the tent.

Gwent had a cut on her leg and went to get help from Dad.

Comments:	2. Text		2. Text	
	DK:	VE:	1st attempt	/88
	SC:	BL:	2nd attempt	/88
	SO:		3rd attempt	/88
	AD:			
	OM:			

Name: **Date:**

3. Comprehension questions

1. Where did Dad set up the tent?
2. Why did Gwen put her hand up?
3. Why did Gwen ask Dad for help?
4. How do you think Gwen felt about her camping experience?

Comments:	3. Comprehension		3. Comprehension	
	DK:	OM:	1st attempt	/4
	SC:	VE:	2nd attempt	/4
	SO:	BL:	3rd attempt	/4
	AD:			

Scores	1st attempt	2nd attempt	3rd attempt
1. Single words			
2. Text			
3. Comprehension			
Total Score / 156			

% score reading text:

% score whole test:

Single VCC and CVCC words

dust	zinc	ink	belt
just	desk	bulb	and
hump	vest	soft	wept
yelp	hulk	band	cups

Single CCVC words

blot	twig	slug	grim
cliff	swum	spot	flag
smell	plot	skid	dwell
frog	glad	dress	snug

Single CCVCC words

bland	stomp	glint	skunk
swift	spend	clamp	stops
scamp	frost	crept	plump
drink	trend	grunt	swept
claps	slept	skimp	crust

Single CVCCC words

hands	limps	jumps	melts
ramps	sinks	costs	tilts

Single CCCVC words

scram	strip	scrub	scrap

High-frequency words

a	for	to	the	out	of

Text

Dad set up a tent for Gwen next to the hut.

The tent had a camp bed. Gwen sat on it.

Jed, the pet dog, crept up to the tent and went in to jump on Gwen. Gwen held a hand up to stop him and fell off the camp bed.

In a blink, a brisk wind swept the camp bed on top of Gwen and Jed.

Jed slunk off out of the tent.

Gwen had a cut on her leg and went to get help from Dad.

Reading Assessment

Dandelion Series

ASSESSMENT FOR DANDELION LAUNCHERS: STAGES 11-15

1. Words with consonant digraphs ch, sh, th, ck, wh, and ng and spellings qu and ve
2. Texts with the spellings listed above.

Response to reading: (For "record" write the appropriate code whilst testing; add the other codes later.)

Choose which codes are appropriate for you.

- ✓: If correct put a check mark above correct sound/word **(score 1)**
- ~~**abc:**~~ If incorrect put a line through the sound/word and write above what was said. **(no score)**
- **DK:** I don't know/no response **("record" and no score)**
- **SC:** Reader self-corrected **("record" and give 1 point)**
- **SO:** Sounded out and read correctly **("record" and give 1 point)**
- **MW:** Missed out a word **("record" and no score)**
- **UH:** Added sound /uh/ after consonant sound **("record" and give 1 point)**
- **AD:** Added a sound: "pond" for "pod" **(no score)**
- **OM:** Omitted a sound: "wet" for "went" **(no score)**
- **VE:** Visual error: "bat" for "pat" **(no score)**
- **GU:** Guessed the word **(no score)**
- **BL:** Sounds out but blends incorrectly **(no score)**

Name: **Date:**

1. Single words

chat	mush	this	rock
bang	when	fish	much
quit	moth	ship	king
bunch	then	luck	quick
crash	truck	broth	swing
chimp	shrub	throb	chick

Comments:	1. Single words	1. Single words	
	DK:	1st attempt	/24
	SC:	2nd attempt	/24
	SO:	3rd attempt	/24
	AD:		
	OM:		
	VE:		
	BL:		

Name:	**Date:**

High-frequency words:

said to is be a the his no

(We are not testing high-frequency words. They are here for you to note whether or not they are recognized by the reader.)

2. Text

Jill said to Mick, "Which is the bus?"

"Quick!" said Mick. "That bus! It will not be a long trip to get to the ranch!"

Jill and Mick had to rush to get on the bus. Mick flung his bag on the bench next to Jill.

When Mick got his lunch box from his bag, the bus had to stop fast. Mick's lunch box fell off his lap with a thud.

Both Jill and Mick had to pick up the mess and dash off the bus with no lunch.

Comments:	2. Text		2. Text	
	DK:	OM:	1st attempt	/88
	SC:	VE:	2nd attempt	/88
	SO:	GU:	3rd attempt	/88
	MW:	BL:		
	AD:			

Name: **Date:**

3. Comprehension questions

1. Where were Mick and Jill going?
2. What did Mick have in his bag?
3. Why did the lunch box fall on the floor?
4. How do you think Mick felt when the lunch box fell on the floor?

Comments:	3. Comprehension		3. Comprehension	
	DK:	OM:	1st attempt	/4
	SC:	VE:	2nd attempt	/4
	SO:	BL:	3rd attempt	/4
	AD:			

Scores	1st attempt	2nd attempt	3rd attempt
1. Single words			
2. Text			
3. Comprehension			
Total Score / 116			

% score reading text:

% score whole test:

Single words

chat	mush	this	rock
bang	when	fish	much
quit	moth	ship	king
bunch	then	luck	quick
crash	truck	broth	swing
chimp	shrub	throb	chick

High-frequency words

said to is be a the his no

Text

Jill said to Mick, "Which is the bus?"

"Quick!" said Mick. "That bus! It will not be a long trip to get to the ranch!"

Jill and Mick had to rush to get on the bus. Mick flung his bag on the bench next to Jill.

When Mick got his lunch box from his bag, the bus had to stop fast. Mick's lunch box fell off his lap with a thud.

Both Jill and Mick had to pick up the mess and dash off the bus with no lunch.

Reading Assessment

Dandelion Series

ASSESSMENT FOR DANDELION LAUNCHERS: STAGES 16–20

1. Spellings tch and ve, two-syllable words, the suffix -ed, the suffix -ing, and le
2. Texts with the spellings listed above.

Response to reading: (For "record" write the appropriate code whilst testing; add the other codes later.)

Choose which codes are appropriate for you.

- ✓: If correct put a check mark above correct sound/word **(score 1)**
- **~~abc~~:** If incorrect put a line through the sound/word and write above what was said. **(no score)**
- **DK:** I don't know/no response **("record" and no score)**
- **SC:** Reader self-corrected **("record" and give 1 point)**
- **SO:** Sounded out and read correctly **("record" and give 1 point)**
- **MW:** Missed out a word **("record" and no score)**
- **UH:** Added sound /uh/ after consonant sound **("record" and give 1 point)**
- **AD:** Added a sound: "pond" for "pod" **(no score)**
- **OM:** Omitted a sound: "wet" for "went" **(no score)**
- **VE:** Visual error: "bat" for "pat" **(no score)**
- **GU:** Guessed the word **(no score)**
- **BL:** Sounds out but blends incorrectly **(no score)**

Name: **Date:**

1. Single words

itch	pocket	fishing	cuddle
catch	bandit	shopping	middle
have	jumped	thinking	live
sniffed	crunching	chicken	hunted
puddle	trumpet	printed	paddle
solve	drumkit	lifted	nettle

Comments:	1. Single words	1. Single words
	DK:	1st attempt /24
	SC:	2nd attempt /24
	SO:	3rd attempt /24
	AD:	
	OM:	
	VE:	
	BL:	

Name:	**Date:**

High-frequency words:

me for you are be go the his

(We are not testing high-frequency words. They are here for you to note whether or not they are recognized by the reader.)

2. Text

Ben and Mitch strolled in the forest. "Are we lost?" said Ben.

Mitch got the map from his pocket. "No. We are not lost. We have to go on this path."

Ben and Mitch jumped over a log. But Ben fell.

"Do not panic!" said Mitch. "I can be a crutch for you."

"I will wobble," said Ben.

"You are the best frog!" Mitch said.

"I can jump into the next puddle," said Ben.

Comments:	2. Text		2. Text	
	DK:	OM:	1st attempt	/74
	SC:	VE:	2nd attempt	/74
	SO:	BL:	3rd attempt	/74
	AD:			

Name: **Date:**

3. Comprehension questions

1. Where were Ben and Mitch?
2. How did Ben hurt his ankle?
3. How do you think Ben felt when he hurt his ankle?
4. Why did Mitch say Ben was the best frog?

Comments:	3. Comprehension		3. Comprehension	
	DK:	OM:	1st attempt	/4
	SC:	VE:	2nd attempt	/4
	SO:	BL:	3rd attempt	/4
	AD:			

Scores	1st attempt	2nd attempt	3rd attempt
1. Single words			
2. Text			
3. Comprehension			
Total Score / 102			

% score reading text:

% score whole test:

Single words

itch	pocket	fishing	cuddle
catch	bandit	shopping	middle
have	jumped	thinking	live
sniffed	crunching	chicken	hunted
puddle	trumpet	printed	paddle
solve	drumstick	lifted	nettle

High-frequency words

me for you are be go the his

Text

Ben and Mitch strolled in the forest.
"Are we lost?" said Ben.

Mitch got the map from his pocket.
"No. We are not lost. We have to go on this path."

Ben and Mitch jumped over a log. But Ben fell.

"Do not panic!" said Mitch. "I can be a crutch for you."

"I will wobble," said Ben.

"You are the best frog!" said Mitch.

"I can jump into the next puddle," said Ben.

Reading Assessment

Dandelion Series

ASSESSMENT FOR DANDELION READERS VOWEL SPELLINGS: LEVEL 1

1. Words with the sounds (and spellings) /ae/: 'ai,' /ee/: 'ee,' /oe/: 'oa,' /er/: 'ur,' /e/: 'ea,' /ow/: 'ow,' b/oo/t: 'oo,' /ie/: 'igh,' l/oo/k: 'oo,' /aw/: 'aw,' /oi/: 'oi,' and / ar/: 'ar'
2. Texts with the spellings listed above.

Response to reading: (For "record" write the appropriate code whilst testing; add the other codes later.)

Choose which codes are appropriate for you.

- ✓: If correct put a check mark above correct sound/word **(score 1)**
- ~~**abc**~~**:** If incorrect put a line through the sound/word and write above what was said. **(no score)**
- **DK:** I don't know/no response **("record" and no score)**
- **SC:** Reader self-corrected **("record" and give 1 point)**
- **SO:** Sounded out and read correctly **("record" and give 1 point)**
- **MW:** Missed out a word **("record" and no score)**
- **UH:** Added sound /uh/ after consonant sound **("record" and give 1 point)**
- **AD:** Added a sound: "pond" for "pod" **(no score)**
- **OM:** Omitted a sound: "wet" for "went" **(no score)**
- **VE:** Visual error: "bat" for "pat" **(no score)**
- **GU:** Guessed the word **(no score)**
- **BL:** Sounds out but blends incorrectly **(no score)**

Name: **Date:**

1. Single words: /ae/: 'ai'

nail	trail	bait	pain
jail	aim	grain	explain
detail	contain	afraid	faint
aid	paint	claim	rail

Comments:	1. Single words	1. Single words
	DK:	1st attempt /16
	SC:	2nd attempt /16
	SO:	3rd attempt /16
	AD:	
	OM:	
	VE:	
	BL:	

Name: **Date:**

2. Single words: /ee/: 'ee'

see	meet	heel	peel
creep	bee	sleep	free
needed	degree	weekend	unseen
coffee	treetop	agree	green

Comments:	2. Single words	2. Single words
	DK:	1st attempt /16
	SC:	2nd attempt /16
	SO:	3rd attempt /16
	AD:	
	OM:	
	VE:	
	BL:	

Name: **Date:**

3. Single words: /oe/: 'oa'

soak	foam	moat	oats
goal	cloak	groan	road
loaded	speedboat	coaches	railroad
soap	roam	coat	moan

Comments:	3. Single words	3. Single words	
	DK:	1st attempt	/16
	SC:	2nd attempt	/16
	SO:	3rd attempt	/16
	AD:		
	OM:		
	VE:		
	BL:		

Name: **Date:**

4. Single words: /er/: ‘ur’

fur	blur	surf	lurk
hurt	burp	purse	urn
purple	disturb	absurd	burger
blurted	turf	lurch	burn

Comments:	4. Single words	4. Single words
	DK:	1st attempt /16
	SC:	2nd attempt /16
	SO:	3rd attempt /16
	AD:	
	OM:	
	VE:	
	BL:	

Name: **Date:**

5. Single words: /e/: 'ea'

head	bread	deaf	thread
tread	ready	sweat	health
leather	breathless	feather	breakfast
weather	heavy	steady	instead

Comments:	5. Single words	5. Single words	
	DK:	1st attempt	/16
	SC:	2nd attempt	/16
	SO:	3rd attempt	/16
	AD:		
	OM:		
	VE:		
	BL:		

Name: **Date:**

6. Single words: /ow/: ‘ow’

cow	now	how	vow
gown	clown	brown	town
power	towel	scowl	vowel
scowl	flower	shower	powder

Comments:	6. Single words	6. Single words
	DK:	1st attempt /16
	SC:	2nd attempt /16
	SO:	3rd attempt /16
	AD:	
	OM:	
	VE:	
	BL:	

Name: **Date:**

7. Single words: b/oo/t: 'oo'

boot	spoon	roof	drool
tool	zoo	cool	soon
igloo	mushroom	cuckoo	balloon
moon	shampoo	root	food

Comments:	7. Single words	7. Single words
	DK:	1st attempt /16
	SC:	2nd attempt /16
	SO:	3rd attempt /16
	AD:	
	OM:	
	VE:	
	BL:	

Name: **Date:**

8. Single words: /ie/: 'igh'

tight	light	might	night
sight	thigh	slight	tonight
higher	alight	highlight	sunlight
midnight	fighting	blight	sigh

Comments:	8. Single words	8. Single words
	DK:	1st attempt /16
	SC:	2nd attempt /16
	SO:	3rd attempt /16
	AD:	
	OM:	
	VE:	
	BL:	

Name: **Date:**

9. Single words: l/oo/k: 'oo'

book	look	took	good
hook	stood	hood	wooden
mistook	cook	foot	nook
rook	brook	shook	looked

Comments:	9. Single words	9. Single words
	DK:	1st attempt /16
	SC:	2nd attempt /16
	SO:	3rd attempt /16
	AD:	
	OM:	
	VE:	
	BL:	

Name: **Date:**

10. Single words: /aw/: 'aw'

jaw	paw	raw	law
claw	hawk	draw	bawl
jigsaw	sawdust	awful	flaw
crawl	yawn	shawl	thaw

Comments:	10. Single words	10. Single words	
	DK:	1st attempt	/16
	SC:	2nd attempt	/16
	SO:	3rd attempt	/16
	AD:		
	OM:		
	VE:		
	BL:		

Name: **Date:**

11. Single words: /oi/: 'oi'

oil	coin	soil	boil
point	noise	join	foil
toilet	avoid	poison	hoisted
joining	boiling	pointless	spoil

Comments:	11. Single words	11. Single words
	DK:	1st attempt /16
	SC:	2nd attempt /16
	SO:	3rd attempt /16
	AD:	
	OM:	
	VE:	
	BL:	

Name: **Date:**

12. Single words: /ar/: ‘ar’

art	jar	far	scar
star	barn	sharp	card
smart	garden	harmless	depart
restart	darker	carpet	artist

Comments:	12. Single words	12. Single words
	DK:	1st attempt /16
	SC:	2nd attempt /16
	SO:	3rd attempt /16
	AD:	
	OM:	
	VE:	
	BL:	

Name: **Date:**

High-frequency words:

the are to go put says my

(We are not testing high-frequency words. They are here for you to note whether or not they are recognized by the reader.)

13. Text

Mark and Joan agree to meet at the weekend.

"Look at the rain!" Joan groans. "I will catch a coach to town."

Mark sees the bad weather too. "I will get the train."

The lawns in the park are soaked. "This is absurd!" Mark sighs and puts up his hood.

"Let's avoid the rain and go for lunch instead," says Joan.

Mark and Joan choose their food. "Do you need a spoon?" asks the waiter.

"Not for a burger!" Mark frowns and rubs his jaw.

Joan hoots. "I need a spoon for my coffee!"

"It is sad the rain spoiled the trip," says Mark. "But now I have got a big lunch, I don't need to cook dinner tonight!"

Comments:	13. Text		13. Text	
	DK:	OM:	1st attempt	/119
	SC:	VE:	2nd attempt	/119
	SO:	BL:	3rd attempt	/119
	AD:			

Name:	**Date:**

14. Comprehension questions

1. How do Joan and Mark travel to town?
2. Why can't they go to the park?
3. Who needed a spoon?
4. Why is Mark happy he is having a big lunch?

Comments:	3. Comprehension		3. Comprehension	
	DK:	OM:	1st attempt	/4
	SC:	VE:	2nd attempt	/4
	SO:	BL:	3rd attempt	/4
	AD:			

Scores	1st attempt	2nd attempt	3rd attempt
1. Single words: /ae/: 'ae'			
2. Single words: /ee/: 'ee'			
3. Single words: /oe/: 'oa'			
4. Single words: /er/: 'ur'			
5. Single words: /e/: 'ea'			
6. Single words: /ow/: 'ow'			
7. Single words: b/oo/t: 'oo'			
8. Single words: /ie/: 'igh'			
9. Single words: l/oo/k: 'oo'			
10. Single words: /aw/: 'aw'			
11. Single words: /oi/: 'oi'			
12. Single words: /ar/: 'ar'			
13. Text			
14. Comprehension			
Total Score / 323			

% score reading text:

% score whole test:

Single words

soap	turf	rail	painted	
seed	spoon	light	spoil	far
now	book	saw	oil	
feet	mail	disturb	instead	
food	tonight	law	jar	
sail	feeling	curd	steady	

High-frequency words

the	are	to	go	put	says	my

Text

Mark and Joan agree to meet at the weekend.

"Look at the rain!" Joan groans. "I will catch a coach to town."

Mark sees the bad weather too. "I will get the train."

The lawns in the park are soaked. "This is absurd!" Mark sighs and puts up his hood.

"Let's avoid the rain and go for lunch instead," says Joan.

Mark and Joan choose their food. "Do you need a spoon?" asks the waiter.

"Not for a burger!" Mark frowns and rubs his jaw.

Joan hoots. "I need a spoon for my coffee!"

"It is sad the rain spoiled the trip," says Mark. "But now I have got a big lunch, I don't need to cook dinner tonight!"

Reading Assessment

Dandelion Series

ASSESSMENT FOR DANDELION READERS: VCe SPELLINGS

1. VCe spellings a–e, e–e, i–e, o–e, and u–e
2. Texts with the spellings listed above

Response to reading: (For "record" write the appropriate code whilst testing; add the other codes later.)

Choose which codes are appropriate for you.

- ✓: If correct put a check mark above correct sound/word **(score 1)**
- ~~**abc**~~**:** If incorrect put a line through the sound/word and write above what was said. **(no score)**
- **DK:** I don't know/no response **("record" and no score)**
- **SC:** Reader self-corrected **("record" and give 1 point)**
- **SO:** Sounded out and read correctly **("record" and give 1 point)**
- **MW:** Missed out a word **("record" and no score)**
- **UH:** Added sound /uh/ after consonant sound **("record" and give 1 point)**
- **AD:** Added a sound: "pond" for "pod" **(no score)**
- **OM:** Omitted a sound: "wet" for "went" **(no score)**
- **VE:** Visual error: "bat" for "pat" **(no score)**
- **GU:** Guessed the word **(no score)**
- **BL:** Sounds out but blends incorrectly **(no score)**

Name: **Date:**

1. Single words: a–e, e–e, i–e, o–e, and u–e

make	snake	plate	tale
inflate	these	eve	theme
meme	delete	athlete	smile
tile	pipe	stripe	bone
stone	globe	joke	flute
cube	plume	rule	volume

Comments:	1. Single words	1. Single words
	DK:	1st attempt /24
	SC:	2nd attempt /24
	SO:	3rd attempt /24
	AD:	
	OM:	
	VE:	
	BL:	

Name: **Date:**

High-frequency words:

is be to I put was my

(We are not testing high-frequency words. They are here for you to note whether or not they are recognized by the reader.)

2. Text

It is June. Pete will be ten. Eve and Steve want to make him a cake.

"Let's compete," said Eve. "I bet I bake the best cake."

"Fine," said Steve. "But I will win!"

The list told them what to include. Steve broke three an egg and dropped it into the bowl. Eve broke six eggs! Steve put in a bit of cake mix. Eve put in a pile.

"I will use the most," she said. "Then my cake will be the biggest!"

The cakes began to bake. Eve's cake began to rise, and rise, and rise… it was going to explode!

"Oh no!" Eve said. "It is like slime!"

Steve was serene. "What is my prize?"

"You get to wipe up the mess," Eve joked.

Comments:	2. Text		2. Text	
	DK:	OM:	1st attempt	/127
	SC:	VE:	2nd attempt	/127
	SO:	BL:	3rd attempt	/127
	AD:			

Name: **Date:**

3. Comprehension questions

1. How old is Pete going to be?
2. Why did Eve want to make the biggest cake?
3. Why do you think the cake exploded?
4. What was Steve's prize?

Comments:	3. Comprehension		3. Comprehension	
	DK:	OM:	1st attempt	/4
	SC:	VE:	2nd attempt	/4
	SO:	BL:	3rd attempt	/4
	AD:			

Scores	1st attempt	2nd attempt	3rd attempt
1. Single words			
2. Text			
3. Comprehension			
Total Score / 155			

% score reading text:

% score whole test:

Single words

make	snake	plate	tale
inflate	these	gene	theme
meme	delete	athlete	smile
tile	pipe	stripe	bone
stone	globe	joke	flute
cube	plume	rule	volume

High-frequency words

is	be	to	I	put	was	my

Text

It is June. Pete will be ten. Eve and Steve want to make him a cake.

“Let’s compete,” said Eve. “I bet I bake the best cake.”

“Fine,” said Steve. “But I will win!”

The list told them what to include. Steve broke an egg and dropped it into the bowl. Eve broke six eggs! Steve put in a bit of cake mix. Eve put in a pile.

“I will use the most,” she said. “Then my cake will be the biggest!”

The cakes began to bake. Eve’s cake began to rise, and rise, and rise … it was going to explode!

“Oh no!” Eve said. “It is like slime!”

Steve was serene. “What is my prize?”

“You get to wipe up the mess,” Eve joked.

LESSON PLANS

Stage 1: s, a, t, i, m

STEP 1
Preparation
20 mins

Learning goal (2 mins)

- Explain the lesson goal: learning the new sounds /s/ /a/ /t/ /i/ /m/
- Introduce the book: Dandelion Launchers Book 1a: Sam, Tam, Tim.
- You will be completing some activities from Dandelion Launchers Stages 1–7 Activities.

Preparation (18 mins)

- Introduce the new focus sounds: /s/ /a/ /t/ /i/ /m/ using sounds cards (Activities, page 7).
- Show the students the sound card with the letter 's.' Model how to say the sound correctly ask students to copy.
- Have students watch you as they say /s/.
- Repeat this process with /a/ /t/ /i/ and /m/.

1 Word building and blending

- First demonstrate how to build a word. Use only three sound cards, e.g. for the word "sit."
- Draw three lines on the whiteboard, and tell the students that you are going to show them how to build the word "sit."
- As you say the word slowly, move your finger under the lines.
- Ask the students to listen to the first sound in the word "sit"—point to the first line. Emphasize the first sound as you say the whole word. The students respond—/s/.
- Then ask the students which letter spells the sound /s/. The students point to the letter (or you can tell them). Bring the letter down to the first line.
- Repeat with the second and last sounds in the word. Now ask the students to sound all three sounds and blend them into a word, moving your finger under the word: /s/ /i/ /t/ → "sit."

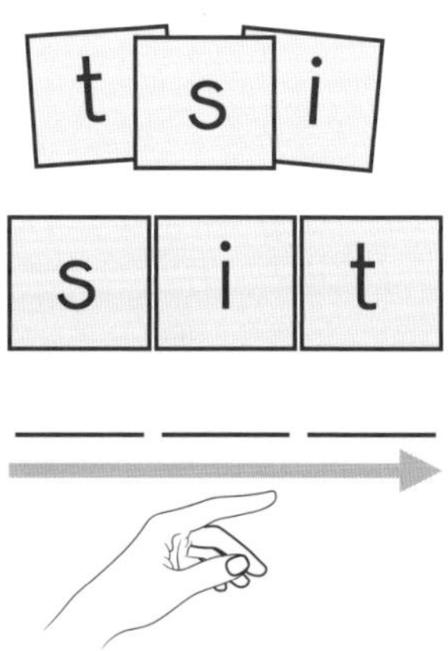

LESSON RESOURCES

- The next time this is done, you can ask a student to participate and identify the sound and then letter and bring it down to the line.

2 Word reading

- Write the words you have created on the whiteboard. Then ask students to blend and read the words.
- Show how to say each sound individually and then blend them together to read the word. Model blending by using a swishing motion with your finger.
- Encourage students to follow your example with these words: "mat," "sit," "sat," "at," "it," and "Sam."

3 Oral segmenting

- Say a word aloud (e.g. "sit") and ask students to a count the sounds in the word (3). Write the number of lines you need for all the sounds. Now ask students to listen to the sounds in the word and write a letter for every sound in the word as you spell the word.

4 Word chain

- Using sound cards or magnetic letters, demonstrate how to build the word "it." Explain to the students that you will be making one change to the word. They must be "sound detectives" and notice if you have added a sound, taken away a sound, or swapped a sound.
- Say that you are going to change the word "it" to "at." Ask the students to listen carefully to where the change has occurred. Move your finger under the word as you say it slowly. Once the change has been identified, invite a student to swap the letter sound or letter. Ask all the students to sound out the word and read the new word, e.g. /a/ /t/ → "at."
- Introduce the new sounds gradually. This allows students to incorporate the letters and sounds they have learned so far.
- Direct students through the following word-chain sequence: it—at—am—sam—sat—sit—it.

STEP 2
Application for reading
25 mins

Before reading (5 mins)

- Revisit the vocabulary taught in Step 1 (e.g. "mat"). Clearly say the word: /m/ /a/ /t/. Then provide a simple definition, e.g. "A mat is fabric we put on the floor."
- Ask questions such as "What is a mat?" and "Where can we put a mat?"
- Then write the word on the whiteboard and refer back to it throughout the week for reinforcement.

Application (10 mins)

- Read Book 1a: Sam, Tam, Tim.
- Encourage students to sound out each word and then blend to read.

Reading fluency (10 mins)

- Once the book is finished, read it again, more fluently.
- As students read more fluently, support them to read with more expression and prosody, changing their pitch, pace, and emphasis according to the words and punctuation.

STEP 3
Application for spelling
15 mins

Segmenting and spelling (5 mins)

- Ask students to complete the following activity to practice writing the graphemes: **Fill in the missing sounds** (Activities, page 9). Encourage the students to say the sounds as they write them and then blend the three sounds in each word together as they write them.

Spelling and dictation (10 mins)

- Ask students to complete **Fill in all the missing sounds** (Activities, page 10) to practice writing whole words.
- Read out the **Sentence dictation** sentences (Activities, page 14): "I am Sam." and "Sam sat."
- Encourage the students to sound out the words as they spell them.
- For students who finish early or need additional practice, create additional sentences and dictate these new passages to them.

STEP 4
Comprehension and consolidation
20 mins

Book reading (5 mins)

- Reread Book 1a: Sam, Tam, Tim.

Comprehension (5 mins)

- Sequencing: Ask students to retell the story, using the pictures and words in the **Retelling the story** activity (Activities, page 16). The word cards on the same page can be used to reinforce vocabulary.
- Comprehension: Check students have understood the story by completing the **Comprehension** activity (Activities, page 18).

Consolidation (10 mins)

- Divide the class into pairs and give each pair a copy of the Dice game (Activities, page 22).
- Have students find and point to these words in Book 1a: Sam, Tam, Tim: "Sam," "Tim," "Tam," "mat," and "sit."

STEP 5
Tracking progress

- Complete the **Bookmark** (Activities, page 21) to make a quick, formative assessment of students' progress.
- Depending on your findings, either revisit some of the activities to reinforce any specific skill gaps, or invite students to complete an additional activity from the Activities book.

PARALLEL BOOKS

In addition to Book 1a: Sam, Tam, Tim, the following books also cover the focus sounds (/s/ /a/ /t/ /i/ /m/) and can be used for more practice of decoding, for book bags to take home.

Dandelion Launchers

Book 1b: Is it Sam?

Dandelion Launchers Extras

Book 1a: I am Sam

Book 1b: On the Mat

Dandelion World

Book 1a: Sit, Tim

Book 1b: At a Mat

Dandelion Readers

Book 1: Sam (Set 1 Units 1–10)

Book 1: Sam and Tim (Set 2 Units 1–10)

Book 1: Sit on It (Set 3 Units 1–10)

LESSON PLANS

Stage 2: n, o, p

STEP 1
Preparation

20 mins

Reviewing sounds (3 mins)

- Using sound cards, review some of the previously learned sounds: /s/ /a/ /t/ /i/ /m/. For example, write the word "mat" on the whiteboard. Model blending "mat," reading it sound by sound and then the whole word. /m/ /a/ /t/ → "mat."

Learning goal (2 mins)

- Explain to the students that you will be teaching them to read and spell new words using the new sounds /n/ /o/ /p/ and the sounds they have previously learned.
- Introduce the book Dandelion Launchers Book 2a: Pam.
- You will be completing some activities from Dandelion Launchers Stages 1–7 Activities.

Preparation (15 mins)

- Model the new focus sounds: /n/ /o/ /p/

1 Word building and blending

- First demonstrate how to build a word. Use only three sound cards, e.g. for "map."
- Draw three lines on the whiteboard, and tell the students that you are going to show them how to build the word "map."
- As you say the word slowly, move your finger under the lines.
- Ask the students to listen to the first sound in the word "map"—point to the first line. Emphasize the first sound as you say the whole word. The students respond—/m/.
- Then ask the students which letter spells the sound /m/. The students point to the letter (or you can tell them). Bring the letter down to the first line.
- Repeat with the second and last sounds in the word. Now ask the students to sound all three sounds and blend them into a word, moving your finger under the word: /m/ /a/ /p/ → "map."

LESSON RESOURCES

- The next time this is done, you can ask a student to participate and identify the sound and then letter and bring it down to the line.

2 Word reading

- Write the words you have created on the whiteboard. Then ask students to blend and read the words.
- Show how to say each sound individually and then blend them together to read the word. Model blending by using a swishing motion with your finger.
- Encourage students to follow your example with these words: "Pam," "pip," and "pot."

3 Oral segmenting

- Say a word aloud (e.g. "pot") and ask students to listen to count the sounds in the word (3). Write the number of lines you need for all the sounds. Now ask students to listen to the sounds in the word and write a letter for every sound in the word as you spell the word.

4 Word chain

- Using sound cards or magnetic letters, demonstrate how to build the word "pip." Explain to the students that you will be making one change to the word. They must be "sound detectives" and notice if you have added a sound, taken away a sound, or swapped a sound.
- Say that you are going to change the word "pip" (moving your finger under the word) to "pit." Ask the students to listen carefully to where the change has occurred. Move your finger under the word as you say it slowly. Once the change has been identified, invite a student to swap the sound card or letter. Ask all the students to sound out the word and read the new word. e.g. /p/ /i/ /t/ → "pit."
- Introduce the new sounds gradually. This allows students to incorporate the letters and sounds they have learned so far.
- Direct students through the following word-chain sequence: pip—pit—pin—pan—tan—tap—tip—pip

STEP 2
Application for reading

15 mins

Before reading (3 mins)

- Revisit the vocabulary taught in Step 1 (e.g. "pot"). Clearly say the word: /p/ /o/ /t/. Then provide a simple definition, e.g. "A pot is a deep pan used for cooking."
- Ask questions such as, "What can we put in a pot?"
- Then write the word on the whiteboard and refer back to it throughout the week for reinforcement.

High-frequency words (2 mins)

- Pre-teach these high-frequency words: "a," "the," "is," and "and."
- Explain that these are high-frequency words that have tricky spellings the students will learn later. Read each high-frequency words aloud.
- Write the words on the board, showing the separate graphemes in each word. As students learn more of the Alphabetic Code, they will be able to decode those graphemes.

Application (10 mins)

- Read Book 2a: Pam.
- Encourage students to sound out each word and then blend to read.

STEP 3
Application for spelling

15 mins

Segmenting and spelling (5 mins)

- Ask students to complete the following activity to practice writing the graphemes: **Fill in the missing sounds** (Activities, page 29). Encourage the students to say the sounds as they write them and then blend the three sounds in each word together as they write them.

Spelling and dictation (10 mins)

- Ask students to complete **Fill in all the missing sounds** (Activities, page 30) to practice writing whole words.
- Read out the **Sentence dictation** sentences (Activities, page 35): "Pam is on top." and "A nap on the mat." Encourage the students to sound out the words as they spell them.
- For students who finish early or need additional practice, create additional sentences and dictate these new passages to them.

STEP 4
Comprehension and consolidation

20 mins

Book reading (5 mins)

- Reread Book 2a: Pam.

Comprehension (5 mins)

- Sequencing: Ask students to retell the story, using the pictures and words in the **Retelling the story** activity (Activities, page 37). The word cards on the same page can be used to reinforce vocabulary.
- Comprehension: Check students have understood the story by completing the **Comprehension** activity (Activities, page 39). Cut out the words on the page. Then ask students to read and match them to the correct pictures.

Consolidation (10 mins)

- Divide the class into pairs and give each pair a copy of the **Stepping stones game** (Activities, page 41).

STEP 5
Tracking progress

- Complete the **Bookmark** (Activities, page 42) to make a quick, formative assessment of students' progress.
- Depending on your findings, either revisit some of the activities to reinforce any specific skill gaps, or invite students to complete an additional activity from the Activities book.

PARALLEL BOOKS

In addition to Book 2a: Pam, the following books also cover the focus sounds (/n/ /o/ /p/) and can be used for more practice of decoding, for book bags to take home.

Dandelion Launchers
Book 2b: The Pot

Dandelion Launchers Extras
Book 2a: The Man
Book 2b: A Map

Dandelion World
Book 2a: At the Top?
Book 2b: A Sap Tap

Dandelion Readers
Book 2: Pip (Set 1)
Book 2: The Nap (Set 2)
Book 2: Pip, Sam, and Tam (Set 3)

LESSON PLANS

Stage 3: b, c, g, h

STEP 1
Preparation

20 mins

Reviewing sounds (3 mins)

- Using sound cards, review some of the previously learned sounds: /s/ /a/ /t/ /i/ /m/ /n/ /o/ /p/. For example, write the word "sip" on the whiteboard. Model blending "sip," reading it sound by sound and then the whole word. /s/ /i/ /p/ → "sip."

Learning goal (2 mins)

- Explain to the students that you will be teaching them to read and spell new words using the new sounds /b/ /c/ /g/ /h/ and the sounds they have previously learned.
- Introduce the book Dandelion Launchers Book 3a: Sam's Bag.
- You will be completing some activities from Dandelion Launchers Stages 1–7 Activities.

Preparation (15 mins)

- Model the new focus sounds: /b/ /c/ /g/ /h/

1 Word building and blending

- First demonstrate how to build a word. Use only three sound cards, e.g. for the word "hat."
- Draw three lines on the whiteboard, and tell the students that you are going to show them how to build the word "hat."
- As you say the word slowly, move your finger under the lines.
- Ask the students to listen to the first sound in the word "hat"—point to the first line. Emphasize the first sound as you say the whole word. The students respond—/h/.
- Then ask the students which letter spells the sound /h/. The students point to the letter (or you can tell them). Bring the letter down to the first line.
- Repeat with the second and last sounds in the word. Now ask the students to sound all three sounds and blend them into a word, moving your finger under the word: /h/ /a/ /t/ → "hat."

LESSON RESOURCES

- The next time this is done, you can ask a student to participate and identify the sound and then letter and bring it down to the line.

2 Word reading

- Write the words you have created on the whiteboard. Then ask students to blend and read the words.
- Show how to say each sound individually and then blend them together to read the word. Model blending by using a swishing motion with your finger.
- Encourage students to follow your example with these words: "cat," "bag," and "bib."

3 Oral segmenting

- Say a word aloud (e.g. "cog") and ask students to count the sounds in the word (3). Write the number of lines you need for all the sounds. Now ask students to listen to the sounds in the word and write a letter for every sound in the word as you spell the word.

4 Word chain

- Using sound cards or magnetic letters, demonstrate how to build the word "cat." Explain to the students that you will be making one change to the word. They must be "sound detectives" and notice if you have added a sound, taken away a sound, or swapped a sound.
- Say that you are going to change the word "cat" (moving your finger under the word) to "bat." Ask the students to listen carefully to where the change has occurred. Move your finger under the word as you say it slowly. Once the change has been identified, invite a student to swap the sound card or letter. Ask all the students to sound out the word and read the new word. e.g. /b/ /a/ /t/ → "bat."
- Introduce the new sounds gradually. This allows students to incorporate the letters and sounds they have learned so far.
- Direct students through the following word-chain sequence: cat—bat—hat—sat—pat—mat—tat—cat

STEP 2
Application for reading
15 mins

Before reading (3 mins)

- Revisit the vocabulary taught in Step 1 (e.g. "bag"). Clearly say the word: /b/ /a/ /g/. Then provide a simple definition, e.g. "A bag is used for carrying things."
- Ask questions such as, "What can we put in a bag?"
- Then write the word on the whiteboard and refer back to it throughout the week for reinforcement.

High-frequency words (2 mins)

- Pre-teach and reiterate these high-frequency words: "Sam's," "has," "a," "get," "the," "is," and "Tam's."
- Explain that these are high-frequency words that have tricky spellings the students will learn later. Read each high-frequency word aloud.
- Write the words on the board, showing the separate graphemes in each word. As students learn more of the Alphabetic Code, they will be able to decode those graphemes.

Application (10 mins)

- Read Book 3a: Sam's Bag.
- Encourage students to sound out each word and then blend to read.

STEP 3
Application for spelling
15 mins

Segmenting and spelling (5 mins)

- Ask students to complete the following activity to practice writing the graphemes: **Fill in the missing sounds** (Activities, page 51). Encourage the students to say the sounds as they write them and then blend the three sounds in each word together as they write them.

Spelling and dictation (10 mins)

- Ask students to complete **Fill in all the missing sounds** (Activities, page 52) to practice writing whole words.
- Read out the **Sentence dictation** sentences (Activities, page 57): "Sam, get the bag!" and "It is Tam's bag." Encourage the students to sound out the words as they spell them.
- For students who finish early or need additional practice, create additional sentences and dictate these new passages to them.

STEP 4
Comprehension and consolidation
20 mins

Book reading (5 mins)

- Reread Book 3a: Sam's Bag.

Comprehension (5 mins)

- Sequencing: Ask students to retell the story, using the pictures and words in the **Retelling the story** activity (Activities, page 59). The word cards on the same page can be used to reinforce vocabulary.
- Comprehension: Check students have understood the story by completing the **Comprehension** activity (Activities, page 61). Cut out the words on the page. Then ask students to read and match them to the correct pictures.

Consolidation (10 mins)

- Divide the class into pairs and give each pair a copy of the **Dice game** (Activities, page 67).

STEP 5
Tracking progress

- Complete the **Bookmark** (Activities, page 66) to make a quick, formative assessment of students' progress.
- Depending on your findings, either revisit some of the activities to reinforce any specific skill gaps, or invite students to complete an additional activity from the Activities book.

PARALLEL BOOKS

In addition to Book 3a: Sam's Bag, the following books also cover the focus sounds (/b/ /c/ /g/ /h/) and can be used for more practice of decoding, for book bags to take home.

Dandelion Launchers

Book 3b: Pip and the Bat

Dandelion Launchers Extras

Book 3a: Bob

Book 3b: Pam and the Cat

Dandelion World

Book 3a: The Cat Can Tag

Book 3b: A Big Hut

Dandelion Readers

Book 3: In the Bag (Set 1 Units 1–10)

Book 3: In the Can (Set 2 Units 1–10)

Book 3: A Hot Cab (Set 3 Units 1–10)

LESSON PLANS

Stage 4: d, e, f, v

STEP 1
Preparation

20 mins

Reviewing sounds (3 mins)

- Using sound cards, review some of the previously learned sounds. For example, write the word "hip" on the whiteboard. Model blending "hip," reading it sound by sound and then the whole word. /h/ /i/ /p/ → "hip."

Learning goal (2 mins)

- Explain to the students that you will be teaching them to read and spell new words using the new sounds /d/ /e/ /f/ /v/ and the sounds they have previously learned.
- Introduce the book Dandelion Launchers Book 4a: Ted.
- You will be completing some activities from Dandelion Launchers Stages 1–7 Activities.

Preparation (15 mins)

- Model the new focus sounds: /d/ /e/ /f/ /v/

1 Word building and blending

- First demonstrate how to build a word. Use only three sound cards, e.g. for the word "dot."
- Draw three lines on the whiteboard, and tell the students that you are going to show them how to build the word "dot."
- As you say the word slowly, move your finger under the lines.
- Ask the students to listen to the first sound in the word "dot"—point to the first line. Emphasize the first sound as you say the whole word. The students respond—/d/.
- Then ask the students which letter spells the sound /d/. The students point to the letter (or you can tell them). Bring the letter down to the first line.
- Repeat with the second and last sounds in the word. Now ask the students to sound all three sounds and blend them into a word, moving your finger under the word: /d/ /o/ /t/ → "dot."

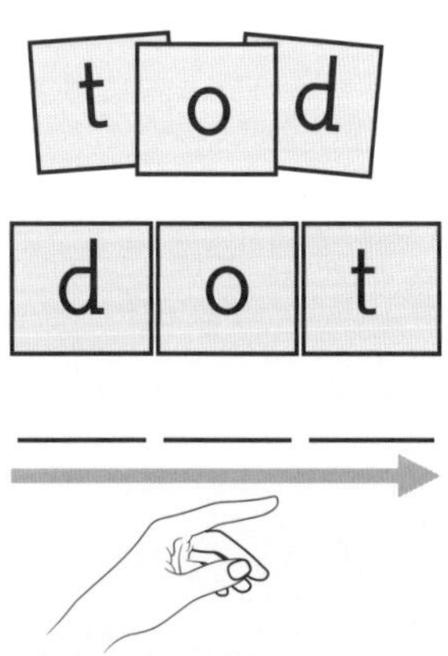

LESSON RESOURCES

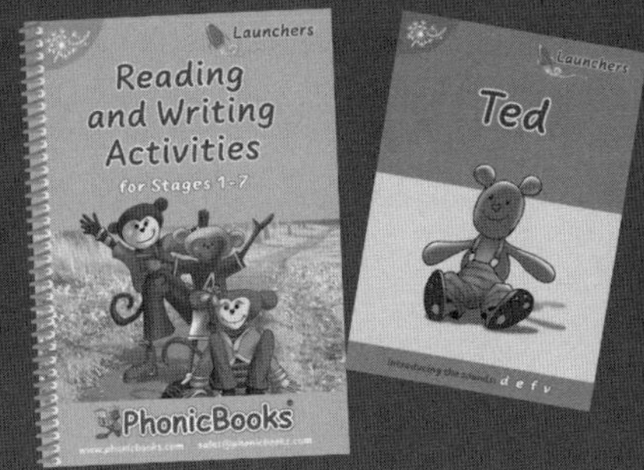

- The next time this is done, you can ask a student to participate and identify the sound and then letter and bring it down to the line.

2 Word reading

- Write the words you have created on the whiteboard. Then ask students to blend and read the words.
- Show how to say each sound individually and then blend them together to read the word. Model blending by using a swishing motion with your finger.
- Encourage students to follow your example with these words: "dot," "fed," and "vet."

3 Oral segmenting

- Say a word aloud (e.g. "dot") and ask students to count the sounds in the word (3). Write the number of lines you need for all the sounds. Now ask students to listen to the sounds in the word and write a letter for every sound in the word as you spell the word.

4 Word chain

- Using sound cards or magnetic letters, demonstrate how to build the word "fed." Explain to the students that you will be making one change to the word. They must be "sound detectives" and notice if you have added a sound, taken away a sound, or swapped a sound.
- Say that you are going to change the word "fed" (moving your finger under the word) to "fad." Ask the students to listen carefully to where the change has occurred. Move your finger under the word as you say it slowly. Once the change has been identified, invite a student to swap the sound card or letter. Ask all the students to sound out the word and read the new word. e.g. /f/ /a/ /d/ → "fad."
- Introduce the new sounds gradually. This allows students to incorporate the letters and sounds they have learned so far.
- Direct students through the following word-chain sequence: fed—fad—bad—sad—sat—set—get—vet—bet—bed—fed

STEP 2
Application for reading
15 mins

Before reading (3 mins)

- Revisit the vocabulary taught in Step 1 (e.g. "bed"). Clearly say the word: /b/ /e/ /d/. Then provide a simple definition, e.g. "A bed is a comfy place where we sleep."
- Ask questions such as, "When do we use a bed?" and "What rhymes with 'bed'?"
- Then write the word on the whiteboard and refer back to it throughout the week for reinforcement.

High-frequency words (2 mins)

- Pre-teach and reiterate these high-frequency words: "the," "up," "off," "into," "is," and "a."
- Explain that these are high-frequency words that have tricky spellings the students will learn later. Read each high-frequency word aloud.
- Write the words on the board, showing the separate graphemes in each word. As students learn more of the Alphabetic Code, they will be able to decode those graphemes.

Application (10 mins)

- Read Book 4a: Ted.
- Encourage students to sound out each word and then blend to read.

STEP 3
Application for spelling
15 mins

Segmenting and spelling (5 mins)

- Ask students to complete the following activity to practice writing the graphemes: **Fill in the missing sounds** (Activities, page 75). Encourage the students to say the sounds as they write them and then blend the three sounds in each word together as they write them.

Spelling and dictation (10 mins)

- Ask students to complete **Fill in all the missing sounds** (Activities, page 76) to practice writing whole words.
- Read out the **Sentence dictation** (Activities, page 81): "Viv got into bed." and "Ted is in the pit!" Encourage the students to sound out the words as they spell them.
- For students who finish early or need additional practice, create additional sentences and dictate these new passages to them.

STEP 4
Comprehension and consolidation
20 mins

Book reading (5 mins)

- Reread Book 4a: Ted.

Comprehension (5 mins)

- Sequencing: Ask students to retell the story, using the pictures and words in the **Retelling the story** activity (Activities, page 83). The word cards on the same page can be used to reinforce vocabulary.
- Comprehension: Check students have understood the story by completing the **Comprehension** activity (Activities, page 85). Cut out the words on the page. Then ask students to read and match them to the correct pictures.

Consolidation (10 mins)

- Divide the class into pairs and give each pair a copy of the **Stepping stones game** (Activities, page 89).

STEP 5
Tracking progress

- Complete the **Bookmark** (Activities, page 90) to make a quick, formative assessment of students' progress.
- Depending on your findings, either revisit some of the activities to reinforce any specific skill gaps, or invite students to complete an additional activity from the Activities book.

PARALLEL BOOKS

In addition to Book 4a: Ted, the following books also cover the focus sounds (/d/ /e/ /f/ /v/) and can be used for more practice of decoding, for book bags to take home.

Dandelion Launchers

Book 4b: Meg and Ted

Dandelion Launchers Extras

Book 4a: The Fib

Book 4b: Bob and the Cod

Dandelion World

Book 4a: Get Fed

Book 4b: A Vet in a Van

Dandelion Readers

Book 4: Bad Cat (Set 1 Units 1–10)

Book 4: At the Vet (Set 2 Units 1–10)

Book 4: In the Van (Set 3 Units 1–10)

LESSON PLANS

Stage 5: k, l, r, u

STEP 1
Preparation

20 mins

Reviewing sounds (3 mins)

- Using sound cards, review some of the previously learned sounds. For example: model blending "fed," reading it sound by sound and then the whole word. /f/ /e/ /d/ → "fed."

Learning goals (2 mins)

- Explain to the students that you will be teaching them to read and spell new words using the new sounds /k/ /l/ /r/ /u/ and the sounds they have previously learned.
- Introduce the book Dandelion Launchers Book 5a: Ken, the Rat.
- You will be completing some activities from Dandelion Launchers Stages 1–7 Activities.

Preparation (15 mins)

- Model the new focus sounds: /k/ /l/ /r/ /u/

1 Word building and blending

- First demonstrate how to build a word. Use only three sound cards, e.g. for the word "rug."
- Draw three lines on the whiteboard, and tell the students that you are going to show them how to build the word "rug."
- As you say the word slowly, move your finger under the lines.
- Ask the students to listen to the first sound in the word "rug"—point to the first line. Emphasize the first sound as you say the whole word. The students respond—/r/.
- Then ask the students which letter spells the sound /r/. The students point to the letter (or you can tell them). Bring the letter down to the first line.
- Repeat with the second and last sounds in the word. Now ask the students to sound all three sounds and blend them into a word, moving your finger under the word: /r/ /u/ /g/ → "rug."

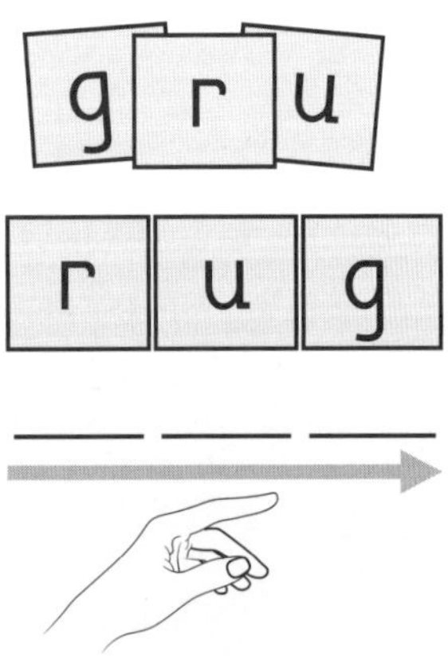

LESSON RESOURCES

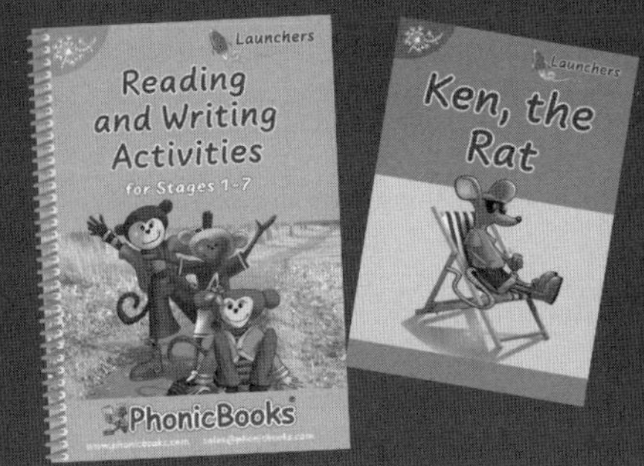

- The next time this is done, you can ask a student to participate and identify the sound and then letter and bring it down to the line.

2 Word reading

- Write the words you have created on the whiteboard . Then ask students to blend and read the words.
- Show how to say each sound individually and then blend them together to read the word. Model blending by using a swishing motion with your finger.
- Encourage students to follow your example with these words: "rug," "cup," and "leg."

3 Oral segmenting

- Say a word aloud (e.g. "kit") and ask students to count the sounds in the word (3). Write the number of lines you need for all the sounds. Now ask students to listen to the sounds in the word and write a letter for every sound in the word as you spell the word.

4 Word chain

- Using sound cards or magnetic letters, demonstrate how to build the word "rag." Explain to the students that you will be making one change to the word. They must be "sound detectives" and notice if you have added a sound, taken away a sound, or swapped a sound.
- Say that you are going to change the word "rag" (moving your finger under the word) to "rug." Ask the students to listen carefully to where the change has occurred. Move your finger under the word as you say it slowly. Once the change has sound identified, invite a student to swap the sound card or letter. Ask all the students to sound out the word and read the new word. e.g. /r/ /u/ /g/ → "rug."
- Introduce the new sounds gradually. This allows students to incorporate the letters and sounds they have learned so far.
- Direct students through the following word-chain sequence: rag—rug—lug—leg—keg—peg—pug—mug—rug—rag

STEP 2
Application for reading
15 mins

Before reading (3 mins)

- Revisit the vocabulary taught in Step 1 (e.g. "rat"). Clearly say the word: /r/ /a/ /t/. Then provide a simple definition, e.g. "A rat is a small animal with a tail."
- Ask questions such as, "What rhymes with 'rat'?"
- Then write the word on the whiteboard and refer back to it throughout the week for reinforcement.

High-frequency words (2 mins)

- Pre-teach and reiterate these high-frequency words: "the," "a," and "it's."
- Explain that these are high-frequency words that have tricky spellings the students will learn later. Read each high-frequency word aloud.
- Write the words on the board, showing the separate graphemes in each word. As students learn more of the Alphabetic Code, they will be able to decode those graphemes.

Application (10 mins)

- Read Book 5a: Ken, the Rat.
- Encourage students to sound out each word and then blend to read.

STEP 3
Application for spelling
15 mins

Segmenting and spelling (5 mins)

- Ask students to complete the following activity to practice writing the graphemes: **Fill in the missing sounds** (Activities, page 99). Encourage the students to say the sounds as they write them and then blend the three sounds in each word together as they write them.

Spelling and dictation (10 mins)

- Ask students to complete **Fill in all the missing sounds** (Activities, page 100) to practice writing whole words.
- Read out the **Sentence dictation** sentences (Activities, page 81): "Ken got a red tan." and "Ken hid in a log." Encourage the students to sound out the words as they spell them.
- For students who finish early or need additional practice, create additional sentences and dictate these new passages to them.

STEP 4
Comprehension and consolidation
20 mins

Book reading (5 mins)

- Reread Book 5a: Ken, the Rat.

Comprehension (5 mins)

- Sequencing: Ask students to retell the story, using the pictures and words in the **Retelling the story** activity (Activities, page 107). The word cards on the same page can be used to reinforce vocabulary.
- Comprehension: Check students have understood the story by completing the **Comprehension** activity (Activities, page 109). Cut out the words on the page. Then ask students to read and match them to the correct pictures.

Consolidation (10 mins)

- Divide the class into pairs and give each pair a copy of the **Dice game** (Activities, page 115).

STEP 5
Tracking progress

- Complete the **Bookmark** (Activities, page 114) to make a quick, formative assessment of students' progress.
- Depending on your findings, either revisit some of the activities to reinforce any specific skill gaps, or invite students to complete an additional activity from the Activities book.

PARALLEL BOOKS

In addition to Book 5a: Ken, the Rat, the following books also cover the focus sounds (/k/ /l/ /r/ /u/) and can be used for more practice of decoding, for book bags to take home.

Dandelion Launchers
Book 5b: Kim, the Bug

Dandelion Launchers Extras
Book 5a: The Bus
Book 5b: Mud

Dandelion World
Book 5a: Up on the Log
Book 5b: A Fun Kid

Dandelion Readers
Book 5: Bun in the Sun (Set 1 Units 1–10)
Book 5: Red Gum (Set 2 Units 1–10)
Book 5: The Hut (Set 3 Units 1–10)

Stage 6: j, w, z

LESSON RESOURCES

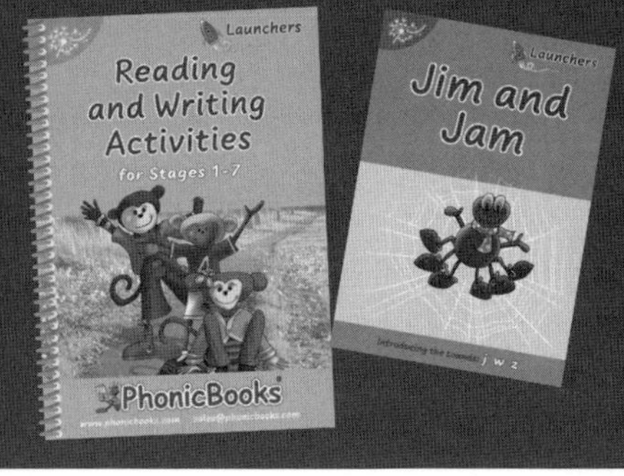

STEP 1
Preparation

20 mins

Reviewing sounds (3 mins)

- Using sound cards, review some of the previously learned sounds. For example: model blending "rug," reading it sound by sound and then the whole word. /r/ /u/ /g/ → "rug."

Learning goal (2 mins)

- Explain to the students that you will be teaching them to read and spell new words using the new sounds /j/ /w/ /z/ and the sounds they have previously learned.
- Introduce the book Dandelion Launchers Book 6a: Jim and Jam.
- You will be completing some activities from Dandelion Launchers Stages 1–7 Activities.

Preparation (15 mins)

- Model the new focus sounds: /j/ /w/ /z/

1 Word building and blending

- First demonstrate how to build a word. Use only three sound cards, e.g. for the word "wig."
- Draw three lines on the whiteboard, and tell the students that you are going to show them how to build the word "wig."
- As you say the word slowly, move your finger under the lines.
- Ask the students to listen to the first sound in the word "wig"—point to the first line. Emphasize the first sound as you say the whole word. The students respond—/w/.
- Then ask the students which letter spells the sound /w/. The students point to the letter (or you can tell them). Bring the letter down to the first line.
- Repeat with the second and last sounds in the word. Now ask the students to sound all three sounds and blend them into a word, moving your finger under the word: /w/ /i/ /g/ → "wig."

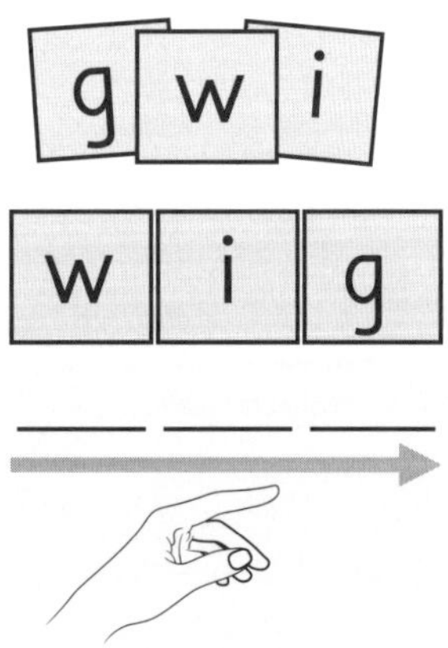

- The next time this is done, you can ask a student to participate and identify the sound and then letter and bring it down to the line.

2 Word reading

- Write the words you have created on the whiteboard. Then ask students to blend and read the words.
- Show how to say each sound individually and then blend them together to read the word. Model blending by using a swishing motion with your finger.
- Encourage students to follow your example with these words: "wig," "zip," and "jet."

3 Oral segmenting

- Say a word aloud (e.g. "zap") and ask students to count the sounds in the word (3). Write the number of lines you need for all the sounds. Now ask students to listen to the sounds in the word and write a letter for every sound in the word as you spell the word.

4 Word chain

- Using sound cards or magnetic letters, demonstrate how to build the word "zap." Explain to the students that you will be making one change to the word. They must be "sound detectives" and notice if you have added a sound, taken away a sound, or swapped a sound.
- Say that you are going to change the word "zap" (moving your finger under the word) to "zip." Ask the students to listen carefully to where the change has occurred. Move your finger under the word as you say it slowly. Once the change has been identified, invite a student to swap the sound card or letter. Ask all the students to sound out the word and read the new word. e.g. /z/ /i/ /p/ → "zip."
- Introduce the new sounds gradually. This allows students to incorporate the letters and sounds they have learned so far.
- Direct students through the following word-chain sequence: zap—zip—pip—ip—ep—wep—wet—pet—pip—zip—zap

STEP 2
Application for reading

15 mins

Before reading (3 mins)

- Revisit the vocabulary taught in Step 1 (e.g. "web"). Clearly say the word: /w/ /e/ /b/.
- Explore different meanings of the word "web." For example: "a spider's web" or "the internet."
- Then write the word on the whiteboard and refer back to it throughout the week for reinforcement.

High-frequency words (2 mins)

- Pre-teach and reiterate these high-frequency words: "and," "was," "his," "I," "have", "a," "of," "to," "the," "legs," and "into."
- Explain that these are high-frequency words that have tricky spellings the students will learn later. Read each high-frequency word aloud.
- Write the words on the board, showing the separate graphemes in each word. As students learn more of the Alphabetic Code, they will be able to decode those graphemes.

Application (10 mins)

- Read Book 6a: Jim and Jam.
- Encourage students to sound out each word and then blend to read.

STEP 3
Application for spelling

15 mins

Segmenting and spelling (5 mins)

- Ask students to complete the following activity to practice writing the graphemes: **Fill in the missing sounds** (Activities, page 123). Encourage the students to say the sounds as they write them and then blend the three sounds in each word together as they write them.

Spelling and dictation (10 mins)

- Ask students to complete **Fill in all the missing sounds** (Activities, page 124) to practice writing whole words.
- Read out the **Sentence dictation** sentences (Activities, page 129): "Jim was in his big web." and "Jim got into a tub." Encourage the students to sound out the words as they spell them.
- For students who finish early or need additional practice, create additional sentences and dictate these new passages to them.

STEP 4
Comprehension and consolidation

20 mins

Book reading (5 mins)

- Reread Book 6a: Jim and Jam.

Comprehension (5 mins)

- Sequencing: Ask students to retell the story, using the pictures and words in the **Retelling the story** activity (Activities, page 131). The word cards on the same page can be used to reinforce vocabulary.
- Comprehension: Check students have understood the story by completing the **Comprehension** activity (Activities, page 133). Cut out the words on the page. Then ask students to read and match them to the correct pictures.

Consolidation (10 mins)

- Divide the class into pairs and give each pair a copy of the **Stepping stones game** (Activities, page 137).

STEP 5
Tracking progress

- Complete the **Bookmark** (Activities, page 138) to make a quick, formative assessment of students' progress.
- Depending on your findings, either revisit some of the activities to reinforce any specific skill gaps, or invite students to complete an additional activity from the Activities book.

PARALLEL BOOKS

In addition to Book 6a: Jim and Jam, the following books also cover the focus sounds (/j/ /w/ /z/) and can be used for more practice of decoding, for book bags to take home.

Dandelion Launchers

Book 6b: Ken Gets Wet

Dandelion Launchers Extras

Book 6a: Viv Can Run

Book 6b: A Bad Job

Dandelion World

Book 6a: Bug in a Jam

Book 6b: Zig, Zag, Tag

Dandelion Readers

Book 6: Zip and Zap (Set 1 Units 1–10)

Book 6: Meg and the Bun (Set 2 Units 1–10)

Book 6: Top Dog (Set 3 Units 1–10)

LESSON PLANS

Stage 7: x, y, ff, ll, ss, zz

LESSON RESOURCES

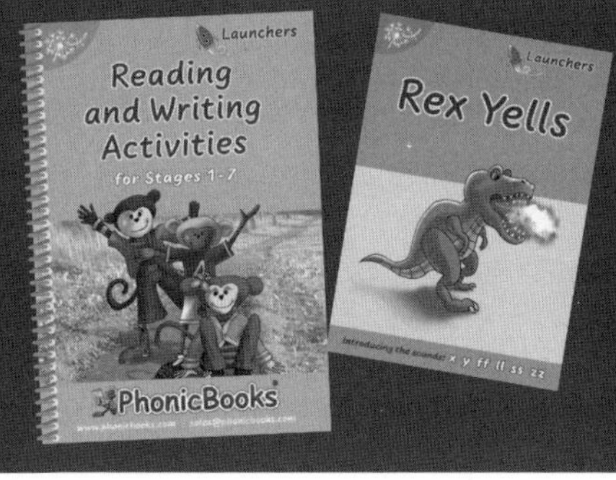

STEP 1
Preparation

20 mins

Reviewing sounds (3 mins)

- Using sound cards, review some of the previously learned sounds.

Learning goal (2 mins)

- Explain to the students that you will be teaching them to read and spell new words using the new sounds /x/ /y/ /ff/ /ll/ /ss/ /zz/ and the sounds they have previously learned.
- Introduce the book Dandelion Launchers Book 7a: Rex Yells
- You will be completing some activities from Dandelion Launchers Stages 1–7 Activities.

Preparation (15 mins)

- Model the new focus sounds.
- Explain that the /x/ sound is two sounds: /k/ and /s/.
- When introducing double consonants, show the student a card with the digraph (e.g. 'ss').
- Explain that the two letters stand for one sound: this is an alternative way to spell the sound /s/.

1 Word building and blending

- First demonstrate how to build a word. Use only three sound cards, e.g. "boss."
- Draw three lines on the whiteboard, and tell the students that you are going to show them how to build the word "boss."
- As you say the word slowly, move your finger under the lines.
- Ask the students to listen to the first sound in the word "boss"—point to the first line. Emphasize the first sound as you say the whole word. The students respond—/b/.
- Then ask the students which letter spells the sound /b/. The students point to the letter (or you can tell them). Bring the letter down to the first line.

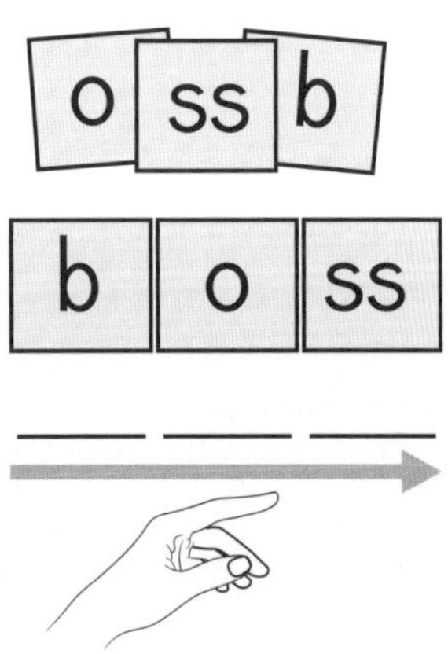

- Repeat with the second and last sounds in the word. Now ask the students to sound all three sounds and blend them into a word, moving your finger under the word: /b/ /o/ /ss/ → "boss."
- The next time this is done, you can ask a student to participate and identify the sound and then letter and bring it down to the line.

2 Word reading

- Write the words you have created on the whiteboard.
- Then ask students to blend and read the words.
- Show how to say each sound individually and then blend them together to read the word. Model blending by using a swishing motion with your finger for blending.

3 Oral segmenting

- Say a word aloud (e.g. "fix") and ask students to count the sounds in the word (3). Write the number of lines you need for all the sounds. Now ask students to listen to the sounds in the word and write a letter for every sound in the word as you spell the word.

4 Word chain

- Using sound cards, demonstrate how to build the word "fox."
- Say that you are going to change the word "fox" (moving your finger under the word) to "box." Ask the students to listen carefully to where the change has occurred. Move your finger under the word as you say it slowly. Once the change has been identified, invite a student to swap the sound card or letter. Ask all the students to sound out the word and read the new word. e.g. /b/ /o/ /x/ → "box."
- Introduce the new sounds gradually. This allows students to incorporate the letters and sounds they have learned so far.
- Direct students through the following word-chain sequence: fox—box—boss—bess—bell—yell—till—tix—tox—box—fox

STEP 2
Application for reading
15 mins

Before reading (3 mins)

- Revisit the vocabulary taught in Step 1 (e.g. "yell"). Clearly say the word: /y/ /e/ /ll/.
- Ask questions such as, "When do you yell?"
- Then write the word on the whiteboard and refer back to it throughout the week for reinforcement.

High-frequency words (2 mins)

- Pre-teach and reiterate these high-frequency words: "yells," "I," "the," "and," "was," "no," "be," "a," and "said."
- Explain that these are high-frequency words that have tricky spellings the students will learn later. Read each high-frequency word aloud.
- Write the words on the board, showing the separate graphemes in each word. As students learn more of the Alphabetic Code, they will be able to decode those graphemes.

Application (10 mins)

- Read Book 7a: Rex Yells.
- Encourage students to sound out each word and then blend to read.

STEP 3
Application for spelling
15 mins

Segmenting and spelling (5 mins)

- Ask students to complete the following activity to practice writing the graphemes: **Fill in the missing sounds** (Activities, page 147). Encourage the students to say the sounds as they write them and then blend the three sounds in each word together as they write them.

Spelling and dictation (10 mins)

- Ask students to complete **Fill in all the missing sounds** (Activities, page 148) to practice writing whole words.
- Read out the **Sentence dictation** sentences (Activities, page 153): "Jill and Fuzz hid in the box." and "Rex was sad. Rex had no pal." Encourage the students to sound out the words as they spell them.
- For students who finish early or need additional practice, create additional sentences and dictate these new passages to them.

STEP 4
Comprehension and consolidation
20 mins

Book reading (5 mins)

- Reread Book 7a: Rex Yells.

Comprehension (5 mins)

- Sequencing: Ask students to retell the story, using the pictures and words in the **Retelling the story** activity (Activities, page 155). The word cards on the same page can be used to reinforce vocabulary.
- Comprehension: Check students have understood the story by completing the **Comprehension** activity (Activities, page 157). Cut out the words on the page. Then ask students to read and match them to the correct pictures.

Consolidation (10 mins)

- Divide the class into pairs and give each pair a copy of the **Dice game** (Activities, page 163).

STEP 5
Tracking progress

- Complete the **Bookmark** (Activities, page 162).
- Revisit some of the activities to reinforce any specific skill gaps, or invite students to complete an additional activity from the Activities book.
- Then for a summative assessment of Stages 1–7, assign the **Reading Assessment** on page 65.

PARALLEL BOOKS

In addition to Book 7a: Rex Yells, the following books also cover the focus sounds (/x/ /y/ /ff/ /ll/ /ss/ /zz/) and can be used for more practice of decoding, for book bags to take home.

Dandelion Launchers

Book 7b: Rex Will Not Sit

Dandelion Launchers Extras

Book 7a: Bob on the Sill

Book 7b: The Hill

Dandelion World

Book 7a: The Jazz Gig

Book 7b: In the Dell

Dandelion Readers

Book 7: Bob is Not Well (Set 1 Units 1–10)

Book 7: Up a Big Hill (Set 2 Units 1–10)

Book 7: I Will Sell (Set 3 Units 1–10)

LESSON PLANS

Stage 8: CVCC

STEP 1
Preparation

20 mins

LESSON RESOURCES

Learning goal (2 mins)

- Explain to the students that you will be teaching them to read and spell words with four sounds using the sounds they have previously learned.
- Introduce the book Dandelion Launchers Book 8a: Junk.
- You will be completing some activities from Dandelion Launchers Stages 8–15 Activities.

Preparation (18 mins)

1 Word building and blending

- First demonstrate how to build a word. Use only four sound cards, e.g. for the word "sand."
- Draw four lines on the whiteboard, and tell the students that you are going to show them how to build the word "sand."
- As you say the word slowly, move your finger under the lines.
- Ask the students to listen to the first sound in the word "sand"—point to the first line. Emphasize the first sound as you say the whole word. The students respond—/s/.
- Then ask the students which letter spells the sound /s/. The students point to the letter (or you can tell them). Bring the letter down to the first line.
- Repeat with the remaining sounds in the word. Now ask the students to sound all four sounds and blend them into a word, moving your finger under the word: /s/ /a/ /n/ /d/ → "sand."
- The next time this is done, you can ask a student to participate and identify the sound and then letter and bring it down to the line.

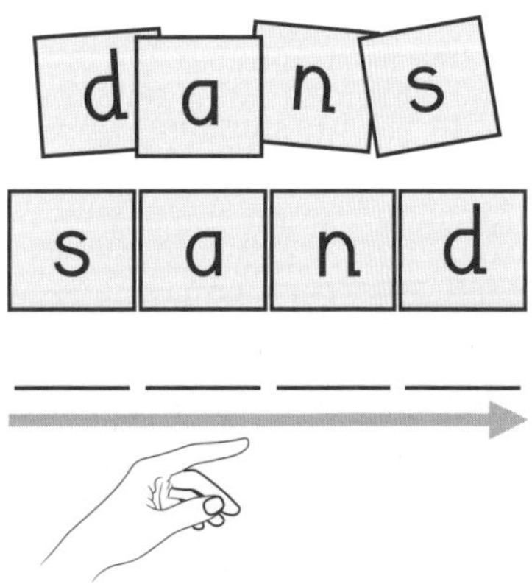

2 Word reading

- Write the words you have created on the whiteboard (if you haven't done so already). Then ask students to blend and read the words.
- Show how to say each sound individually and then blend them together to read the word. Model blending by using a swishing motion with your finger.
- Encourage students to follow your example with these words: "must," "tent," "hand," and "went."

3 Oral segmenting

- Say the word aloud (e.g. "mend") and count the sounds in the word (4). Write the number of lines you need for all the sounds. Now ask students to listen to the sounds in the word and write a letter for every sound in the word as you spell the word.

4 Word chain

- Using sound cards or magnetic letters, demonstrate how to build the word "tend." Explain to the students that you will be making one change to the word. They must be "sound detectives" and notice if you have added a sound, taken away a sound, or swapped a sound.
- Say that you are going to change the word "tend" (moving your finger under the word) to "tent." Ask the students to listen carefully to where the change has occurred. Move your finger under the word as you say it slowly. Once the change has been identified, invite a student to swap the sound card or letter. Ask all the students to sound out the word and read the new word. e.g. /t/ /e/ /n/ /t/ → "tent."
- Direct students through the following word-chain sequence: tend—tent—ten—tan—ban—band—hand—had—bad—bed—bend—tend

STEP 2
Application for reading
15 mins

Before reading (3 mins)

- Revisit the vocabulary taught in Step 1 (e.g. "tent"). Clearly say the word: /t/ /e/ /n/ /t/. Then provide a simple definition, e.g. "A tent is a shelter made of canvas or nylon that you can use outside."
- Ask questions such as "When do you use a tent?" and "What rhymes with 'tent'?"
- Then write the word on the whiteboard and refer back to it throughout the week for reinforcement.

High-frequency words (2 mins)

- Pre-teach or revisit these high-frequency words: "I," "of," "this," "old," "said," "to," "the," and "that."
- Explain that these are high-frequency words that have tricky spellings the students will learn later.
- Write the words on the board, showing the separate graphemes in each word. As students learn more of the Alphabetic Code, they will be able to decode those graphemes.

Application (10 mins)

- Read Book 8a: Junk.
- Encourage students to sound out each word and then blend to read.

STEP 3
Application for spelling
15 mins

Segmenting and spelling (5 mins)

- Ask students to complete the following activity to practice writing the graphemes: **Fill in initial missing sounds** (Activities, page 9). Encourage the students to say the sounds as they write them and then blend the four sounds in each word together as they write them.

Spelling and dictation (10 mins)

- Ask students to complete **Fill in all the missing sounds** (Activities, page 10) to practice writing whole words.
- Read out the **Sentence dictation** sentences (Activities, page 13): "Alf went to the dump." and "Hank and Alf went off to camp."
- Encourage the students to sound out the words as they spell them.
- For students who finish early or need additional practice, create additional sentences and dictate these new passages to them.

STEP 4
Comprehension and consolidation
20 mins

Book reading (5 mins)

- Reread 8a: Junk.

Comprehension (5 mins)

- Sequencing: Ask students to retell the story, using the pictures and words in the **Retelling the story** activity (Activities, page 15). The word cards on the same page can be used to reinforce vocabulary.
- Comprehension: Check students have understood the story by completing the **Comprehension** activity (Activities, page 17). Cut out the words on the page. Then ask students to read and match them to the correct pictures.

Consolidation (10 mins)

- Divide the class into pairs and give each pair a copy of the **Stepping stones game** (Activities, page 21).

STEP 5
Tracking progress

- Complete the **Spelling assessmen**t (Activities, page 26) to make a quick, formative assessment of students' progress.
- Depending on your findings, either revisit some of the activities to reinforce any specific skill gaps, or invite students to complete an additional activity from the Activities book.

PARALLEL BOOKS

In addition to Book 8a: Junk, the following books also cover CVCC words and can be used for more practice of decoding, for book bags to take home.

Dandelion Launchers
Book 8b: The Gift

Dandelion Launchers Extras
Book 8a: Lost
Book 8b: Jump!

Dandelion World
Book 8a: Kids at Camp
Book 8b: At Dusk

Dandelion Readers
Book 8: The Lost Box (Set 1 Units 1–10)
Book 8: Lost in the Pond (Set 2 Units 1–10)
Book 8: The Best Gift (Set 3 Units 1–10)

LESSON PLANS

Stage 9: CCVC

STEP 1
Preparation

20 mins

Reviewing sounds (3 mins)

- Using sound cards or a whiteboard, review some previously learned CVCC words.

Learning goal (2 mins)

- Explain to the students that you will be teaching them to read and spell words with four sounds using the sounds they have previously learned.
- Introduce the book Dandelion Launchers Book 9a: Don't Spill.
- You will be completing some activities from Dandelion Launchers Stages 8–15 Activities.

Preparation (15 mins)

1 Word building and blending

- First demonstrate how to build a word. Use only four sound cards, e.g. for the word "step."
- Draw four lines on the whiteboard, and tell the students that you are going to show them how to build the word "step."
- As you say the word slowly, move your finger under the lines.
- Ask the students to listen to the first sound in the word "step"—point to the first line. Emphasize the first sound as you say the whole word. The students respond—/s/.
- Then ask the students which letter spells the sound /s/. The students point to the letter (or you can tell them). Bring the letter down to the first line.
- Repeat with the remaining sounds in the word. Now ask the students to sound all four sounds and blend them into a word, moving your finger under the word: /s/ /t/ /e/ /p/ → "step."
- The next time this is done, you can ask a student to participate and identify the sound and then letter and bring it down to the line.

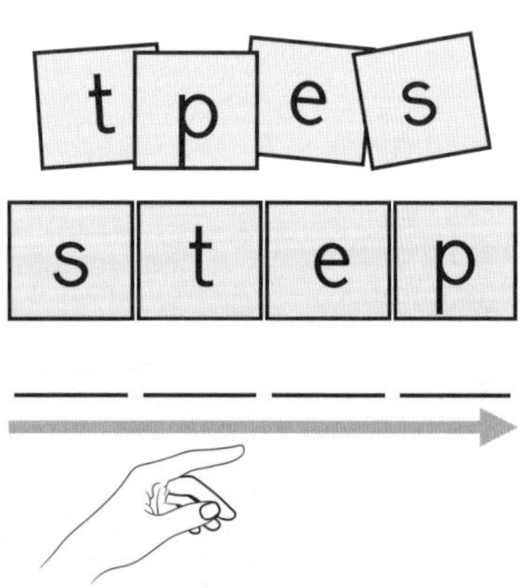

LESSON RESOURCES

2 Word reading

- Write the words you have created on the whiteboard (if you haven't done so already). Then ask students to blend and read the words.
- Show how to say each sound individually and then blend them together to read the word. Model blending by using a swishing motion with your finger.
- Encourage students to follow your example with these words: "step," "frog," "sled," and "grab."

3 Oral segmenting

- Say the word aloud (e.g. "spot") and count the sounds in the word (4). Write the number of lines you need for all the sounds. Now ask students to listen to the sounds in the word and write a letter for every sound in the word as you spell the word.

4 Word chain

- Using sound cards or magnetic letters, demonstrate how to build the word "slot." Explain to the students that you will be making one change to the word. They must be "sound detectives" and notice if you have added a sound, taken away a sound, or swapped a sound.
- Say that you are going to change the word "slot" (moving your finger under the word) to "slat." Ask the students to listen carefully to where the change has occurred. Move your finger under the words as you say it slowly. Once the change has been identified, invite a student to swap the sound card or letter. Ask all the students to sound out the word and read the new word. e.g. /s/ /l/ /a/ /t/ → "slat."
- Direct students through the following word-chain sequence: slot—slat—slap—lap—clap—cap—camp—lamp—limp—lip—slip—slop—slot

STEP 2
Application for reading
15 mins

Before reading (3 mins)

- Pre-teach difficult vocabulary in the book (e.g. "glum" and "brim"). Clearly say the word: /g/ /l/ /u/ /m/. Then provide a simple definition, e.g. "Glum describes a feeling of sadness."
- Ask questions such as, "Can you think of a book where a character felt glum?"
- Then write the word on the whiteboard and refer back to it throughout the week for reinforcement.

High-frequency words (2 mins)

- Pre-teach or revisit these high-frequency words: "have," "a," "of," "don't," "says," "the," "to," and "is."
- Explain that these are high-frequency words that have tricky spellings the students will learn later.
- Write the words on the board, showing the separate graphemes in each word. As students learn more of the Alphabetic Code, they will be able to decode those graphemes.

Application (10 mins)

- Read Book 9a: Don't Spill.
- Encourage students to sound out each word and then blend to read.

STEP 3
Application for spelling
15 mins

Segmenting and spelling (5 mins)

- Ask students to complete the following activity to practice writing the graphemes: **Fill in initial missing sounds** (Activities, page 31). Encourage the students to say the sounds as they write them and then blend the four sounds in each word together as they write them.

Spelling and dictation (10 mins)

- Ask students to complete **Fill in all the missing sounds** (Activities, page 32) to practice writing whole words.
- Read out the **Sentence dictation** sentences (Activities, page 35): "Viv fills the cups to the brim." and "Viv and Fred trip and spill the milk."
- Encourage the students to sound out the words as they spell them.
- For students who finish early or need additional practice, create additional sentences and dictate these new passages to them.

STEP 4
Comprehension and consolidation
20 mins

Book reading (5 mins)

- Reread Book 9a: Don't Spill.

Comprehension (5 mins)

- Sequencing: Ask students to retell the story, using the pictures and words in the **Retelling the story** activity (Activities, page 37). The word cards on the same page can be used to reinforce vocabulary.
- Comprehension: Check students have understood the story by completing the **Comprehension** activity (Activities, page 39). Cut out the words on the page. Then ask students to read and match them to the correct pictures.

Consolidation (10 mins)

- Divide the class into pairs and give each pair a copy of the **Dice game** (Activities, page 45).

STEP 5
Tracking progress

- Complete the **Spelling assessmen**t (Activities, page 48) to make a quick, formative assessment of students' progress.
- Depending on your findings, either revisit some of the activities to reinforce any specific skill gaps, or invite students to complete an additional activity from the Activities book.

PARALLEL BOOKS

In addition to Book 9a: Don't Spill, the following books also cover CCVC words and can be used for more practice of decoding, for book bags to take home.

Dandelion Launchers
Book 9b: Floss

Dandelion Launchers Extras
Book 9a: Bob is Glum
Book 9b: Stop the Pram!

Dandelion World
Book 9a: Up the Cliff
Book 9b: Clam, Crab, Gull

Dandelion Readers
Book 9: Flip and Flop Slip (Set 1 Units 1–10)
Book 9: The Trap (Set 2 Units 1–10)
Book 9: Fred Has a Plan (Set 3 Units 1–10)

LESSON PLANS

Stage 10: CCVCC

STEP 1
Preparation

20 mins

LESSON RESOURCES

Reviewing sounds (3 mins)

- Using sound cards or a whiteboard, review some previously learned CCVC words.

Learning goal (2 mins)

- Explain to the students that you will be teaching them to read and spell words with five sounds using the sounds they have previously learned.
- Introduce the book Dandelion Launchers Book 10a: Stunt Rat.
- You will be completing some activities from Dandelion Launchers Stages 8–15 Activities.

Preparation (15 mins)

1 Word building

- First demonstrate how to build a word. Use only five sound cards, e.g. for the word "drink."
- Draw five lines on the whiteboard, and tell the students that you are going to show them how to build the word "drink."
- As you say the word slowly, move your finger under the lines.
- Ask the students to listen to the first sound in the word "drink"—point to the first line. Emphasize the first sound as you say the whole word. The students respond—/d/.
- Then ask the students which letter spells the sound /d/. The students point to the letter (or you can tell them). Bring the letter down to the first line.
- Repeat with the remaining sounds in the word. Now ask the students to sound all four sounds and blend them into a word, moving your finger under the word: /d/ /r/ /i/ /n/ /k/ → "drink."
- The next time this is done, you can ask a student to participate and identify the sound and then letter and bring it down to the line.

2 Word reading

- Write the words you have created on the whiteboard (if you haven't done so already). Then ask blend and read the words.
- Show how to say each sound individually and then blend them together to read the word. Model blending by using a swishing motion with your finger for blending.
- Encourage students to follow your example with these words: "drink," "stunt," and "trunk."

3 Oral segmenting

- Say the word aloud (e.g. "print") and count the sounds in the word (5). Write the number of lines you need for all the sounds. Now ask students to listen to the sounds in the word and write a letter for every sound in the word as you spell the word.

4 Word chain

- Using sound cards or magnetic letters, demonstrate how to build the word "brand." Explain to the students that you will be making one change to the word. They must be "sound detectives" and notice if you have added a sound, taken away a sound, or swapped a sound.
- Say that you are going to change the word "brand" (moving your finger under the word) to "bland." Ask the students to listen carefully to where the change has occurred. Swish your finger under the words as you say it slowly. Once the change has been identified, invite a student to swap the sound card or letter. Ask all the students to sound out the word and read the new word. e.g. /b/ /l/ /a/ /n/ /d/ → "bland."
- Direct students through the following word-chain sequence: brand—bland—land—sand—stand—stan—clan—clam—clamp—cramp—cram—ram—ran—bran—brand

STEP 2
Application for reading
15 mins

Before reading (3 mins)

- Revisit the vocabulary taught in Step 1 (e.g. "stunt"). Clearly say the word: /s/ /t/ /u/ /n/ /t/. Then provide a simple definition, e.g. "A stunt is an action that shows skill or bravery."
- Ask questions such as "What rhymes with stunt?" and "Who performs stunts?"
- Then write the word on the whiteboard and refer back to it throughout the week for reinforcement.

High-frequency words (2 mins)

- Pre-teach or revisit these high-frequency words: "he," "as," "I," "be," "a," "says," and "the."
- Explain that these are high-frequency words that have tricky spellings the students will learn later.
- Write the words on the board, showing the separate graphemes in each word. As students learn more of the Alphabetic Code, they will be able to decode those graphemes.

Application (10 mins)

- Read Book 10a: Stunt Rat.
- Encourage students to sound out each word and then blend to read.

STEP 3
Application for spelling
15 mins

Segmenting and spelling (5 mins)

- Ask students to complete the following activity to practice writing the graphemes: **Fill in initial missing sounds** (Activities, page 53). Encourage the students to say the sounds as they write them and then blend the five sounds in each word together as they write them.

Spelling and dictation (10 mins)

- Ask students to complete **Fill in all the missing sounds** (Activities, page 54) to practice writing whole words.
- Read out the **Sentence dictation** sentences (Activities, page 57): "Ken lifts up the twigs." and "Ken springs off and Bob pants." Encourage the students to sound out the words as they spell them.
- For students who finish early or need additional practice, create additional sentences and dictate these new passages to them.

STEP 4
Comprehension and consolidation
20 mins

Book reading (5 mins)

- Reread 10a: Stunt Rat.

Comprehension (5 mins)

- Sequencing: Ask students to retell the story, using the pictures and words in the **Retelling the story** activity (Activities, page 59).
- Comprehension: Check students have understood the story by completing the **Comprehension** activity (Activities, page 61). Cut out the words on the page. Then ask students to read and match them to the correct pictures.

Consolidation (10 mins)

- Divide the class into pairs and give each pair a copy of the **Dice game** (Activities, page 67).
- Have students find and point to these words in Book 10a: Stunt Rat: "stunt" and "swims."

STEP 5
Tracking progress

- Complete the **Spelling assessment** (Activities, page 71) to make a quick, formative assessment of students' progress.
- Then for a summative assessment of Stages 8–10, assign the **Reading Assessment** on page 73.

PARALLEL BOOKS

In addition to Book 10a: Stunt Rat, the following books also cover CCVCC words and can be used for more practice of decoding, for book bags to take home.

Dandelion Launchers

Book 10b: Frank Swims

Dandelion Launchers Extras

Book 10a: Punk Smells Crisp Chips

Book 10b: Mom Gets Strict

Dandelion World

Book 10a: Frost Melts

Book 10b: Frank and the Skunk

Dandelion Readers

Book 10: The Stink (Set 1 Units 1–10)

Book 10: Punk and the Plums (Set 2 Units 1–10)

Book 10: The Stilts (Set 3 Units 1–10)

LESSON PLANS

Stage 11: ch

STEP 1
Preparation

20 mins

Reviewing sounds (3 mins)

- Using sound cards or a whiteboard, review some previously learned CCVCC words.

Learning goal (2 mins)

- Explain to the students that you will be teaching them to read and spell words using the consonant digraph /ch/ and sounds they have previously learned.
- Introduce the book Dandelion Launchers Book 11a: Nuts for Lunch.
- You will be completing some activities from Dandelion Launchers Stages 8–15 Activities.

Preparation (15 mins)

- Introduce and model the new focus sound: /ch/.

1 Word building and blending

- First demonstrate how to build a word. Use only three sound cards, e.g. for the word "chip."
- Draw three lines on the whiteboard, and tell the students that you are going to show them how to build the word "chip."
- As you say the word slowly, move your finger under the lines.
- Ask the students to listen to the first sound in the word "chip"—point to the first line. Emphasize the first sound as you say the whole word. The students respond—/ch/.
- Then ask the students which letters spell the sound /ch/. Remind students that two letters 'c' and 'h' spell the sound /ch/. Bring the letters down to the first line.
- Repeat with the second and last sounds in the word. Now ask the students to sound all three sounds and blend them into a word, moving your finger under the word: /ch/ /i/ /p/ → "chip."

LESSON RESOURCES

- The next time this is done, you can ask a student to participate and identify the sound and then letter and bring it down to the line.

2 Word reading

- Write the words you have created on the whiteboard (if you haven't done so already). Then ask students to blend and read the words.
- Show how to say each sound individually and then blend them together to read the word. Model blending by using a swishing motion with your finger for blending.
- Encourage students to follow your example with these words: "chest," "lunch," "bench."

3 Oral segmenting

- Say the word aloud (e.g. "munch") and count the sounds in the word (4). Write the number of lines you need for all the sounds. Now ask students to listen to the sounds in the word and write a letter for every sound in the word as you spell the word.

4 Word chain

- Using sound cards or magnetic letters, demonstrate how to build the word "lunch." Explain to the students that you will be making one change to the word. They must be "sound detectives" and notice if you have added a sound, taken away a sound, or swapped a sound.
- Say that you are going to change the word "lunch" (moving your finger under the word) to "munch." Ask the students to listen carefully to where the change has occurred. Move your finger under the word as you say it slowly. Once the change has been identified, invite a student to swap the sound card or letter. Ask all the students to sound out the word and read the new word. e.g. /m/ /u/ /n/ /ch/ → "munch."
- Direct students through the following word-chain sequence: lunch—munch—punch—bunch—hunch—lunch

STEP 2
Application for reading
15 mins

Before reading (3 mins)

- Revisit the vocabulary taught in Step 1 (e.g. "lunch"). Clearly say the word: /l/ /u/ /n/ /ch/. Then provide a simple definition, e.g. "Lunch is a meal eaten in the middle of the day."
- Ask questions such as "What do you eat for lunch?" and "What do squirrels eat?"
- Then write the word on the whiteboard and refer back to it throughout the week for reinforcement.

High-frequency words (2 mins)

- Pre-teach or revisit these high-frequency words: "a," "was," "to," "the," "for," "his," "I," "have," "said," "plant," and "off."
- Explain that these are high-frequency words that have tricky spellings the students will learn later.
- Write the words on the board, showing the separate graphemes in each word. As students learn more of the Alphabetic Code, they will be able to decode those graphemes.

Application (10 mins)

- Read Book 11a: Nuts for Lunch.
- Encourage students to sound out each word and then blend to read.

STEP 3
Application for spelling
15 mins

Segmenting and spelling (5 mins)

- Ask students to complete the following activity to practice writing the graphemes: **Fill in the ch sound** (Activities, page 75). Encourage the students to say the sounds as they write them and then blend the sounds in each word together as they write them.

Spelling and dictation (10 mins)

- Ask students to complete **Fill in all the missing sounds** (Activities, page 76) to practice writing whole words.
- Read out the **Sentence dictation** sentences (Activities, page 79): "I have nuts to munch." and "Let's plant a nut next to the bench."
- Encourage the students to sound out the words as they spell them.
- For students who finish early or need additional practice, create additional sentences and dictate these new passages to them.

STEP 4
Comprehension and consolidation
20 mins

Book reading (5 mins)

- Reread Book 11a: Nuts for Lunch.

Comprehension (5 mins)

- Sequencing: Ask students to retell the story, using the pictures and words in the **Retelling the story** activity (Activities, page 81). The word cards on the same page can be used to reinforce vocabulary.
- Comprehension: Check students have understood the story by completing the **Comprehension** activity (Activities, page 83). Cut out the words on the page. Then ask students to read and match them to the correct pictures.

Consolidation (10 mins)

- Divide the class into pairs and give each pair a copy of the **Dice game** (Activities, page 89)

STEP 5
Tracking progress

- Complete the **Spelling assessment** (Activities, page 92) to make a quick, formative assessment of students' progress.
- Depending on your findings, either revisit some of the activities to reinforce any specific skill gaps, or invite students to complete an additional activity from the Activities book.

PARALLEL BOOKS

In addition to Book 11a: Nuts for Lunch, the following books also cover the /ch/ sound and can be used for more practice of decoding, for book bags to take home.

Dandelion Launchers
Book 11b: The Champ

Dandelion Launchers Extras
Book 11a: The Big Chip
Book 11b: Chit Chat

Dandelion World
Book 11a: Crunch, Munch!
Book 11b: Chimp Chums

Dandelion Readers
Book 11: Pip Gets Rich (Set 1 Units 11–20)
Book 11: Twin Chimps (Set 2 Units 11–20)

LESSON PLANS

Stage 12: sh

STEP 1
Preparation

20 mins

Reviewing sounds (3 mins)

- Using sound cards or a whiteboard, review some previously learned words containing the /ch/ sound.

Learning goal (2 mins)

- Explain to the students that you will be teaching them to read and spell words using the consonant digraph /sh/ and sounds they have previously learned.
- Introduce the book Dandelion Launchers Book 12a: Shep and Tosh.
- You will be completing some activities from Dandelion Launchers Stages 8–15 Activities.

Preparation (15 mins)

- Introduce and model the new focus sound: /sh/.

1 Word building and blending

- First demonstrate how to build a word. Use only three sound cards, e.g. for the word "ship."
- Draw three lines on the whiteboard, and tell the students that you are going to show them how to build the word "ship."
- As you say the word slowly, move your finger under the lines.
- Ask the students to listen to the first sound in the word "ship"—point to the first line. Emphasize the first sound as you say the whole word. The students respond—/sh/.
- Then ask the students which letters spell the sound /sh/. Remind students that two letters 's' and 'h' spell the sound /sh/. Bring the letters down to the first line.
- Repeat with the second and last sounds in the word. Now ask the students to sound all three sounds and blend them into a word, moving your finger under the word: /sh/ /i/ /p/ → "ship"

LESSON RESOURCES

- The next time this is done, you can ask a student to participate and identify the sound and then letter and bring it down to the line.

2 Word reading

- Write the words you have created on the whiteboard (if you haven't done so already). Then ask students to blend and read the words.
- Show how to say each sound individually and then blend them together to read the word. Model blending by using a swishing motion with your finger for blending.
- Encourage students to follow your example with these words: "wish" and "shrub."

3 Oral segmenting

- Say the word aloud (e.g. "wish") and count the sounds in the word (3). Write the number of lines you need for all the sounds. Now ask students to listen to the sounds in the word and write a letter for every sound in the word as you spell the word.

4 Word chain

- Using sound cards or magnetic letters, demonstrate how to build the word "wish." Explain to the students that you will be making one change to the word. They must be "sound detectives" and notice if you have added a sound, taken away a sound, or swapped a sound.
- Say that you are going to change the word "wish" (moving your finger under the word) to "dish." Ask the students to listen carefully to where the change has occurred. Move your finger under the words as you say it slowly. Once the change has been identified, invite a student to swap the sound card or letter. Ask all the students to sound out the word and read the new word. e.g. /d/ /i/ /sh/ → "dish."
- Direct students through the following word-chain sequence: wish—dish—dash—ash—cash—clash—flash—flush—lush—blush—brush—rush—mush—mash—dash—dish—wish

STEP 2
Application for reading
15 mins

Before reading (3 mins)

- Pre-teach difficult vocabulary in the book (e.g. "shrub"). Clearly say the word: /sh/ /r/ /u/ /b/. Then provide a simple definition, e.g. "A shrub is a type of small, woody plant."
- Ask questions such as, "Can you name a type of shrub you know?"
- Then write the word on the whiteboard and refer back to it throughout the week for reinforcement.

High-frequency words (2 mins)

- Pre-teach or revisit these high-frequency words: "I," "a," "was," "you," "be," "my," "to," "no," "yelled," and "said."
- Explain that these are high-frequency words that have tricky spellings the students will learn later.
- Write the words on the board, showing the separate graphemes in each word. As students learn more of the Alphabetic Code, they will be able to decode those graphemes.

Application (10 mins)

- Read Book 12a: Shep and Tosh.
- Encourage students to sound out each word and then blend to read.

STEP 3
Application for spelling
15 mins

Segmenting and spelling (5 mins)

- Ask students to complete the following activity to practice writing the graphemes: **Fill in the sh sound** (Activities, page 97). Encourage the students to say the sounds as they write them and then blend the sounds in each word together as they write them.

Spelling and dictation (10 mins)

- Ask students to complete **Fill in all the missing sounds** (Activities, page 98) to practice writing whole words.
- Read out the **Sentence dictation** sentences (Activities, page 101): "The big dog yelled at Shep." and "Shep ran and hid in a shrub."
- Encourage the students to sound out the words as they spell them.
- For students who finish early or need additional practice, create additional sentences and dictate these new passages to them.

STEP 4
Comprehension and consolidation
20 mins

Book reading (5 mins)

- Reread Book 12a: Shep and Tosh.

Comprehension (5 mins)

- Sequencing: Ask students to retell the story, using the pictures and words in the **Retelling the story** activity (Activities, page 103). The word cards on the same page can be used to reinforce vocabulary.
- Comprehension: Check students have understood the story by completing the **Comprehension** activity (Activities, page 105). Cut out the words on the page. Then ask students to read and match them to the correct pictures.

Consolidation (10 mins)

- Divide the class into pairs and give each pair a copy of the **Stepping stones game** (Activities, page 113).

STEP 5
Tracking progress

- Complete the **Spelling assessment** (Activities, page 110) to make a quick, formative assessment of students' progress.
- Depending on your findings, either revisit some of the activities to reinforce any specific skill gaps, or invite students to complete an additional activity from the Activities book.

PARALLEL BOOKS

In addition to Book 12a: Shep and Tosh, the following books also cover the /sh/ sound and can be used for more practice of decoding, for book bags to take home.

Dandelion Launchers

Book 12b: Fresh Fish

Dandelion Launchers Extras

Book 12a: The Shop

Book 12b: Fish Pond

Dandelion World

Book 12a: Trash in the Trench

Book 12b: Sled Dogs Dash

Dandelion Readers

Book 12: "Hush!" (Set 1 Units 11–20)

Book 12: The Cash (Set 2 Units 11–20)

LESSON PLANS

Stage 13: th

STEP 1
Preparation

20 mins

Reviewing sounds (3 mins)

- Using sound cards or a whiteboard, review some previously learned words containing the /sh/ sound.

Learning goal (2 mins)

- Explain to the students that you will be teaching them to read and spell words using the consonant digraph /th/ and sounds they have previously learned.
- Introduce the book Dandelion Launchers Book 13a: This and That.
- You will be completing some activities from Dandelion Launchers Stages 8–15 Activities.

Preparation (15 mins)

- Introduce and model the new focus sound: /th/.
- 'th' can spell two different sounds: /th/ as in "that" which is voiced, and /th/ as in "thin" which is non-voiced. Ask students to listen to you say the word "that" and hear the voiced sound /th/ at the beginning of the word. Then ask them to listen to the word "thin" and hear just the air flowing at the beginning of the word.

1 Word building and blending

- First demonstrate how to build a word. Use only three sound cards, e.g. for the word "that."
- Draw three lines on the whiteboard, and tell the students that you are going to show them how to build the word "that."
- As you say the word slowly, move your finger under the lines.
- Ask the students to listen to the first sound in the word "that"—point to the first line. Emphasize the first sound as you say the whole word. The students respond—/th/.
- Then ask the students which letters spell the sound /th/. Remind students that two letters 't' and 'h' spell the sound /th/. Bring the letters down to the first line.
- Repeat with the second and last sounds in the word. Now ask the students to sound all three sounds and blend them into a word, moving your finger under the word: /th/ /a/ /t/ → "that"

LESSON RESOURCES

- The next time this is done, you can ask a student to participate and identify the sound and then letter and bring it down to the line.

2 Word reading

- Write the words you have created on the whiteboard (if you haven't done so already). Then ask students to blend and read the words.
- Show how to say each sound individually and then blend them together to read the word. Model blending by using a swishing motion with your finger for blending.
- Encourage students to follow your example with these words: "this," "that," and "think."

3 Oral segmenting

- Say a word aloud (e.g. "this") and ask students to count the sounds in the word (3). Write the number of lines you need for all the sounds. Now ask students to listen to the sounds in the word and write a letter for every sound in the word as you spell the word.

4 Word chain

- Using sound cards or magnetic letters, demonstrate how to build the word "that." Explain to the students that you will be making one change to the word. They must be "sound detectives" and notice if you have added a sound, taken away a sound, or swapped a sound.
- Say that you are going to change the word "that" (moving your finger under the word) to "at." Ask the students to listen carefully to where the change has occurred. Move your finger under the word as you say it slowly. Once the change has been identified, invite a student to swap the sound card or letter. Ask all the students to sound out the word and read the new word. e.g. /a/ /t/ → "at."
- Direct students through the following word-chain sequence: that—at—bat—bit—bin—thin—think—thank—bank—ban—than—that

STEP 2
Application for reading
15 mins

Before reading (3 mins)

- Revisit the vocabulary in Step 1 (e.g. "think"). Clearly say the word: /th/ /i/ /n/ /k/. Then provide a simple definition, e.g. "To think is to have an idea about something or someone."
- Ask questions such as "What rhymes with 'think'?" and "What might you be thinking when holding an ice cream?"
- Then write the word on the whiteboard and refer back to it throughout the week for reinforcement.

High-frequency words (2 mins)

- Pre-teach or revisit these high-frequency words: "to," "I," "have," "a," "of," and "the."
- Explain that these are high-frequency words that have tricky spellings the students will learn later.
- Write the words on the board, showing the separate graphemes in each word. As students learn more of the Alphabetic Code, they will be able to decode those graphemes.

Application (10 mins)

- Read Book 13a: This and That.
- Encourage students to sound out each word and then blend to read.

STEP 3
Application for spelling
15 mins

Segmenting and spelling (5 mins)

- Ask students to complete the following activity to practice writing the graphemes: **Fill in the th sound** (Activities, page 121). Encourage the students to say the sounds as they write them and then blend the sounds in each word together as they write them.

Spelling and dictation (10 mins)

- Ask students to complete **Fill in all the missing sounds** (Activities, page 122) to practice writing whole words.
- Read out the **Sentence dictation** sentences (Activities, page 125): "and with nuts on the top..." and "'I think that's it. Thanks. Yum!'" Encourage the students to sound out the words as they spell them.
- For students who finish early or need additional practice, create additional sentences and dictate these new passages to them.

STEP 4
Comprehension and consolidation
20 mins

Book reading (5 mins)

- Reread Book 13a: This and That.

Comprehension (5 mins)

- Sequencing: Ask students to retell the story, using the pictures and words in the **Retelling the story** activity (Activities, page 127). The word cards on the same page can be used to reinforce vocabulary.
- Comprehension: Check students have understood the story by completing the **Comprehension** activity (Activities, page 129). Cut out the words on the page. Then ask students to read and match them to the correct pictures.

Consolidation (10 mins)

- Divide the class into pairs and give each pair a copy of the **Dice game** (Activities, page 135).

STEP 5
Tracking progress

- Complete the **Spelling assessment** (Activities, page 138) to make a quick, formative assessment of students' progress.
- Depending on your findings, either revisit some of the activities to reinforce any specific skill gaps, or invite students to complete an extension activity.

PARALLEL BOOKS

In addition to Book 13a: This and That, the following books also cover the /th/ sound and can be used for more practice of decoding, for book bags to take home.

Dandelion Launchers
Book 13b: Will This Fit?

Dandelion Launchers Extras
Book 13a: Thud! Crash!
Book 13b: That's It!

Dandelion World
Book 13a: Sloths
Book 13b: The Thrill of a Run

Dandelion Readers
Book 13: The Path Up the Hill (Set 1 Units 11–20)
Book 13: Thump, Thump (Set 2 Units 11–20)

Stage 14: ck, wh

STEP 1
Preparation 20 mins

Reviewing sounds (3 mins)

- Using sound cards or a whiteboard, review some previously learned words containing the two sounds for the spelling 'th'.

Learning goal (2 mins)

- Explain to the students that you will be teaching them to read and spell words using the consonant digraphs ck and wh and sounds they have previously learned.
- Introduce the book Dandelion Launchers Book 14b: Which Shall I Pick?
- You will be completing some activities from Dandelion Launchers Stages 8–15 Activities.

Preparation (15 mins)

- Introduce the new focus spellings: 'ck' and 'wh.'
- Model how to say each sound correctly (/k/ and /w/).
- Explain that we have already learned two other ways to spell the sound /k/ (e.g. "cat" and "king").
- Explain that we have already learned another way to spell the sound /w/ as in "wind."

1 Word building and blending

- First demonstrate how to build a word. Use only three sound cards, e.g. for "duck."
- Draw three lines on the whiteboard, and tell the students that you are going to show them how to build the word "duck."
- As you say the word slowly, move your finger under the lines.
- Ask the students to listen to the first sound in the word "duck"—point to the first line. Emphasize the first sound as you say the whole word. The students respond—/d/.
- Then ask the students which letter spells the sound /d/. The students point to the letter (or you can tell them). Bring the letter down to the first line.
- Repeat with the second and last sounds in the word. Now ask the students to sound all three sounds and blend them into a word, moving your finger under the word: /d/ /u/ /ck/ → "duck"

LESSON RESOURCES

- The next time this is done, you can ask a student to participate and identify the sound and then letter and bring it down to the line.

2 Word reading

- Write the words you have created on the whiteboard (if you haven't done so already). Then ask students to blend and read the words.
- Show how to say each sound individually and then blend them together to read the word. Model blending by using a swishing motion with your finger for blending.
- Encourage students to follow your example with these words: "pack," "thick," "when."

3 Oral segmenting

- Say a word aloud (e.g. "thick") and ask students to count the sounds in the word (3). Write the number of lines you need for all the sounds. Now ask students to listen to the sounds in the word and write a letter for every sound in the word as you spell the word.

4 Word chain

- Using sound cards or magnetic letters, demonstrate how to build the word "lick." Explain to the students that you will be making one change to the word. They must be "sound detectives" and notice if you have added a sound, taken away a sound, or swapped a sound.
- Say that you are going to change the word "lick" (moving your finger under the word) to "click." Ask the students to listen carefully to where the change has occurred. Move your finger under the word as you say it slowly. Once the change has been identified, invite a student to swap the sound card or letter. Ask all the students to sound out the word and read the new word. e.g. /c/ /l/ /i/ /ck/ → "click."
- Direct students through the following word-chain sequence: lick—click—slick—slack—lack—lock—clock—clack—black—back—rack—track—trick—tick—lick

STEP 2
Application for reading

15 mins

Before reading (3 mins)

- Revisit the vocabulary taught in Step 1 (e.g. "sock"). Clearly say the word: "sock." Then provide a simple definition, e.g. "A sock is a piece of clothing for the foot."
- Ask questions such as "What patterns can socks have?" and "What else do you wear on your feet?"
- Then write the word on the whiteboard and refer back to it throughout the week for reinforcement.

High-frequency words (2 mins)

- Pre-teach or revisit these high-frequency words: "cold," "he," "to," "the," "I," and "put."
- Write the words on the board, showing the separate graphemes in each word. As students learn more of the Alphabetic Code, they will be able to decode those graphemes.

Application (10 mins)

- Read Book 14b: Which Shall I Pick?
- Encourage students to sound out each word and then blend to read.

STEP 3
Application for spelling

15 mins

Segmenting and spelling (5 mins)

- Ask students to complete the following activity to practice writing the graphemes: **Fill in the ck sound** (Activities, page 145). Encourage the students to say the sounds as they write them and then blend the four sounds in each word together as they write them.

Spelling and dictation (10 mins)

- Ask students to complete **Fill in all the missing sounds** (Activities, page 146) to practice writing whole words.
- Read out the **Sentence dictation** sentences (Activities, page 151): "'Jim put on the thick socks and the black socks." and "When Jim left the sock shop, he had lots of socks!" Encourage the students to sound out the words as they spell them.
- For students who finish early or need additional practice, create additional sentences and dictate these new passages to them.

STEP 4
Comprehension and consolidation

20 mins

Book reading (5 mins)

- Reread Book 14b: Which Shall I Pick?

Comprehension (5 mins)

- Sequencing: Ask students to retell the story, using the pictures and words in the **Retelling the story** activity (Activities, page 153). The word cards on the same page can be used to reinforce vocabulary.
- Comprehension: Check students have understood the story by completing the **Comprehension** activity (Activities, page 155). Cut out the words on the page. Then ask students to read and match them to the correct pictures.

Consolidation (10 mins)

- Divide the class into pairs and give each pair a copy of the **Dice game** (Activities, page 161).

STEP 5
Tracking progress

- Complete the **Spelling assessment** (Activities, page 164) to make a quick, formative assessment of students' progress.
- Depending on your findings, either revisit some of the activities to reinforce any specific skill gaps, or invite students to complete another activity from the Activities book.

PARALLEL BOOKS

In addition to Book 14b: Which Shall I Pick?, the following books also cover the 'ck' or 'wh' spellings and can be used for more practice of decoding, for book bags to take home.

Dandelion Launchers

Book 14a: The Back Pack

Dandelion Launchers Extras

Book 14a: The Clock

Book 14b: When Can I Get On?

Dandelion World

Book 14a: Shells and Rocks

Book 14b: Flick the Puck

Dandelion Readers

Book 14: The Trick (Set 1 Units 11–20)

Book 14: Raj Gets a Shock (Set 2 Units 11–20)

Stage 15: ng, qu

STEP 1
Preparation

20 mins

Reviewing sounds (3 mins)

- Using sound cards or a whiteboard, review some previously learned words containing the 'ck' and 'wh' spellings.

Learning goal (2 mins)

- Explain to the students that you will be teaching them to read and spell words using the consonant digraphs ng and qu and sounds they have previously learned.
- Introduce the book Dandelion Launchers Book 15b: The Strong Wind.
- You will be completing some activities from Dandelion Launchers Stages 8–15 Activities.

Preparation (15 mins)

- Introduce and model the new focus sounds: /ng/ and /qu/. Note: the letters 'qu' spell two sounds (/k/ and /w/), but we teach them together because they usually appear together in words.

1 Word building and blending

- First demonstrate how to build a word. Use only three sound cards, e.g. for the word "quip."
- Draw three lines on the whiteboard, and tell the students that you are going to show them how to build the word "quip."
- As you say the word slowly, move your finger under the lines.
- Ask the students to listen to the first sound in the word "quip"—point to the first line. Emphasize the first sound as you say the whole word. The students respond—/qu/.
- Then ask the students which letters spell this sound. The students point to the letters (or you can tell them). Bring the letters down to the first line.
- Repeat with the second and last sounds in the word. Now ask the students to sound all three sounds and blend them into a word, moving your finger under the word: /qu/ /i/ /p/ → "quip"
- The next time this is done, you can ask a student to participate and identify the sound and then letter and bring it down to the line.

LESSON RESOURCES

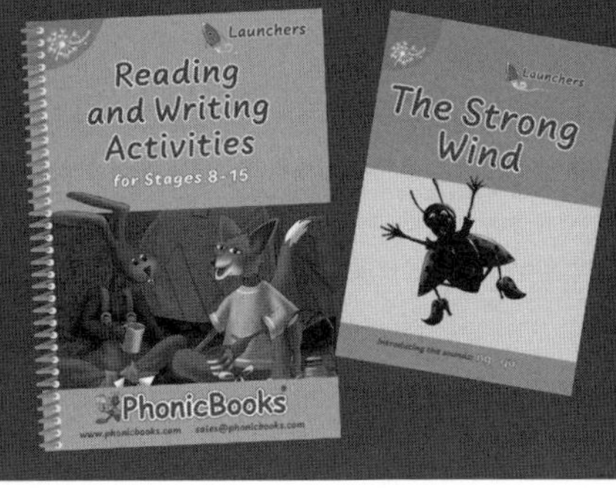

2 Word reading

- Write the words you have created on the whiteboard (if you haven't done so already). Then ask students to blend and read the words.
- Show how to say each sound individually and then blend them together to read the word. Model blending by using a swishing motion with your finger for blending.
- Encourage students to follow your example with these words: "ding," "rings," "quit," and "quick."

3 Oral segmenting

- Say a word aloud (e.g. "quilt") and ask students to count to sounds in the word (4). Write the number of lines you need for all the sounds. Now ask students to listen to the sounds in the word and write a letter for every sound in the word as you spell the word.
- You may need to explain that /qu/ is two sounds: /k/ and /w/.

4 Word chain

- Using sound cards or magnetic letters, demonstrate how to build the word "sing." Explain to the students that you will be making one change to the word. They must be "sound detectives" and notice if you have added a sound, taken away a sound, or swapped a sound.
- Say that you are going to change the word "sing" (moving your finger under the word) to "sling." Ask the students to listen carefully to where the change has occurred. Move your finger under the word as you say it slowly. Once the change has been identified, invite a student to swap the sound card or letter. Ask all the students to sound out the word and read the new word. e.g. /s/ /l/ /i/ /ng/ → "sling."
- Direct students through the following word-chain sequence: sing—sling—slang—sang—song—pong—ping—wing—swing—sing

STEP 2
Application for reading
15 mins

Before reading (3 mins)

- Revisit the vocabulary in Step 1 (e.g. "sing"). Clearly say the word: /s/ /i/ /ng/. Then provide a simple definition, e.g. "To sing is to make a musical sound with your voice."
- Ask questions such as "What is your favorite song?" and "When might you sing on someone's birthday?"
- Then write the word on the whiteboard and refer back to it throughout the week for reinforcement.

High-frequency words (2 mins)

- Pre-teach or revisit these high-frequency words: "I," "have," "you," "do," "to," "was," "he," "said," "the," "a," "she," "cannot," and "yelled."
- Write the words on the board, showing the separate graphemes in each word. As students learn more of the Alphabetic Code, they will be able to decode those graphemes.

Application (10 mins)

- Read Book 15b: The Strong Wind.
- Encourage students to sound out each word and then blend to read.

STEP 3
Application for spelling
15 mins

Segmenting and spelling (5 mins)

- Ask students to complete the following activity to practice writing the graphemes: **Fill in the ng sound** (Activities, page 169). Encourage the students to say the sounds as they write them and then blend the sounds in each word together as they write them.

Spelling and dictation (10 mins)

- Ask students to complete **Fill in all the missing sounds** (Activities, page 170) to practice writing whole words.
- Read out the **Sentence dictation** sentences (Activities, page 174): "Dot ran up a long stem. Dot did not quit the song." and "Then Dot felt a strong wind. She hung from the stem." Encourage the students to sound out the words as they spell them.
- For students who finish early or need additional practice, create additional sentences and dictate these new passages to them.

STEP 4
Comprehension and consolidation
20 mins

Book reading (5 mins)

- Reread Book 15b: The Strong Wind.

Comprehension (5 mins)

- Sequencing: Ask students to retell the story, using the pictures and words in the **Retelling the story** activity (Activities, page 176). The word cards on the same page can be used to reinforce vocabulary.
- Comprehension: Check students have understood the story by completing the **Comprehension** activity (Activities, page 178). Cut out the words on the page. Then ask students to read and match them to the correct pictures.

Consolidation (10 mins)

- Divide the class into pairs and give each pair a copy of the **Stepping stones game** (Activities, page 181).

STEP 5
Tracking progress

- Complete the **Spelling assessment** (Activities, page 186) to make a quick, formative assessment of students' progress.
- Invite students to complete an additional activity from the Activities book.
- For a summative assessment of each student's progress, assign the Stages 11–15 Assessment (page 83).

PARALLEL BOOKS

In addition to Book 15b: The Strong Wind, the following books also cover the /ng/ or /qu/ sounds and can be used for more practice of decoding, for book bags to take home.

Dandelion Launchers

Book 15a: Ding Dong!

Dandelion Launchers Extras

Book 15a: Spring

Book 15b: Ting-a-ling

Dandelion World

Book 15a: Spring has Sprung

Book 15b: Long Bat Wings

Dandelion Readers

Book 15: The Ring (Set 1 Units 11–20)

Book 15: the Sting (Set 2 Units 11–20)

Stage 16: tch, ve

LESSON RESOURCES

STEP 1
Preparation

20 mins

Reviewing sounds (3 mins)

- Using sound cards or a whiteboard, review some previously learned words containing the /ng/ or /qu/ sounds.

Learning goal (2 mins)

- Explain to the students that you will be teaching them to read and spell words using 'tch' and 've' and sounds they have previously learned.
- Introduce the book Dandelion Launchers Book 16a: The Itch.
- You will be completing some activities from Dandelion Launchers Stages 16–20 Activities.

Preparation (15 mins)

- Introduce the spelling 'tch' for the sound /ch/ and the spelling 've' for the sound /v/.
- Explain that they already know one way to spell the sound /ch/ as in the word "chips." They also already know how to spell the sound /v/ as in the word "vet."
- Model the sounds /ch/ and /v/ for words with these spellings.

1 Word building

- First demonstrate how to build a word. Use only three sound cards, e.g. for the word "give."
- Draw three lines on the whiteboard, and tell the students that you are going to show them how to build the word "give."
- As you say the word slowly, move your finger under the lines.
- Ask the students to listen to the first sound in the word "give"—point to the first line. Emphasize the first sound as you say the whole word. The students respond—/g/.
- Then ask the students which letter spells this sound. The students point to the letter (or you can tell them). Bring the letter down to the first line.
- Repeat with the second and last sounds in the word. Now ask the students to sound all three sounds and blend them into a word, moving your finger under the word: /g/ /i/ /ve/ → "give"
- The next time this is done, you can ask a student to participate and identify the sound and then letter and bring it down to the line.

2 Word reading

- Write the words you have created on the whiteboard (if you haven't done so already). Then ask students to blend and read the words.
- Show how to say each sound individually and then blend them together to read the word. Model blending by using a swishing motion with your finger for blending.
- Encourage students to follow your example with these words: "patch," "fetch," "have," and "give."

3 Oral segmenting

- Say a word aloud (e.g. "fetch") and ask students to count the sounds in the word (3). Write the number of lines you need for all the sounds. Now ask students to listen to the sounds in the word and write a letter for every sound in the word as you spell the word.

4 Word chain

- Using sound cards or magnetic letters, demonstrate how to build the word "patch." Explain to the students that you will be making one change to the word. They must be "sound detectives" and notice if you have added a sound, taken away a sound, or swapped a sound.
- Say that you are going to change the word "patch" (moving your finger under the word) to "hatch." Ask the students to listen carefully to where the change has occurred. Swish your finger under the word as you say it slowly. Once the change has been identified, invite a student to swap the sound card or letter. Ask all the students to sound out the word and read the new word. e.g. /h/ /a/ /tch/ → "hatch."
- Direct students through the following word-chain sequence: patch—hatch—hutch—hitch—pitch—ditch—itch—etch—fetch

STEP 2
Application for reading
20 mins

Before reading (3 mins)

- Revisit the vocabulary taught in Step 1 (e.g. "stretch"). Clearly say the word: /s/ /t/ /r/ /e/ /tch/. Then provide a simple definition, e.g. "To stretch is to straighten your body or part of your body."
- Ask questions such as "What is the opposite of 'stretch'?" and "When might you stretch?"
- Then write the word on the whiteboard and refer back to it throughout the week for reinforcement.

High-frequency words (2 mins)

- Pre-teach or revisit these high-frequency words: "of," "the," "to," "you," "I'll," "says," "has," "begins," "too," "I," and "for."
- Explain that these are high-frequency words that have tricky spellings the students will learn later.
- Write the words on the board, showing the separate graphemes in each word. As students learn more of the Alphabetic Code, they will be able to decode those graphemes.

Application (10 mins)

- Read Book 16a: The Itch.
- Encourage students to sound out each word and then blend to read.

Reading for fluency and expression (5 mins)

- Ask each student to complete the **Fluency** activity (Activities, page 21).
- Ask each student to read the passage twice.
- The first reading is for fluency.
- The second reading is for reading with expression.
- Put a check, sticker or stamp in the box once this is done.

STEP 3
Application for spelling
15 mins

- Read out the **Sentence dictation** sentences (Activities, page 13): "Alf has a stretch." and "Alf gets a nip. Itch and scratch!" Encourage the students to sound out the words as they spell them.
- For students who finish early or need additional practice, create additional sentences and dictate these new passages to them.

STEP 4
Comprehension and consolidation
20 mins

Book reading (5 mins)

- Reread Book 16a: The Itch.

Comprehension (5 mins)

- Sequencing: Ask students to retell the story, using the pictures and words in the **Retelling the story** activity (Activities, page 15). The word cards on the same page can be used to reinforce vocabulary.
- Comprehension: Check students have understood the story by completing the **Find the untruths** activity (Activities, page 19). Cut out the words on the page. Then ask students to read and match them to the correct pictures.

Consolidation (10 mins)

- Divide the class into pairs and give each pair a copy of the **Stepping stones game** (Activities, page 23).

STEP 5
Tracking progress

- Assign the **Timed word reading** activity (Activities, page 16). Students can repeat this activity to improve their reading speed.
- Complete the **Spelling assessment** (Activities, page 27) to make a quick, formative assessment of students' progress.
- Depending on your findings, either revisit some of the activities to reinforce any specific skill gaps, or invite students to complete an additional activity from the Activities book.

PARALLEL BOOKS

In addition to Book 16a: The Itch, the following books also cover 'tch' and 've' and can be used for more practice of decoding, for book bags to take home.

Dandelion Launchers

Book 16b: The Ditch

Dandelion World

Book 16a: Catch the Fun!

Book 16b: A Clutch in the Hutch

Dandelion Readers

Book 15: The Ring (Set 1 Units 11–20)

Book 16: The Quest (Set 1 Units 11–20)

Book 15: The Sting (Set 2 Units 11–20)

Book 16: The Quilt (Set 2 Units 11–20)

Stage 17: Two-syllable words

LESSON RESOURCES

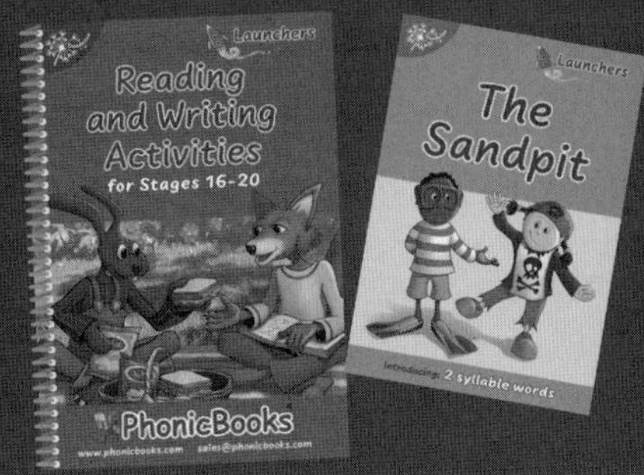

STEP 1
Preparation

20 mins

Reviewing sounds (3 mins)

- Using sound cards or a whiteboard, review some previously learned words containing 'tch' or 've' spellings for /ch/ and /v/ sounds, respectively.
- For example, model blending "batch." /b/ /a/ /tch/ → "batch."

Learning goal (2 mins)

- Explain to the students that you will be teaching them to read and spell two-syllable words using the sounds they have previously learned. They will be learning how two-syllable words are formed and how to blend their sounds smoothly.
- Introduce the book Dandelion Launchers Book 17a: The Sandpit.
- You will be completing some activities from Dandelion Launchers Stages 16–20 Activities.

Preparation (15 mins)

- Provide a brief explanation of what a syllable is. For example: "A syllable is like a beat in music but for words. Each syllable has one vowel sound. A word can be easier to read and write by breaking it down into syllables."
- Clap or tap out each syllable for a simple two-syllable word, for example ("sand-pit" to show how words can be split.
- Ask students to clap out syllables for a few more simple two-syllable words, for example "picnic" or "lunchbox."

1 Word building

- Choose a number of two-syllable words, e.g. "laptop" and "handbag."
- Place sound cards or magnetic letters needed to spell the word on the board. Draw two lines on the board—one for each syllable. Ask the students to listen to the word. You say "laptop." Move your finger under the two lines as you say the word. Point to the first line—what is the first syllable in the word laptop?
- Students say "lap." Ask a student to build the syllable 'lap' with the letters on the board.
- Now listen to the second syllable.
- You say "lap top." Move your finger under the word. Students say "top."
- Ask a student to build the word "top" with the letters on the board. Now ask the students to read the syllables together. "lap" "top" and say the word quickly "laptop."
- Now ask the students to spell the word "laptop" by drawing two lines on the board, writing each syllable they hear and then writing the whole word underneath without a gap.

2 Segmenting and spelling two-syllable words

- Move on to the **Segmenting and spelling: two-syllable words** activity (Activities, page 32).
- Dictate two-syllable words to the students. In this activity, each word is associated with a picture as a visual clue.
- Task students with filling in the squares with the appropriate spelling for each sound, paying attention to the syllable break indicated by a line.
- This activity further reinforces their understanding of syllable segmentation and sound–spelling correspondence.
- Assist students in identifying where one syllable ends and the next begins, emphasizing the importance of accurate segmentation for both reading and spelling.

Extension activities

- Play the game in Book 17a: The Sandpit (pages 7–8) to familiarize students with the vocabulary in the books.

a	o	l	t	p	p

________________ ________________

STEP 2
Application for reading
20 mins

Before reading (3 mins)

- Revisit the vocabulary in Step 1 (e.g. "sandpit"). Clearly say the word: /s/ /a/ /n/ /d/ /p/ /i/ /t/. Then provide a simple definition, e.g. "A sandpit is a box filled with sand."
- Ask questions such as "What do we use sandpits for?" and "Where might you find a sandpit?"
- Then write the word on the whiteboard and refer back to it throughout the week for reinforcement.

High-frequency words (2 mins)

- Pre-teach or revisit these high-frequency words: "are," "the," "pretend," "is," "island," "says," "has," "her," "I'll," "you," and "for."
- Explain that these are high-frequency words that have tricky spellings the students will learn later.
- Write the words on the board, showing the separate graphemes in each word. As students learn more of the Alphabetic Code, they will be able to decode those graphemes.

Application (10 mins)

- Read Book 17a: The Sandpit.
- Encourage students to sound out each word and then blend to read.

Reading for fluency and expression (5 mins)

- Ask each student to complete the **Fluency** activity (Activities, page 45).
- Ask each student to read the passage twice.
- The first reading is for fluency.
- The second reading is for reading with expression.
- Put a check, sticker or stamp in the box once this is done.

STEP 3
Application for spelling
10 mins

- Read out the **Sentence dictation** sentences (Activities, page 37): "Fred is a frogman." and "'Bandit!' yells Viv as Meg runs off." Encourage the students to sound out the words as they spell them.
- For students who finish early or need additional practice, create additional sentences and dictate these new passages to them.

STEP 4
Comprehension and consolidation
20 mins

Book reading (5 mins)

- Reread Book 17a: The Sandpit.

Comprehension (5 mins)

- Sequencing: Ask students to retell the story, using the pictures and words in the **Retelling the story** activity (Activities, page 39). The word cards on the same page can be used to reinforce vocabulary.
- Comprehension: Check students have understood the story by completing the **Find the untruths** activity (Activities, page 43). Cut out the words on the page. Then ask students to read and match them to the correct pictures.

Consolidation (10 mins)

- Divide the class into pairs and give each pair a copy of the **4-in-a-row game** (Activities, page 48).

STEP 5
Tracking progress

- Assign the **Timed word reading** activity (Activities, page 34). Students can repeat this activity to improve their reading speed.
- Complete the **Spelling assessment** (Activities, page 51) to make a quick, formative assessment of students' progress.
- Depending on your findings, either revisit some of the activities to reinforce any specific skill gaps, or invite students to complete an extension activity.

PARALLEL BOOKS

In addition to Book 17a: The Sandpit, the following books also cover simple two-syllable words and can be used for more practice of decoding, for book bags to take home.

Dandelion Launchers

Book 17b: The Muffin Shop

Dandelion World

Book 17a: Selling Crops

Book 17b: The Bandit Kittens

Dandelion Readers

Book 17: When Meg was a Pup (Set 1 Units 11–20)

Book 17: What a Bad Dog! (Set 2 Units 11–20)

Stage 18: Two-syllable words, -ed

LESSON RESOURCES

STEP 1
Preparation
20 mins

Reviewing sounds (3 mins)

- Using sound cards or a whiteboard, review some previously learned two-syllable words.
- For example, for the word "handbag," clap or tap out each syllable.
- Ask students to clap out syllables for a few simpler two-syllable words like "chopstick" or "cabin."

Learning goal (2 mins)

- Explain to the students that you will be teaching them to read and spell two-syllable words using the suffix -ed and sounds they have previously learned.
- Introduce the book Dandelion Launchers Book 18a: Stranded.
- You will be completing some activities from Dandelion Launchers Stages 16–20 Reading and Writing Activities.

Preparation (15 mins)

1 Introducing the three sounds of -ed

- Explain to students that the suffix -ed indicates that something has happened in the past. In the next activity, they are going to be "sound detectives" because -ed doesn't always sound the same.
- Introduce the three sounds: /t/ /d/ and /id/. Explain that the sound of -ed depends on the last sound of the verb before the -ed is added. For example, for words ending in a voiced sound, the -ed sounds like /d/ (e.g. "hummed"); for words ending in a voiceless sound, the -ed sounds like /t/ ("kissed"); and for words ending in /t/ or /d/, the -ed is an extra syllable /id/ (e.g. "wanted").
- Next play the **Three sounds of -ed** game (Activities, page 55). In this activity, say the list of -ed words aloud and then the students sort them into the correct column depending on the sounds they make.

2 Word building

- Choose a number of two-syllable words, e.g. "hunted" and "chipmunk."
- Place two-syllable cards or magnetic letters needed to spell the word on the board. Draw two lines on the board—one for each syllable. Ask the students to listen to the word. You say "hunted." Move your finger under the two lines as you say the word. Point to the first line—what is the first syllable in the word "hunted"?
- Students say "hunt." Ask a student to build the syllable 'hunt' with the letters on the board.
- Now listen to the second syllable.
- You say "hunt ed." Move your finger under the word. Students say "ed."
- Ask a student to build "ed" with the letters on the board. Now ask the students to read the syllables together. "hunt" "ed" and say the word quickly "hunted."
- Now ask the students to spell the word "hunted" by drawing two lines on the board, writing each syllable they hear and then writing the whole word underneath without a gap.

3 Segmenting and spelling

- Assign the **Segmenting and spelling** activity (Activities, page 56).
- Dictate two-syllable words to the students. In this activity, each word is associated with a picture as a visual clue.
- Task students with filling in the squares with the appropriate spelling for each sound, paying attention to the syllable break indicated by a line.
- This activity further reinforces their understanding of syllable segmentation and sound–spelling correspondence.
- Assist students in identifying where one syllable ends and the next begins, emphasizing the importance of accurate segmentation for both reading and spelling.

Extension activities

- Play the game in Book 18a: Stranded (pages 7–8) to familiarize students with the vocabulary in the books.
- Use the **Reading practice** cards (Activities, page 57) to expand vocabulary and reinforce recognition of words ending with -ed. The words can be cut out to make a simple matching game.

STEP 2
Application for reading

20 mins

Before reading (3 mins)

- Revisit the vocabulary taught in Step 1 (e.g. "stranded"). Clearly say the word: /s/ /t/ /r/ /a/ /n/ d/ /ed/.
- Explain the meaning of "stranded": left helpless, without transport.
- Then write the word on the whiteboard and refer back to it throughout the week for reinforcement.

High-frequency words (2 mins)

- Pre-teach or revisit these high-frequency words: "the," "his," "he," "I," "to," "onto," "tree," "began," "all," and "of."
- Write the words on the board, showing the separate graphemes in each word. As students learn more of the Alphabetic Code, they will be able to decode those graphemes.

Application (10 mins)

- Read Book 18a: Stranded.
- Encourage students to sound out each word and then blend to read.

Reading for fluency and expression (5 mins)

- Ask each student to complete the **Fluency** activity (Activities, page 69).
- Ask each student to read the passage twice.
- The first reading is for fluency.
- The second reading is for reading with expression.
- Put a check, sticker or stamp in the box once this is done.

STEP 3
Application for spelling

10 mins

- Read out the **Sentence dictation** sentences (Activities, page 61): "Dennis hatched a plan." and "Dennis began to swing! Panic!" Encourage the students to sound out the words as they spell them.
- For students who finish early or need additional practice, create additional sentences and dictate these new passages to them.

STEP 4
Comprehension and consolidation

20 mins

Book reading (5 mins)

- Reread Book 18a: Stranded.

Comprehension (5 mins)

- Sequencing: Ask students to retell the story, using the pictures and words in the **Retelling the story** activity (Activities, page 63). The word cards on the same page can be used to reinforce vocabulary.
- Comprehension: Check students have understood the story by completing the **Find the untruths** activity (Activities, page 43). Cut out the words on the page. Then ask students to read and match them to the correct pictures.

Consolidation (10 mins)

- Divide the class into pairs and give each pair a copy of the **Stepping stones game** (Activities, page 71).

STEP 5
Tracking progress

- Assign the **Timed word reading** activity (Activities, page 58). Students can repeat this activity to improve their reading speed.
- Complete the **Spelling assessment** (Activities, page 75) to make a quick, formative assessment of students' progress.
- Depending on your findings, either revisit some of the activities to reinforce any specific skill gaps, or invite students to complete an additional activity from the Activities book.

PARALLEL BOOKS

In addition to Book 18a: Stranded, the following books also cover simple two-syllable words and -ed, and can be used for more practice of decoding, for book bags to take home.

Dandelion Launchers

Book 18b: Stan is Shocked

Dandelion World

Book 18a: Planted in Space

Book 18b: The Bobcat Hunted

Dandelion Readers

Book 18: A Wicked Snack (Set 1 Units 11–20)

Book 18: Dan Is Trapped (Set 2 Units 11–20)

Stage 19: Two-syllable words, -ing

STEP 1
Preparation

20 mins

Reviewing sounds (3 mins)

- Using sound cards or a whiteboard, review some previously learned words ending in -ed.
- Choose words that have the three different sounds of -ed. For example, "lifted," "drummed," and "slipped."
- Use visual aids or gestures to help students remember the sounds of -ed.

Learning goal (2 mins)

- Explain to the students that you will be teaching them to read and spell two-syllable words using the suffix -ing and sounds they have previously learned.
- Introduce the book Dandelion Launchers Book 19a: Thinking of a Gift.
- You will be completing some activities from Dandelion Launchers Stages 16–20 Reading and Writing Activities.

Preparation (15 mins)

1 Introducing the suffix -ing

- Explain that we add -ing to the end of verbs to talk about different things.
- The -ing suffix can be used to tell us about something we do, for example, "Singing is fun." (Here, "singing" acts as a noun.)
- The -ing suffix can tell us about what someone is doing now. For example: "She is swimming." (The sentence is in the present continuous tense and -ing is the present participle of the verb.)
- The -ing suffix can also be used to describe things or how they make us feel. For example: "This book is interesting." (Here, "interesting" is an adjective that describes the book.)
- Explain that -ing is made up of two sounds /i/ and /ng/.
- Model how to say the sounds correctly and ask students to copy.
- Have students watch you as they pronounce /i/ /ng/.
- Read this list of words: "singing," "ringing," and "running."

2 Word building

- Choose a number of two-syllable words, e.g. "fishing" and "handing."
- Place sound cards or magnetic letters needed to spell the word on the board. Draw two lines on the board—one for each syllable. Ask the students to listen to the word. You say "fishing." Move your finger under the two lines as you say the word. Point to the first line—what is the first syllable in the word fishing?
- Students say "fish." Ask a student to build the syllable 'fish' with the letters on the board.
- Now listen to the second syllable.
- You say "fish ing." Move your finger under the word. Students say "ing."
- Ask a student to build "ing" with the letters on the board. Now ask the students to read the syllables together. "fish" "ing" and say the word quickly "fishing."
- Now ask the students to spell the word "fishing" by drawing two lines on the board, writing each syllable they hear and then writing the whole word underneath without a gap.

3 Segmenting and spelling

- Assign the **Segmenting and spelling** activity (Activities, page 80).
- Dictate two-syllable words to the students. In the activity each word is associated with a picture as a visual clue.
- Task students with filling in the squares with the appropriate spelling for each sound, paying attention to the syllable break indicated by a line.
- This activity further reinforces their understanding of syllable segmentation and sound–spelling correspondence.
- Assist students in identifying where one syllable ends and the next begins, emphasizing the importance of accurate segmentation for both reading and spelling.

Extension activities

- Play the game in Book 19a: Thinking of a Gift (pages 7–8) to familiarize students with the vocabulary in the books.

LESSON RESOURCES

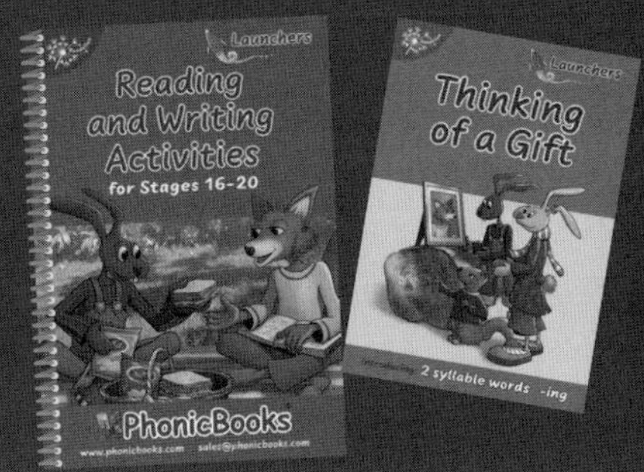

STEP 2
Application for reading
20 mins

Before reading (3 mins)

- Revisit the vocabulary in Step 1 (e.g. "fixing"). Clearly say the word: /f/ /i/ /x/ /i/ /ng/.
- Explore different meanings of "fixing".
- Ask questions such as "What is another word for 'fixing'?" and "What is the opposite of 'fixing'?"
- Then write the word on the whiteboard and refer back to it throughout the week for reinforcement.

High-frequency words (2 mins)

- Pre-teach or revisit these high-frequency words: "his," "are," "of," "for," "I," "says," "into," "surprise," "to," "the," "is," "coming," "fingers," and "my."
- Explain that these are high-frequency words that have tricky spellings the students will learn later.
- Write the words on the board, showing the separate graphemes in each word. As students learn more of the Alphabetic Code, they will be able to decode those graphemes.

Application (10 mins)

- Read Book 19a: Thinking of a Gift.
- Encourage students to sound out each word and then blend to read.

Reading for fluency and expression (5 mins)

- Ask each student to complete the Fluency activity (Activities, page 93).
- Ask each student to read the passage twice.
- The first reading is for fluency.
- The second reading is for reading with expression.
- Put a check, sticker or stamp in the box once this is done.

STEP 3
Application for spelling
10 mins

- Read out the **Sentence dictation** sentences (Activities, page 85): "I am getting him a whisk and a brush." and "I am stitching this fabric into a hat." Encourage the students to sound out the words as they spell them
- For students who finish early or need additional practice, create additional sentences and dictate these new passages to them.

STEP 4
Comprehension and consolidation
20 mins

Book reading (5 mins)

- Reread Book 19a: Thinking of a Gift.

Comprehension (5 mins)

- Sequencing: Ask students to retell the story, using the pictures and words in the **Retelling the story** activity (Activities, page 87). The word cards on the same page can be used to reinforce vocabulary.
- Comprehension: Check students have understood the story by completing the **Find the untruths** activity (Activities, page 91). Cut out the words on the page. Then ask students to read and match them to the correct pictures.

Consolidation (10 mins)

- Divide the class into pairs and give each pair a copy of the **4-in-a-row game** (Activities, page 96).

STEP 5
Tracking progress

- Assign the **Timed word reading** activity (Activities, page 82). Students can repeat this activity to improve their reading speed.
- Complete the **Spelling assessment** (Activities, page 99) to make a quick, formative assessment of students' progress.
- Depending on your findings, either revisit some of the activities to reinforce any specific skill gaps, or invite students to complete an additional activity from the Activities book.

PARALLEL BOOKS

In addition to Book 19a: Thinking of a Gift, the following books also cover simple two-syllable words and -ing, and can be used for more practice of decoding, for book bags to take home.

Dandelion Launchers

Book 19b: Swimming

Dandelion World

Book 19a: Sharks Swimming

Book 19b: At the Fun Park

Dandelion Readers

Book 19: Sinking Sand (Set 1 Units 11–20)

Book 19: A Red Jacket (Set 2 Units 11–20)

Stage 20: Two-syllable words, le

LESSON RESOURCES

STEP 1
Preparation 20 mins

Reviewing sounds (3 mins)

- Review some previously learned words that end in -ing using sound cards or writing them on a whiteboard.
- For example, write or show the word "blending." Model how to say it by splitting it into its individual sounds and syllables: "blend" (/b/ /l/ /e/ /n/ /d/) and "ing" (/i/ /ng/).
- After modeling, guide the students to practice by themselves. They should say each sound and syllable, then blend them together to read the whole word.
- Encourage students to repeat after you, and then try it on their own with other -ing words.

Learning goal (2 mins)

- Explain to the students that you will be teaching them to read and spell two-syllable words with the spelling 'le' and sounds they have previously learned.
- Introduce the book Dandelion Launchers Book 20: Cuddles.
- You will be completing some activities from Dandelion Launchers Stages 16–20 Activities.

Preparation (15 mins)

- Introduce the spelling 'le'.
- Read this list of words: "puddle," "cuddle," and "riddle."

1 Word building

- Place sound cards or magnetic letters needed to spell an le word on the board (for example, "apple.")
- Draw two lines on the board—one for each syllable. Ask the students to listen to the word. You say "apple." Move your finger under the two lines as you say the word. Point to the first line—what is the first syllable in the word "apple"?

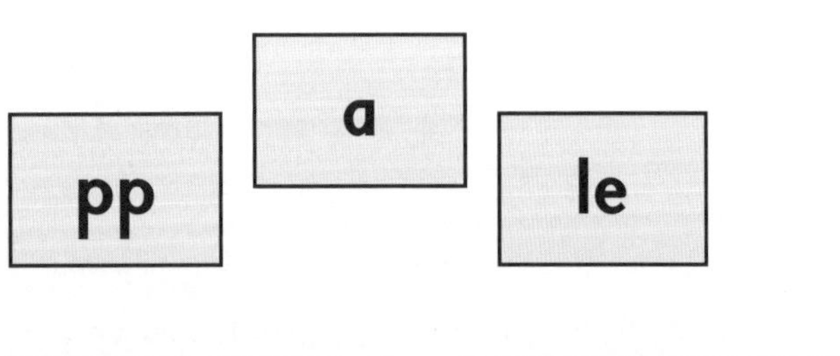

- Students say "app." Ask a student to build the syllable 'app' with the letters on the board.
- Now listen to the second syllable.
- You say "apple." Move your finger under the word. Students say "le."
- Ask a student to build the syllable "le" with the letters on the board. Now ask the students to read the syllables together. "app" "le" and say the word quickly "apple."
- Now ask the students to spell the word "apple" by drawing two lines on the board, writing each syllable they hear and then writing the whole word underneath without a gap.

2 Segmenting and spelling

- Assign the **Segmenting and spelling** activity (Activities, page 104).
- Dictate two-syllable words to the students. In the activity each word is associated with a picture as a visual clue.
- Task students with filling in the squares with the appropriate spelling for each sound, paying attention to the syllable break indicated by a line.
- This activity further reinforces their understanding of syllable segmentation and sound–spelling correspondence.
- Assist students in identifying where one syllable ends and the next begins, emphasizing the importance of accurate segmentation for both reading and spelling.

Extension activities

- Play the game in Book 20: Cuddles (pages 7–8) to familiarize students with the vocabulary in the books.
- Use the **Reading practice** cards (Activities, page 105) to expand vocabulary and reinforce recognition of words containing 'le'. The words can be cut out to make a simple matching game.
- Have students find and point to these words in Book 20: Cuddles: "snuggle," "cuddle," and "paddle."

STEP 2
Application for reading
20 mins

Before reading (3 mins)

- Revisit the vocabulary (e.g. "guzzle"). Clearly say the word. Then provide a simple definition, e.g. "To guzzle is to eat or drink something quickly or greedily."
- Ask questions such as "What is another word for 'guzzle'?" and "What rhymes with 'guzzle'?"
- Then write the word on the whiteboard and refer back to it throughout the week for reinforcement.

High-frequency words (2 mins)

- Pre-teach or revisit these high-frequency words: "has," "was," "the," "adopted," "her," "is," "to," "she," and "into."
- Explain that these are high-frequency words that have tricky spellings the students will learn later.
- Write the words on the board, showing the separate graphemes in each word. As students learn more of the Alphabetic Code, they will be able to decode those graphemes.

Application (10 mins)

- Read Book 20: Cuddles.
- Encourage students to sound out each word and then blend to read.

Reading for fluency and expression (5 mins)

- Ask each student to complete the **Fluency** activity (Activities, page 117).
- Ask each student to read the passage twice.
- The first reading is for fluency.
- The second reading is for reading with expression.
- Put a check, sticker or stamp in the box once this is done.

STEP 3
Application for spelling
10 mins

- Read out the **Sentence dictation** sentences (Activities, page 109): "Gran has a little dog, Floss." and "Floss snuggles up to Gran." Encourage the students to sound out the words as they spell them.
- For students who finish early or need additional practice, create additional sentences and dictate these new passages to them.

STEP 4
Comprehension and consolidation
20 mins

Book reading (5 mins)

- Reread Book 20: Cuddles.

Comprehension (5 mins)

- Sequencing: Ask students to retell the story, using the pictures and words in the **Retelling the story** activity (Activities, page 111). The word cards on the same page can be used to reinforce vocabulary.
- Comprehension: Check students have understood the story by completing the **Find the untruths** activity (Activities, page 115). Cut out the words on the page. Then ask students to read and match them to the correct pictures.

Consolidation (10 mins)

- Divide the class into pairs and give each pair a copy of **Stepping stones game** (Activities, page 119).

STEP 5
Tracking progress

- Assign the **Timed word reading** activity (Activities, page 106). Students can repeat this activity to improve their reading speed.
- Complete the **Spelling assessment** (Activities, page 123) to make a quick, formative assessment of students' progress.
- Then for a summative assessment of Stages 16–20, assign the **Reading Assessment** on page 89.

PARALLEL BOOKS

In addition to Book 20: Cuddles, the following books also cover simple two-syllable words containing 'le' and can be used for more practice of decoding, for book bags to take home.

Dandelion Launchers

Book 20b: Muddle in the Middle

Dandelion World

Book 20a: Apple Fest Fun!

Book 20b: Cuddle Pup

Dandelion Readers

Book 20: The Paddle (Set 1 Units 11–20)

Book 20: Apple Crumble (Set 2 Units 11–20)

/ae/

STEP 1
Preparation

20 mins

Learning goal (2 mins)

- Explain to the students that you will be teaching them to read and spell new words using the spelling ‘ai’ for the sound /ae/.
- Introduce the book Dandelion Readers Level 1 Book 1: The Mail.
- You will be completing some activities from Dandelion Readers Level 1 Activities.

Preparation (18 mins)

- Introduce the spelling ‘ai’ for the sound /ae/.
- Show the students a sound card with the letters ‘ai.’ Tell students that these two letters spell one sound: /ae/. Model the sound correctly and ask students to copy.

1 Word building and blending

- Tell the students that you are going to build the word “rain.” Use only the sound cards for the word “rain.”
- Draw three lines on the board and ask the students to listen to the sound in the word “rain.” Move your finger under the word as you pronounce it.
- Ask the students to tell you which is the first sound in the word (move your finger again under the word as you say it). Students respond: /r/.
- Ask a student to show you the spelling for the sound /r/ and to place it on the first line.
- Now ask the students to listen to the next sound in the word “rain”: /ae/. Ask a student to find the spelling for the sound /ae/.
- Complete with the third sound. Then ask the students to sound out all the sounds and blend them into a word. /r/ /ae/ /n/ → “rain.”

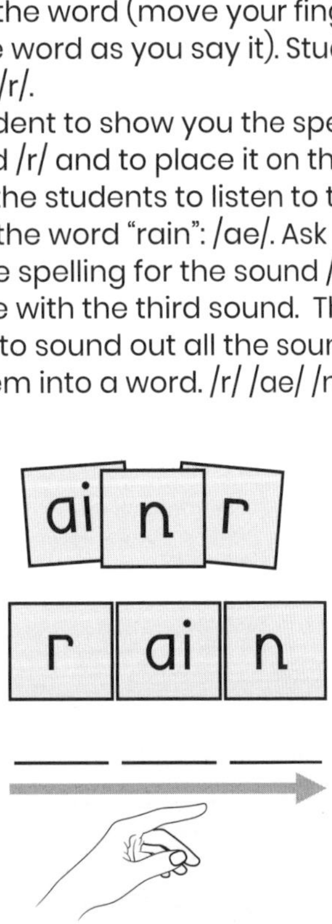

LESSON RESOURCES

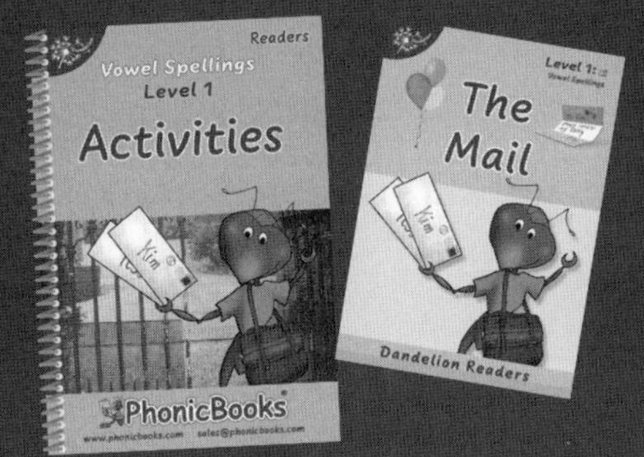

2 Word reading

- Write the words you have created on the board (if you haven’t done so already). Then ask students to blend and read the words.
- Show how to say each sound individually and then blend them together to read the word. Model blending by using a swishing motion with your finger.
- Encourage students to follow your example with these words: “wait,” “tail,” and “main.”

3 Oral segmenting

- Say a word aloud (e.g. “pail”) and ask students to count the sounds in the word (3). Students then spell the word sound by sound. This is important as it links reading and spelling. Write the number of lines you need for all the sounds. Now ask students to listen to the sounds in the word and write a letter for every sound in the word as you spell the word.

4 Word chain

- Use sound cards or magnetic letters that represent the graphemes in the word “rain.” This word chain would need the sound cards: ‘r,’ ‘ai,’ ‘n,’ ‘t,’ ‘l,’ ‘p,’ and ‘s.’ Explain to the students that you will be making one change to the word. They must be “sound detectives” and notice if you have added a sound, taken away a sound, or swapped a sound.
- Say that you are going to change the word “rain” (moving your finger under the word) to “pain.” Ask the students to listen carefully to where the change has occurred. Move your finger under the words as you say it slowly. Once the change has been identified, invite a student to swap the sound card or letter. Ask all the students to sound out the word and read the new word. e.g. /p/ /ae/ /n/ → “pain.”
- Direct students through the following word-chain sequence: rain—pain—plain—slain—stain—strain—train—rain

STEP 2 Application for reading

15 mins

Before reading (3 mins)

- Revisit the vocabulary taught in Step 1 (e.g. "wail"). Clearly say the word: /w/ /ae/ /l/. Provide a simple definition: "The word 'wail' means a long cry when someone is upset, angry, or in pain."
- Ask questions such as "What is another word for 'wail'?" and "What rhymes with 'wail'?"
- Then write the word on the whiteboard and refer back to it throughout the week for reinforcement.

High-frequency words (2 mins)

- Pre-teach or reiterate these high-frequency words: "has," "his," "is," "begins," "to," "the," "I," "this," "my," "he," "says," "open," "we," "they," and "say."
- Explain that these are high-frequency words that have tricky spellings the students will learn later.
- Write the words on the board, showing the separate graphemes in each word. As students learn more of the Alphabetic Code, they will be able to decode those graphemes.

Application (10 mins)

- Read Book 1: The Mail.
- Encourage students to sound out each word and then blend to read.

Extension activities

- Complete the **Fluency** activity (Activities, page 14) to develop students' fluency and prosody skills.

STEP 3 Application for spelling

15 mins

Segmenting and spelling (15 mins)

- Ask students to complete the following activity to practice writing whole words: **Segmenting and spelling** (Activities, page 7).
- Dictate the words to the students. In the activity each word is associated with a picture as a visual clue.
- Task students with filling in the squares with the appropriate spelling for each sound.
- Read out the **Sentence dictation** sentences (Activities, page 15): "It rains and rains. Can Pip get the mail to his pals?"

STEP 4 Comprehension and consolidation

20 mins

Book reading (5 mins)

- Reread Book 1: The Mail.

Comprehension (5 mins)

- Ask students to complete **What happens next?** (Activities, page 11).
- Check students have understood the story by completing **Find the untruths** (Activities, page 12).

Consolidation (10 mins)

- Divide the class into pairs and give each pair a copy of the **4-in-a-row game** (Activities, page 20).

STEP 5 Tracking progress

15 mins

- Assign the **Timed word reading** (Activities, page 13). Students can repeat this activity to improve their reading speed.
- Complete the **Spelling assessment** (Activities, page 21) to make a quick, formative assessment of students' progress. A second list of words is provided for additional practice for more advanced students.
- Hide the words and ask students to write them out as you read them, encouraging them to segment each sound.
- Depending on your findings, either revisit some of the activities to reinforce any specific skill gaps, or invite students to complete an additional activity from the Activities book.

Extension activities

- Ask students to complete the **Make a book** activity (Activities, page 10).
- Play the **Reading game** (Activities, page 19).
- Ask students to complete the **Write the story in your own words** activity (Activities, page 17).

/ee/

LESSON RESOURCES

STEP 1
Preparation

20 mins

Reviewing sounds (3 mins)

- Using sound cards or a whiteboard, review some previously learned words containing the 'ai' spelling for the /ae/ sound.

Learning goal (2 mins)

- Explain to the students that you will be teaching them to read and spell new words using the spelling 'ee' for the sound /ee/.
- Introduce the book Dandelion Readers Level 1 Book 2: The Tree.
- You will be completing some activities from Dandelion Readers Level 1 Activities.

Preparation (15 mins)

- Introduce the spelling 'ee' for the sound /ee/.
- Show the students a sound card with the letters 'ee.' Tell students that these two letters spell one sound: /ee/. Model the sound correctly and ask students to copy.

1 Word building and blending

- Tell the students that you are going to build the word "tree." Use only the sound cards for the word "tree."
- Draw three lines on the board and ask the students to listen to the sound in the word "tree." Move your finger under the word as you pronounce it.
- Ask the students to tell you which is the first sound in the word (move your finger again under the word as you say it). Students respond: /t/.
- Ask a student to show you the spelling for the sound /t/ and to place it on the first line.
- Now ask the students to listen to the next sound in the word "tree": /r/. Ask a student to find the spelling for the sound /r/.
- Complete with the third sound. Then ask the students to sound out all the sounds and blend them into a word. /t/ /r/ /ee/ → "tree"

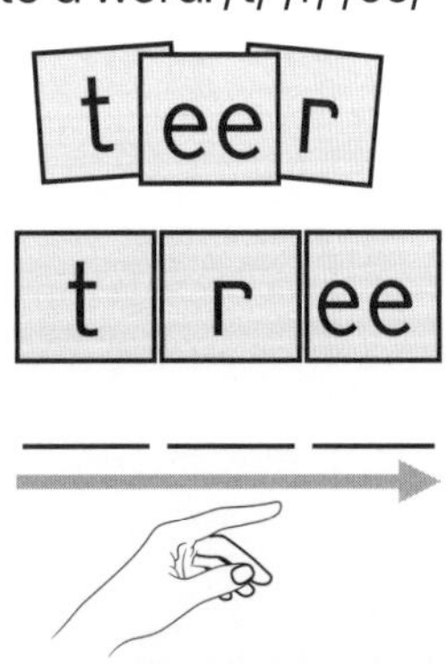

2 Word reading

- Write the words you have created on the board (if you haven't done so already). Then ask students to blend and read the words.
- Show how to say each sound individually and then blend them together to read the word. Model blending by using a swishing motion with your finger.
- Encourage students to follow your example with these words: "free," "eel," and "sleep."

3 Oral segmenting

- Say a word aloud (e.g. "free") and ask students to count the sounds in the word (3). Write the number of lines you need for all the sounds. Now ask students to listen to the sounds in the word and write a letter for every sound in the word as you spell the word.

4 Word chain

- Use sound cards or magnetic letters that represent the graphemes in the word "heel." This word chain would need the sound cards: 'h,' 'ee,' 'l,' 'k,' 'p,' and 'r.' Explain to the students that you will be making one change to the word. They must be "sound detectives" and notice if you have added a sound, taken away a sound, or swapped a sound.
- Say that you are going to change the word "heel" (moving your finger under the word) to "eel." Ask the students to listen carefully to where the change has occurred. Move your finger under the word as you say it slowly. Once the change has been identified, invite a student to swap the sound card or letter. Ask all the students to sound out the word and read the new word. e.g. /ee/ /l/ → "eel."
- Direct students through the following word-chain sequence: heel—eel—keel—keep—seep—seek—leek—reek—reel—heel

STEP 2
Application for reading
15 mins

Before reading (3 mins)

- Revisit the vocabulary taught in Step 1 (e.g. "seed"). Clearly say the word: /s/ /ee/ /d/. Provide a simple definition: "A seed is a small part of a plant that can grow into a new plant."
- Ask questions such as, "What can you plant seeds of?"
- Then write the word on the whiteboard and refer back to it throughout the week for reinforcement.

High-frequency words (2 mins)

- Pre-teach or reiterate these high-frequency words: "is," "buzzes," "we," "as," "to," "the," "says," "be," and "are."
- Write the words on the board, showing the separate graphemes in each word. As students learn more of the Alphabetic Code, they will be able to decode those graphemes.

Application (10 mins)

- Read Book 2: The Tree.
- Encourage students to sound out each word and then blend to read.

Extension activities

- Complete the **Fluency** activity (Activities, page 32) to develop students' fluency and prosody skills.

STEP 3
Application for spelling
15 mins

Segmenting and spelling (15 mins)

- Ask students to complete the following activity to practice writing whole words: **Segmenting and spelling** (Activities, page 25).
- Dictate the words to the students. In the activity each word is associated with a picture as a visual clue.
- Task students with filling in the squares with the appropriate spelling for each sound.
- Read out the **Sentence dictation** sentences (Activities, page 33): "Tess keeps the seed wet. It will be a big green tree."

Extension activities

- Assign the **Splitting two-syllable words** activity (Activities, page 36) to practice syllable division, and decoding and writing longer words.

STEP 4
Comprehension and consolidation
20 mins

Book reading (5 mins)

- Reread Book 2: The Tree.

Comprehension (5 mins)

- Ask students to complete **What happens next?** (Activities, page 29).
- Check students have understood the story by completing **Find the untruths** (Activities, page 30).

Consolidation (10 mins)

- Divide the class into pairs and give each pair a copy of the **Reading game** (Activities, page 37).
- Have students find and point to these words in Book 2: The Tree: "tree," "deep," and "seed."

STEP 5
Tracking progress
15 mins

- Assign the **Timed word reading** (Activities, page 31). Students can repeat this activity to improve their reading speed.
- Complete the **Spelling assessment** (Activities, page 39) to make a quick, formative assessment of students' progress. A second list of words is provided for additional practice for more advanced students.
- Hide the words and ask students to write them out as you read them, encouraging them to segment each sound.
- Depending on your findings, either revisit some of the activities to reinforce any specific skill gaps, or invite students to complete an additional activity from the Activities book.

Extension activities

- Ask students to complete the **Make a book** activity (Activities, page 28).
- Play the **4-in-a-row game** (Activities, page 38).
- Ask students to complete the **Write the story in your own words** activity (Activities, page 35).

/oe/

LESSON RESOURCES

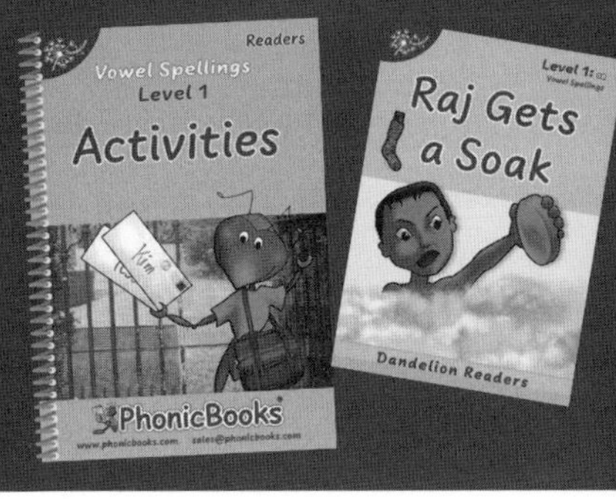

STEP 1
Preparation

20 mins

Reviewing sounds (3 mins)

- Using sound cards or a whiteboard, review some previously learned words containing the 'ee' spelling for the /ee/ sound.

Learning goal (2 mins)

- Explain to the students that you will be teaching them to read and spell new words using the spelling 'oa' for the sound /oe/.
- Introduce the book Dandelion Readers Level 1 Book 3: Raj Gets a Soak.
- You will be completing some activities from Dandelion Readers Level 1 Activities.

Preparation (15 mins)

- Introduce the spelling 'oa' for the sound /oe/.
- Show the students a sound card with the letters 'oa.' Tell students that these two letters spell one sound: /oe/. Model the sound correctly and ask students to copy.

1 Word building and blending

- Tell the students that you are going to build the word "boat." Use only the sound cards for the word "boat."
- Draw three lines on the board and ask the students to listen to the sound in the word "boat." Move your finger under the word as you pronounce it.
- Ask the students to tell you which is the first sound in the word (move your finger again under the word as you say it). Students respond: /b/.
- Ask a student to show you the spelling for the sound /b/ and to place it on the first line.
- Now ask the students to listen to the next sound in the word "boat": /oe/. Ask a student to find the spelling for /oe/.
- Complete with the third sound. Then ask the students to sound out all sounds and blend them into a word. /b/ /oe/ /t/ → "boat."

2 Word reading

- Write the words you have created on the board (if you haven't done so already). Then ask students to blend and read the words.
- Show how to say each sound individually and then blend them together to read the word. Model blending by using a swishing motion with your finger.
- Encourage students to follow your example with these words: "goat," "loaf," and "soap."

3 Oral segmenting

- Say a word aloud (e.g. "moat") and ask students to count the sounds in the word (3). Write the number of lines you need for all the sounds. Now ask students to listen to the sounds in the word and write a letter for every sound in the word as you spell the word.

4 Word chain

- Use sound cards or magnetic letters that represent the graphemes in the word "coat." This word chain would need the sound cards: 'c,' 'oa,' 't,' 'b,' 'f,' 'l,' 'm,' and 'n.' Explain to the students that you will be making one change to the word. They must be "sound detectives" and notice if you have added a sound, taken away a sound, or swapped a sound.
- Say that you are going to change the word "coat" (moving your finger under the word) to "boat." Ask the students to listen carefully to where the change has occurred. Move your finger under the word as you say it slowly. Once the change has been identified, invite a student to swap the sound card or letter. Ask all the students to sound out the word and read the new word. e.g. /b//oe/ /t/ → "boat."
- Direct students through the following word-chain sequence: coat—boat—oat—oaf—loaf—loan—moan—moat—coat

STEP 2
Application for reading
15 mins

Before reading (3 mins)

- Revisit the vocabulary taught in Step 1 (e.g. "coat"). Clearly say the word: /c/ /oa/ /t/. Explore different meanings for the word "coat," such as clothing or a layer that covers something.
- Ask questions such as, "When would you need to wear a coat?"
- Then write the word on the whiteboard and refer back to it throughout the week for reinforcement.

High-frequency words (2 mins)

- Pre-teach or reiterate these high-frequency words: "is," "he," "the," "no," "has," "of," "his," "says," "your," "she," and "day."
- Write the words on the board, showing the separate graphemes in each word. As students learn more of the Alphabetic Code, they will be able to decode those graphemes.

Application (10 mins)

- Read Book 3: Raj Gets a Soak.
- Encourage students to sound out each word and then blend to read.

Extension activities

- Complete the **Fluency** activity (Activities, page 50) to develop students' fluency and prosody skills.

STEP 3
Application for spelling
15 mins

Segmenting and spelling (15 mins)

- Ask students to complete the following activity to practice writing whole words: **Segmenting and spelling** (Activities, page 43).
- Dictate the words to the students. In the activity each word is associated with a picture as a visual clue.
- Task students with filling in the squares with the appropriate spelling for each sound.
- Read out the **Sentence dictation** sentences (Activities, page 51): "Raj has loads of mud on his coat. His mom groans."

Extension activities

- Assign the **Splitting two-syllable words** activity (Activities, page 54) to practice syllable division, and decoding and writing longer words.

STEP 4
Comprehension and consolidation
20 mins

Book reading (5 mins)

- Reread Book 3: Raj Gets a Soak.

Comprehension (5 mins)

- Ask students to complete **What happens next?** (Activities, page 47).
- Check students have understood the story by completing **Find the untruths** (Activities, page 48).

Consolidation (10 mins)

- Divide the class into pairs and give each pair a copy of the **4-in-a-row game** (Activities, page 56).
- Have students find and point to these words in Book 3: Raj Gets a Soak: "groan," "moan," and "foam."

STEP 5
Tracking progress
15 mins

- Assign the **Timed word reading** (Activities, page 49). Students can repeat this activity to improve their reading speed.
- Complete the **Spelling assessment** (Activities, page 57) to make a quick, formative assessment of students' progress. A second list of words is provided for additional practice for more advanced students.
- Hide the words and ask students to write them out as you read them, encouraging them to segment each sound.
- Depending on your findings, either revisit some of the activities to reinforce any specific skill gaps, or invite students to complete an additional activity from the Activities book.

Extension activities

- Ask students to complete the **Make a book** activity (Activities, page 46).
- Play the **Reading game** (Activities, page 55).
- Ask students to complete the **Write the story in your own words** activity (Activities, page 53).

/er/

STEP 1
Preparation

20 mins

LESSON RESOURCES

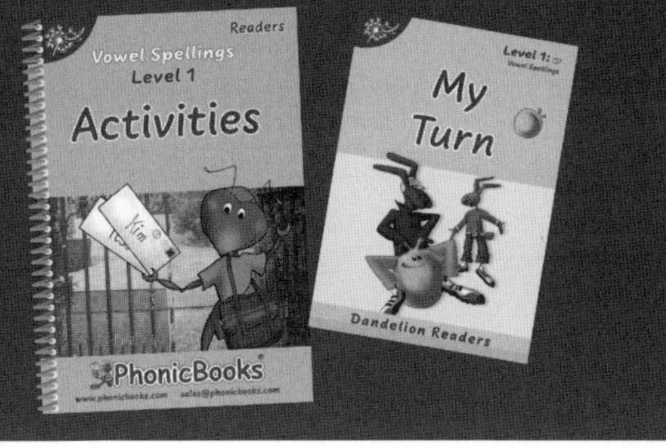

Reviewing sounds (3 mins)

- Using sound cards or a whiteboard, review some previously learned words containing the 'oa' spelling for the /oe/ sound.

Learning goal (2 mins)

- Explain to the students that you will be teaching them to read and spell new words using the spelling 'ur' for the sound /er/.
- Introduce the book Dandelion Readers Level 1 Book 4: My Turn.
- You will be completing some activities from Dandelion Readers Level 1 Activities.

Preparation (15 mins)

- Introduce the spelling 'ur' for the sound /er/.
- Show the students a sound card with the letters 'ur.' Tell students that these two letters spell one sound: /er/. Model the sound correctly and ask students to copy.

1 Word building and blending

- Tell the students that you are going to build the word "surf." Use only the sound cards for the word "surf."
- Draw three lines on the board and ask the students to listen to the sound in the word "surf." Move your finger under the word as you pronounce it.
- Ask the students to tell you which is the first sound in the word (move your finger again under the word as you say it). Students respond: /s/.
- Ask a student to show you the spelling for the sound /s/ and to place it on the first line.
- Now ask the students to listen to the next sound in the word "surf": /er/. Ask a student to find the spelling for the sound /er/.
- Complete with the third sound. Then ask the students to sound out all the sounds and blend them into a word. /s/ /er/ /f/ → "surf."

2 Word reading

- Write the words you have created on the board (if you haven't done so already). Then ask students to blend and read the words.
- Show how to say each sound individually and then blend them together to read the word. Model blending by using a swishing motion with your finger.
- Encourage students to follow your example with these words: "surf," "hurt," and "burn."

3 Oral segmenting

- Say a word aloud (e.g. "turn") and ask students to listen to the sounds in the word. Write the number of lines you need for all the sounds. Now ask students to listen to the sounds in the word and write a letter for every sound in the word as you spell the word.

4 Word chain

- Use sound cards or magnetic letters that represent the graphemes in the word "hurt." This word chain would need the sound cards: 'h,' 'ur,' 't,' 'l,' 'c,' and 'f.' Explain to the students that you will be making one change to the word. They must be "sound detectives" and notice if you have added a sound, taken away a sound, or swapped a sound.
- Say that you are going to change the word "hurt" (moving your finger under the word) to "hurl." Ask the students to listen carefully to where the change has occurred. Move your finger under the word as you say it slowly. Once the change has been identified, invite a student to swap the sound card or letter. Ask all the students to sound out the word and read the new word. e.g. /h/ /ur/ /l/ → "hurl."
- Direct students through the following word-chain sequence: hurt—hurl—furl—curl—curt—hurt

STEP 2
Application for reading
15 mins

Before reading (3 mins)

- Revisit the vocabulary taught in Step 1 (e.g. "turn"). Clearly say the word: /t/ /ur/ /n/. Explore different meanings for the word "turn", such as moving or changing direction, or waiting for your chance to do something.
- Ask questions such as, "Why do you think it's important to take turns in games?" and "What happens in a game if everyone tries to go at the same time?"
- Then write the word on the whiteboard and refer back to it throughout the week for reinforcement.

High-frequency words (2 mins)

- Pre-teach or reiterate these high-frequency words: "is," "my," "says," "me," "have," "give," "you're," "hurled," "his," and "to."
- Write the words on the board, showing the separate graphemes in each word. As students learn more of the Alphabetic Code, they will be able to decode those graphemes.

Application (10 mins)

- Read Book 4: My Turn.
- Encourage students to sound out each word and then blend to read.

Extension activities

- Complete the **Fluency** activity (Activities, page 68) to develop students' fluency and prosody skills.

STEP 3
Application for spelling
15 mins

Segmenting and spelling (15 mins)

- Ask students to complete the following activity to practice writing whole words: **Segmenting and spelling** (Activities, page 61).
- Dictate the words to the students. In the activity each word is associated with a picture as a visual clue.
- Task students with filling in the squares with the appropriate spelling for each sound.
- Read out the **Sentence dictation** sentences (Activities, page 69): "Burt curls up and yells. His hand hurts. His leg hurts."

STEP 4
Comprehension and consolidation
20 mins

Book reading (5 mins)

- Reread Book 4: My Turn.

Comprehension (5 mins)

- Ask students to complete **What happens next?** (Activities, page 65).
- Check students have understood the story by completing **Find the untruths** (Activities, page 66).

Consolidation (10 mins)

- Divide the class into pairs and give each pair a copy of the **Reading game** (Activities, page 73).
- Have students find and point to these words in Book 4: My Turn: "turn," "Burt," "hurled," and "hurts."

STEP 5
Tracking progress
15 mins

- Assign the **Timed word reading** (Activities, page 67). Students can repeat this activity to improve their reading speed.
- Complete the **Spelling assessment** (Activities, page 75) to make a quick, formative assessment of students' progress. A second list of words is provided for additional practice for more advanced students.
- Hide the words and ask students to write them out as you read them, encouraging them to segment each sound.
- Depending on your findings, either revisit some of the activities to reinforce any specific skill gaps, or invite students to complete an additional activity from the Activities book.

Extension activities

- Ask students to complete the **Make a book** activity (Activities, page 64).
- Play the **4-in-a-row game** (Activities, page 74).
- Ask students to complete the **Write the story in your own words** activity (Activities, page 71).

LESSON PLANS

/e/

LESSON RESOURCES

STEP 1
Preparation

20 mins

Reviewing sounds (3 mins)

- Using sound cards or a whiteboard, review some previously learned words containing the 'ur' spelling for the /er/ sound.

Learning goal (2 mins)

- Explain to the students that you will be teaching them to read and spell new words using the spelling 'ea' for the sound /e/.
- Introduce the book Dandelion Readers Level 1 Book 5: Bread and Jam.
- You will be completing some activities from Dandelion Readers Level 1 Activities.

Preparation (15 mins)

- Introduce the spelling 'ea' for the sound /e/.
- Show the students a sound card with the letters 'ea.' Tell students that these two letters spell one sound: /e/. Model the sound correctly and ask students to copy.

1 Word building and blending

- Tell the students that you are going to build the word "head." Use only the sound cards for the word "head."
- Draw three lines on the board and ask the students to listen to the sound in the word "head." Move your finger under the word as you pronounce it.
- Ask the students to tell you which is the first sound in the word (move your finger again under the word as you say it). Students respond: /h/.
- Ask a student to show you the spelling for the sound /h/ and to place it on the first line.
- Now ask the students to listen to the next sound in the word "head": /e/. Ask a student to find the spelling for the sound /e/.
- Complete with the third sound. Then ask the students to sound out all the sounds and blend them into a word. /h/ /e/ /d/ → "head."

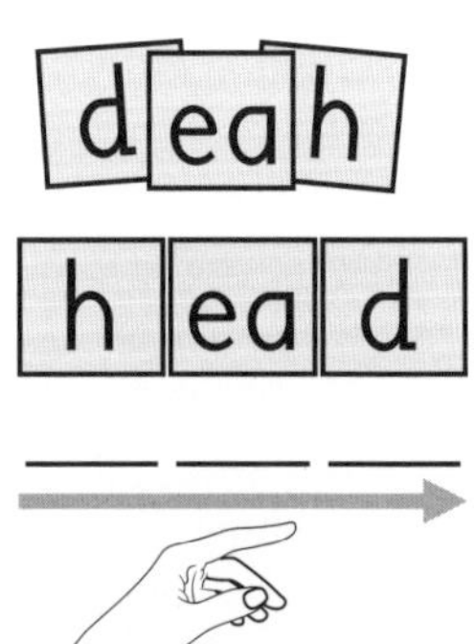

2 Word reading

- Write the words you have created on the board (if you haven't done so already). Then ask students to blend and read the words.
- Show how to say each sound individually and then blend them together to read the word. Model blending by using a swishing motion with your finger.
- Encourage students to follow your example with these words: "wealth," "sweat," and "bread."

3 Segmenting and spelling

- Say a word aloud (e.g. "health") and ask students to count the sounds in the word (4). Write the number of lines you need for all the sounds. Now ask students to listen to the sounds in the word and write a letter for every sound in the word as you spell the word.

4 Word chain

- Use sound cards or magnetic letters that represent the graphemes in the word "tread." This word chain would need the sound cards: 't,' 'r,' 'ea,' 'd,' 'b,' and 'h.' Explain to the students that you will be making one change to the word. They must be "sound detectives" and notice if you have added a sound, taken away a sound, or swapped a sound.
- Say that you are going to change the word "tread" (moving your finger under the word) to "read." Ask the students to listen carefully to where the change has occurred. Move your finger under the word as you say it slowly. Once the change has been identified, invite a student to swap the sound card or letter. Ask all the students to sound out the word and read the new word. e.g. /r/ /e/ /d/ → "read."
- Direct students through the following word-chain sequence: tread—read—head—dead—dread—bread—read—tread

STEP 2
Application for reading
15 mins

Before reading (3 mins)

- Revisit the vocabulary taught in Step 1 (e.g. "read"). Clearly say the word: /r/ /e/ /d/. Provide a simple definition of "read," such as having read something in the past.
- Explain how "read" can be pronounced /r/ /e/ /d/ when talking about something that was read in the past and /r/ /ee/ /d/ when referring to reading in the present or future.
- Then write the word on the whiteboard and refer back to it throughout the week for reinforcement.

High-frequency words (2 mins)

- Pre-teach or reiterate these high-frequency words: "of," "the," "said," "I," "don't," "you'll," "his," "he," "was," "began," "to," "me," "yanked," and "my."
- Explain that these are high-frequency words that have tricky spellings the students will learn later.
- Write the words on the board, showing the separate graphemes in each word. As students learn more of the Alphabetic Code, they will be able to decode those graphemes.

Application (10 mins)

- Read Book 5: Bread and Jam.
- Encourage students to sound out each word and then blend to read.

Extension activities

- Complete the **Fluency** activity (Activities, page 86) to develop students' fluency and prosody skills.

STEP 3
Application for spelling
15 mins

Segmenting and spelling (15 mins)

- Ask students to complete the following activity to practice writing whole words: **Segmenting and spelling** (Activities, page 79).
- Dictate the words to the students. In the activity each word is associated with a picture as a visual clue.
- Task students with filling in the squares with the appropriate spelling for each sound.
- Read out the **Sentence dictation** sentences (Activities, page 87): "Pip landed with his head in the jam. He began to sweat."

STEP 4
Comprehension and consolidation
20 mins

Book reading (5 mins)

- Reread Book 5: Bread and Jam.

Comprehension (5 mins)

- Ask students to complete **What happens next?** (Activities, page 83).
- Check students have understood the story by completing **Find the untruths** (Activities, page 84).

Consolidation (10 mins)

- Divide the class into pairs and give each pair a copy of the **4-in-a-row game** (Activities, page 92).
- Have students find and point to these words in Book 5: Bread and Jam: "bread," "spread," "tread," and "head."

STEP 5
Tracking progress
15 mins

- Assign the **Timed word reading** (Activities, page 85). Students can repeat this activity to improve their reading speed.
- Complete the **Spelling assessment** (Activities, page 93) to make a quick, formative assessment of students' progress. A second list of words is provided for additional practice for more advanced students.
- Hide the words and ask students to write them out as you read them, encouraging them to segment each sound.
- Depending on your findings, either revisit some of the activities to reinforce any specific skill gaps, or invite students to complete an extension activity.

Extension activities

- Ask students to complete the **Make a book** activity (Activities, page 82).
- Play the **Reading game** (Activities, page 91).
- Ask students to complete the **Write the story in your own words** activity (Activities, page 89).

LESSON PLANS

/ow/

LESSON RESOURCES

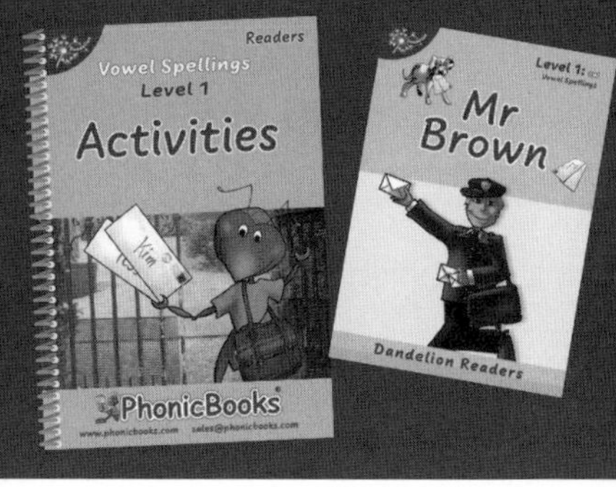

STEP 1

Preparation

20 mins

Reviewing sounds (3 mins)

- Using sound cards or a whiteboard, review some previously learned words containing the 'ea' spelling for the /e/ sound.

Learning goal (2 mins)

- Explain to the students that you will be teaching them to read and spell new words using the spelling 'ow' for the sound /ow/.
- Introduce the book Dandelion Readers Level 1 Book 6: Mr Brown.
- You will be completing some activities from Dandelion Readers Level 1 Activities.

Preparation (15 mins)

- Introduce the spelling 'ow' for the sound /ow/.
- Show the students the sound card with the letters 'ow.' Tell students that these two letters spell one sound: /ow/. Model the sound correctly and ask students to copy.

1 Word building and blending

- Tell the students that you are going to build the word "cow." Use only the sound cards for the word "cow."
- Draw two lines on the board and ask the students to listen to the sound in the word "cow." Move your finger under the word as you pronounce it.
- Ask the students to tell you which is the first sound in the word (move your finger again under the word as you say it). Students respond: /c/.
- Ask a student to show you the spelling for the sound /c/ and to place it on the first line.
- Now ask the students to listen to the next sound in the word "cow": /ow/. Ask a student to find the spelling for the sound /ow/.
- Ask the students to sound out all the sounds and blend them into a word. /c/ /ow/ → "cow."

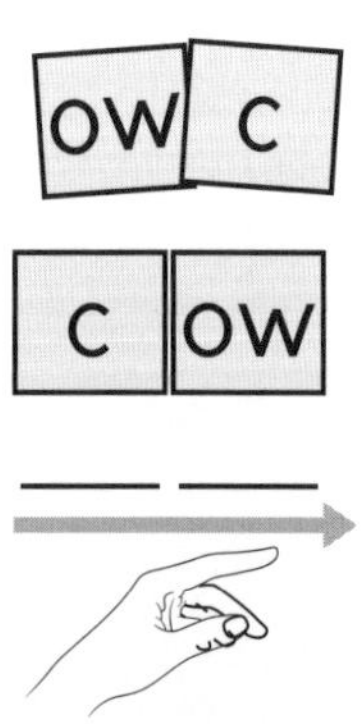

2 Word reading

- Write the words you have created on the whiteboard (if you haven't done so already). Then ask students to blend and read the words.
- Show how to say each sound individually and then blend them together to read the word. Model blending by using a swishing motion with your finger.
- Encourage students to follow your example with these words: "owl," "crown," and "clown."

3 Oral segmenting

- Say a word aloud (e.g. "clown") and ask students to count the sounds in the word (4). Write the number of lines you need for all the sounds. Now ask students to listen to the sounds in the word and write a letter for every sound in the word as you spell the word.

4 Word chain

- Using sound cards or magnetic letters, demonstrate how to build the word "cow." This word chain would need the sound cards: 'c,' 'ow,' 'n,' 'h,' and 'l.'
- Explain to the students that you will be making one change to the word. They must be "sound detectives" and notice if you have added a sound, taken away a sound, or swapped a sound.
- Say that you are going to change the word "cow" (moving your finger under the word) to "now." Ask the students to listen carefully to where the change has occurred. Move your finger under the word as you say it slowly. Once the change has been identified, invite a student to swap the sound card or letter. Ask all the students to sound out the word and read the new word. e.g. /n/ /ow/ → "now."
- Direct students through the following word-chain sequence: cow—now—how—howl—cowl—owl—ow—cow

STEP 2
Application for reading
15 mins

Before reading (3 mins)

- Revisit the vocabulary taught in Step 1 (e.g. "frown"). Clearly say the word: /f/ /r/ /ow/ /n/. Provide a simple definition of "frown," such as to bring your eyebrows together.
- Ask questions such as, "Why do you frown?" and "How do you feel when you are frowning?"
- Then write the word on the whiteboard and refer back to it throughout the week for reinforcement.

High-frequency words (2 mins)

- Pre-teach or reiterate these high-frequency words: "Mr," "was," "the," "mailman," "growled," "mopped," "his," "frowned," "I," "to," "he," and "asked."
- Write the words on the board, showing the separate graphemes in each word. As students learn more of the Alphabetic Code, they will be able to decode those graphemes.

Application (10 mins)

- Read Book 6: Mr Brown.
- Encourage students to sound out each word and then blend to read.

Extension activities

- Complete the **Fluency** activity (Activities, page 104) to develop students' fluency and prosody skills.

STEP 3
Application for spelling
15 mins

Segmenting and spelling (15 mins)

- Ask students to complete the following activity to practice writing whole words: **Segmenting and spelling** (Activities, page 97).
- Dictate the words to the students. In the activity each word is associated with a picture as a visual clue.
- Task students with filling in the squares with the appropriate spelling for each sound.
- Read out the **Sentence dictation** sentences (Activities, page 105): "'Now, how can I get past that growling dog?' asked Mr Brown."

Extension activities

- Assign the **Splitting two-syllable words** activity (Activities, page 108) to practice syllable division, and decoding and writing longer words.

STEP 4
Comprehension and consolidation
20 mins

Book reading (5 mins)

- Reread Book 6: Mr Brown.

Comprehension (5 mins)

- Ask students to complete **What happens next?** (Activities, page 101).
- Check students have understood the story by completing **Find the untruths** (Activities, page 102).

Consolidation (10 mins)

- Divide the class into pairs and give each pair a copy of the **Reading game** (Activities, page 109).
- Have students find and point to these words in Book 6: Mr Brown: "brown," "town," "growled," "brow," and "frowned."

STEP 5
Tracking progress
15 mins

- Assign the **Timed word reading** (Activities, page 103). Students can repeat this activity to improve their reading speed.
- Complete the **Spelling assessment** (Activities, page 111) to make a quick, formative assessment of students' progress. A second list of words is provided for additional practice for more advanced students.
- Hide the words and ask students to write them out as you read them, encouraging them to segment each sound.
- Depending on your findings, either revisit some of the activities to reinforce any specific skill gaps, or invite students to complete an extension activity.

Extension activities

- Ask students to complete the **Make a book** activity (Activities, page 100).
- Play the **4-in-a-row game** (Activities, page 110).
- Ask students to complete the **Write the story in your own words** activity (Activities, page 107).

b/oo/t

STEP 1
Preparation

20 mins

Reviewing sounds (3 mins)

- Using sound cards or a whiteboard, review some previously learned words containing the 'ow' spelling for the /ow/ sound.

Learning goal (2 mins)

- Explain to the students that you will be teaching them to read and spell new words using the spelling 'oo' for the sound b/oo/t.
- Introduce the book Dandelion Readers Level 1 Book 7: The Cocoon.
- You will be completing some activities from Dandelion Readers Level 1 Activities.

Preparation (15 mins)

- Introduce the spelling 'oo' for the sound b/oo/t.
- Show the students a sound card with the letters 'oo.' Tell students that these two letters spell one sound: b/oo/t. Model the sound correctly and ask students to copy.

1 Word building and blending

- Tell the students that you are going to build the word "boot." Use only the sound cards for the word "boot."
- Draw three lines on the board and ask the students to listen to the sound in the word "boot." Move your finger under the word as you pronounce it.
- Ask the students to tell you which is the first sound in the word (move your finger again under the word as you say it). Students respond: /b/.
- Ask a student to show you the spelling for the sound /b/ and to place it on the first line.
- Now ask the students to listen to the next sound in the word "boot": /oo/. Ask a student to find the spelling for the sound /oo/.
- Complete with the third sound. Then ask the students to sound out all the sounds and blend them into a word. /b/ /oo/ /t/ → "boot."

LESSON RESOURCES

2 Word reading

- Write the words you have created on the board (if you haven't done so already). Then ask students to blend and read the words.
- Show how to say each sound individually and then blend them together to read the word. Model blending by using a swishing motion with your finger.
- Encourage students to follow your example with these words: "roof," "moon," and "spoon."

3 Oral segmenting

- Say a word aloud (e.g. "cool") and ask students to count the sounds in the word (3). Write the number of lines you need for all the sounds. Now ask students to listen to the sounds in the word and write a letter for every sound in the word as you spell the word.

4 Word chain

- Using sound cards or magnetic letters, demonstrate how to build the word "too." This word chain would need the sound cards: 't,' 'oo,' 'l,' 'c,' 'p,' 'm,' 'r,' and 't.' Explain to the students that you will be making one change to the word. They must be "sound detectives" and notice if you have added a sound, taken away a sound, or swapped a sound.
- Say that you are going to change the word "too" (moving your finger under the word) to "tool." Ask the students to listen carefully to where the change has occurred. Move your finger under the word as you say it slowly. Once the change has been identified, invite a student to swap the sound card or letter. Ask all the students to sound out the word and read the new word. e.g. /t/ /oo/ /l/ → "tool."
- Direct students through the following word-chain sequence: too—tool—cool—coop—loop—loom—room—root—toot—too

STEP 2 Application for reading

15 mins

Before reading (3 mins)

- Revisit the vocabulary taught in Step 1 (e.g. "cocoon"). Clearly say the word:/k/ /u/ /k/ /oo/ /n/. Note the 'o' in "cocoon" makes the schwa sound.
- Explore different meanings of the word "cocoon," such as a protective case spun by insects or to describe a place that feels protected.
- Ask questions such as, "Have you ever seen a cocoon in nature? What did it look like?"
- Then write the word on the whiteboard and refer back to it throughout the week for reinforcement.

High-frequency words (2 mins)

- Pre-teach or reiterate these high-frequency words: "night," "swooped," "the," "hatched," "out," "popped," "he," "began," "to," "look," "there," "was," "no," "open," and "into."
- Write the words on the board, showing the separate graphemes in each word. As students learn more of the Alphabetic Code, they will be able to decode those graphemes.

Application (10 mins)

- Read Book 7: The Cocoon.
- Encourage students to sound out each word and then blend to read.

Extension activities

- Complete the **Fluency** activity (Activities, page 122) to develop students' fluency and prosody skills.

STEP 3 Application for spelling

15 mins

Segmenting and spelling (15 mins)

- Ask students to complete the following activity to practice writing whole words: **Segmenting and spelling** (Activities, page 115).
- Dictate the words to the students. In the activity each word is associated with a picture as a visual clue.
- Task students with filling in the squares with the appropriate spelling for each sound.
- Read out the **Sentence dictation** sentences (Activities, page 123): "Sid began to look for food. Soon there was no room in his skin."

STEP 4 Comprehension and consolidation

20 mins

Book reading (5 mins)

- Reread Book 7: The Cocoon.

Comprehension (5 mins)

- Ask students to complete **What happens next?** (Activities, page 119).
- Check students have understood the story by completing **Find the untruths** (Activities, page 120).

Consolidation (10 mins)

- Divide the class into pairs and give each pair a copy of the **4-in-a-row game** (Activities, page 128).
- Have students find and point to these words in Book 7: The Cocoon: "moonlit," "food," "cool," "room," and "soon."

STEP 5 Tracking progress

15 mins

- Assign the **Timed word reading** (Activities, page 121). Students can repeat this activity to improve their reading speed.
- Complete the **Spelling assessment** (Activities, page 129) to make a quick, formative assessment of students' progress. A second list of words is provided for additional practice for more advanced students.
- Hide the words and ask students to write them out as you read them, encouraging them to segment each sound.
- Depending on your findings, either revisit some of the activities to reinforce any specific skill gaps, or invite students to complete an extension activity.

Extension activities

- Ask students to complete the **Make a book** activity (Activities, page 118).
- Play the **Reading game** (Activities, page 127).
- Ask students to complete the **Write the story in your own words** activity (Activities, page 125).

/ie/

STEP 1
Preparation

20 mins

Reviewing sounds (3 mins)

- Using sound cards or a whiteboard, review some previously learned words containing the 'oo' spelling for the b/oo/t sound.

Learning goal (2 mins)

- Explain to the students that you will be teaching them to read and spell new words using the spelling 'igh' for the sound /ie/.
- Introduce the book Dandelion Readers Level 1 Book 8: A Fright in the Night.
- You will be completing some activities from Dandelion Readers Level 1 Activities.

Preparation (15 mins)

- Introduce the spelling 'igh' for the sound /ie/.
- Show the students the sound card with the letters 'ie.' Tell students that these two letters spell one sound: /ie/. Model the sound correctly and ask students to copy.

1 Word building and blending

- Tell the students that you are going to build the word "light." Use only the sound cards for the word "light."
- Draw three lines on the board and ask the students to listen to the sound in the word "light." Move your finger under the word as you pronounce it.
- Ask the students to tell you which is the first sound in the word (move your finger again under the word as you say it). Students respond: /l/.
- Ask a student to show you the spelling for the sound /l/ and to place it on the first line.
- Now ask the students to listen to the next sound in the word "light": /ie/. Ask a student to find the spelling for the sound /ie/.
- Complete with the third sound. Then ask the students to sound out all the sounds and blend them into a word. /l/ /ie/ /t/ → "light."

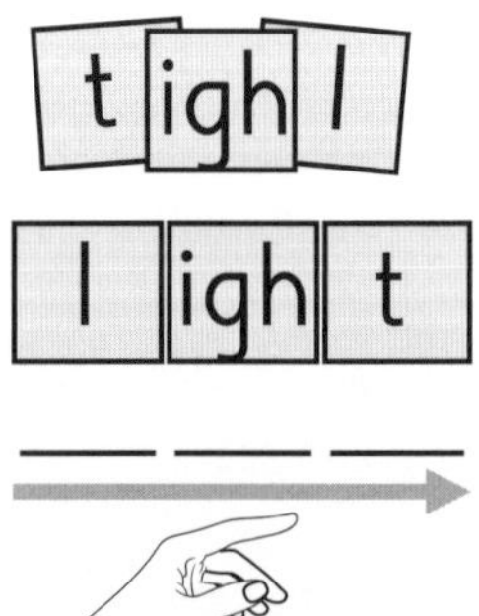

LESSON RESOURCES

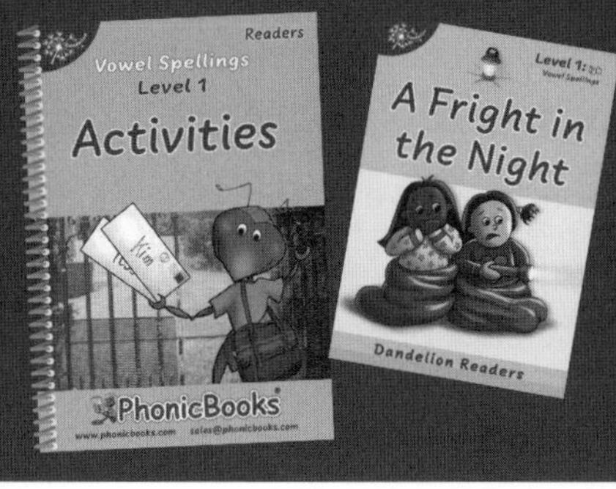

2 Word reading

- Write the words you have created on the board (if you haven't done so already). Then ask students to blend and read the words.
- Show how to say each sound individually and then blend them together to read the word. Model blending by using a swishing motion with your finger.
- Encourage students to follow your example with these words: "sight," "night," and "flight."

3 Oral segmenting

- Say a word aloud (e.g. "fight") and ask students to listen to the sounds in the word (3). Write the number of lines you need for all the sounds. Now ask students to listen to the sounds in the word and write a letter for every sound in the word as you spell the word.

4 Word chain

- Using sound cards or magnetic letters, demonstrate how to build the word "high." This word chain would need the sound cards: 'r,' 'igh,' 't,' 'f,' 'l,' 'n,' 's,' and 'b.' Explain to the students that you will be making one change to the word. They must be "sound detectives" and notice if you have added a sound, taken away a sound, or swapped a sound.
- Say that you are going to change the word "right" (moving your finger under the word) to "fright." Ask the students to listen carefully to where the change has occurred. Move your finger under the word as you say it slowly. Once the change has been identified, invite a student to swap the sound card or letter. Ask all the students to sound out the word and read the new word. e.g. /f/ /r/ /ie/ /t/ → "fright."
- Direct students through the following word-chain sequence: right—fright—flight—light—night—sight—slight—blight—bright—right

STEP 2
Application for reading

15 mins

Before reading (3 mins)

- Revisit the vocabulary taught in Step 1 (e.g. "bright"). Clearly say the word: /b/ /r/ /ie/ /t/.
- Explore different meanings of the word "bright," such as something that shines with a dazzling light or smart.
- Ask questions such as, "Can you name a few objects that are bright?"
- Then write the word on the whiteboard and refer back to it throughout the week for reinforcement.

High-frequency words (2 mins)

- Pre-teach or reiterate these high-frequency words: "we," "the," "tonight," "asked," "settled," "switched," "was," "flashed," "to," and "stretched."
- Explain that these are high-frequency words that have tricky spellings the students will learn later.
- Write the words on the board, showing the separate graphemes in each word. As students learn more of the Alphabetic Code, they will be able to decode those graphemes.

Application (10 mins)

- Read Book 8: A Fright in the Night.
- Encourage students to sound out each word and then blend to read.

Extension activities

- Complete the **Fluency** activity (Activities, page 140) to develop students' fluency and prosody skills.

STEP 3
Application for spelling

15 mins

Segmenting and spelling (15 mins)

- Ask students to complete the following activity to practice writing whole words: **Segmenting and spelling** (Activities, page 133).
- Dictate the words to the students. In the activity each word is associated with a picture as a visual clue.
- Task students with filling in the squares with the appropriate spelling for each sound.
- Read out the **Sentence dictation** sentences (Activities, page 141): "Scratch, scratch! Ella sat upright. Viv flashed the flashlight."

STEP 4
Comprehension and consolidation

20 mins

Book reading (5 mins)

- Reread Book 8: A Fright in the Night.

Comprehension (5 mins)

- Ask students to complete **What happens next?** (Activities, page 137).
- Check students have understood the story by completing **Find the untruths** (Activities, page 138).

Consolidation (10 mins)

- Divide the class into pairs and give each pair a copy of the **Reading game** (Activities, page 145).
- Have students find and point to these words in Book 8: A Fright in the Night: "night," "light," "bright," and "tonight."

STEP 5
Tracking progress

15 mins

- Assign the **Timed word reading** (Activities, page 139). Students can repeat this activity to improve their reading speed.
- Complete the **Spelling assessment** (Activities, page 147) to make a quick, formative assessment of students' progress. A second list of words is provided for additional practice for more advanced students.
- Hide the words and ask students to write them out as you read them, encouraging them to segment each sound.
- Depending on your findings, either revisit some of the activities to reinforce any specific skill gaps, or invite students to complete an extension activity.

Extension activities

- Ask students to complete the **Make a book** activity (Activities, page 136).
- Play the **4-in-a-row game** (Activities, page 146).
- Ask students to complete the **Write the story in your own words** activity (Activities, page 143).

LESSON PLANS

l/oo/k

STEP 1
Preparation

20 mins

LESSON RESOURCES

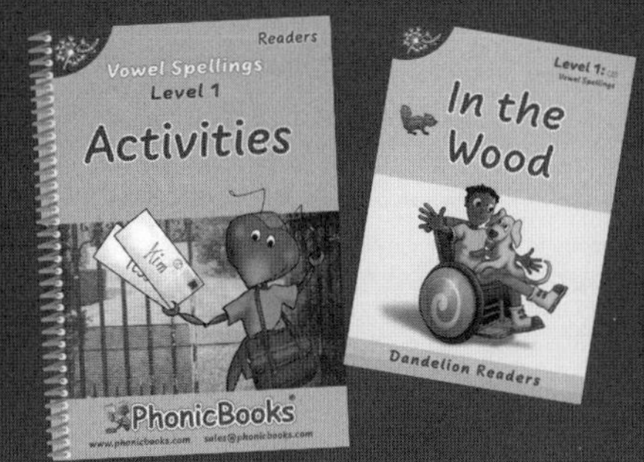

Reviewing sounds (3 mins)

- Using sound cards or a whiteboard, review some previously learned words containing the 'igh' spelling for the /ie/ sound.

Learning goal (2 mins)

- Explain to the students that you will be teaching them to read and spell new words using the spelling 'oo' for the sound l/oo/k.
- Introduce the book Dandelion Readers Level 1 Book 9: In the Wood.
- You will be completing some activities from Dandelion Readers Level 1 Activities.

Preparation (15 mins)

- Introduce the spelling 'oo' for the sound l/oo/k.
- Show the students a sound card with the letters 'oo.' Tell students that these two letters spell one sound: l/oo/k. Model the sound correctly and ask students to copy.

1 Word building and blending

- Tell the students that you are going to build the word "cook." Use only the sound cards for the word "cook."
- Draw three lines on the board and ask the students to listen to the sound in the word "cook." Move your finger under the word as you pronounce it.
- Ask the students to tell you which is the first sound in the word (move your finger again under the word as you say it). Students respond: /k/.
- Ask a student to show you the spelling for the sound /k/ and to place it on the first line.
- Now ask the students to listen to the next sound in the word "cook": /oo/. Ask a student to find the spelling for /oo/.
- Complete with the third sound. Then ask the students to sound out all the sounds and blend them into a word. /k/ /oo/ /k/ → "cook."

2 Word reading

- Write the words you have created on the board (if you haven't done so already). Then ask students to blend and read the words.
- Show how to say each sound individually and then blend them together to read the word. Model blending by using a swishing motion with your finger.
- Encourage students to follow your example with these words: "book," "wood," and "foot."

3 Oral segmenting

- Say a word aloud (e.g. "book") and ask students to count to the sounds in the word (3). Write the number of lines you need for all the sounds. Now ask students to listen to the sounds in the word and write a letter for every sound in the word as you spell the word.

4 Word chain

- Using sound cards or magnetic letters, demonstrate how to build the word "book." This word chain would need the sound cards: 'b,' 'oo,' 'k,' 'c,' 'l,' 't,' 'h,' and 'r.' Explain to the students that you will be making one change to the word. They must be "sound detectives" and notice if you have added a sound, taken away a sound, or swapped a sound.
- Say that you are going to change the word "book" (moving your finger under the word) to "cook." Ask the students to listen carefully to where the change has occurred. Move your finger under the word as you say it slowly. Once the change has been identified, invite a student to swap the sound card or letter. Ask all the students to sound out the word and read the new word. e.g. /c/ /oo/ k/ → "cook."
- Direct students through the following word-chain sequence: book—cook—look—took—hook—rook—brook—book

STEP 2 Application for reading

15 mins

Before reading (3 mins)

- Revisit the vocabulary taught in Step 1 (e.g. "wood"). Clearly say the word: /w/ /oo/ /d/.
- Explore different meanings of the word "wood", such as an area of land covered with trees or a building material made from trees.
- Ask questions such as, "Is there anything in the classroom made of wood?" or "Have you ever visited a wood?"
- Then write the word on the whiteboard and refer back to it throughout the week for reinforcement.

High-frequency words (2 mins)

- Pre-teach or reiterate these high-frequency words: "his," "to," "the," "said," "was," "into," "looked," "he," "vanished," "limped," "you," and "jumped."
- Explain that these are high-frequency words that have tricky spellings the students will learn later.
- Write the words on the board, showing the separate graphemes in each word. As students learn more of the Alphabetic Code, they will be able to decode those graphemes.

Application (10 mins)

- Read Book 9: In the Wood.
- Encourage students to sound out each word and then blend to read.

Extension activities

- Complete the **Fluency** activity (Activities, page 158) to develop students' fluency and prosody skills.

STEP 3 Application for spelling

15 mins

Segmenting and spelling (15 mins)

- Ask students to complete the following activity to practice writing whole words: **Segmenting and spelling** (Activities, page 151).
- Dictate the words to the students. In the activity each word is associated with a picture as a visual clue.
- Task students with filling in the squares with the appropriate spelling for each sound.
- Read out the **Sentence dictation** sentences (Activities, page 159): "Baz spotted a chipmunk and took off into the wood. 'Woof!'"

STEP 4 Comprehension and consolidation

20 mins

Book reading (5 mins)

- Reread Book 9: In the Wood.

Comprehension (5 mins)

- Ask students to complete **What happens next?** (Activities, page 155).
- Check students have understood the story by completing **Find the untruths** (Activities, page 156).

Consolidation (10 mins)

- Divide the class into pairs and give each pair a copy of the **4-in-a-row game** (Activities, page 164).
- Have students find and point to these words in Book 9: In the Wood: "wood" and "brook."

STEP 5 Tracking progress

15 mins

- Assign the **Timed word reading** (Activities, page 157). Students can repeat this activity to improve their reading speed.
- Complete the **Spelling assessment** (Activities, page 165) to make a quick, formative assessment of students' progress. A second list of words is provided for additional practice for more advanced students.
- Hide the words and ask students to write them out as you read them, encouraging them to segment each sound.
- Depending on your findings, either revisit some of the activities to reinforce any specific skill gaps, or invite students to complete an extension activity.

Extension activities

- Ask students to complete the **Make a book** activity (Activities, page 154).
- Play the **Reading game** (Activities, page 163).
- Ask students to complete the **Write the story in your own words** activity (Activities, page 161).

LESSON PLANS

/aw/

STEP 1
Preparation

20 mins

Reviewing sounds (3 mins)

- Using sound cards or a whiteboard, review some previously learned words containing the 'oo' spelling for the l/oo/k sound.

Learning goal (2 mins)

- Explain to the students that you will be teaching them to read and spell new words using the spelling 'aw' for the sound /aw/.
- Introduce the book Dandelion Readers Level 1 Book 10: Paw Prints.
- You will be completing some activities from Dandelion Readers Level 1 Activities.

Preparation (15 mins)

- Introduce the spelling 'aw' for the sound /aw/.
- Show the students a sound card with the letters 'aw.' Tell students that these two letters spell one sound: /aw/. Model the sound correctly and ask students to copy.

1 Word building and blending

- Tell the students that you are going to build the word "paw." Use only the sound cards for the word "paw."
- Draw two lines on the board and ask the students to listen to the sound in the word "paw." Move your finger under the word as you pronounce it.
- Ask the students to tell you which is the first sound in the word (move your finger again under the word as you say it).
- Students respond: /p/.
- Ask a student to show you the spelling for the sound /p/ and to place it on the first line.
- Now ask the students to listen to the next sound in the word "paw": /aw/. Ask a student to find the spelling for the sound /aw/.
- Ask the students to sound out all the sounds and blend them into a word. /p/ /aw/ → "paw."

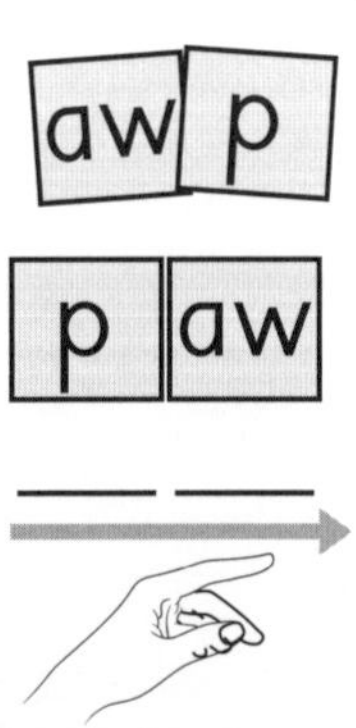

LESSON RESOURCES

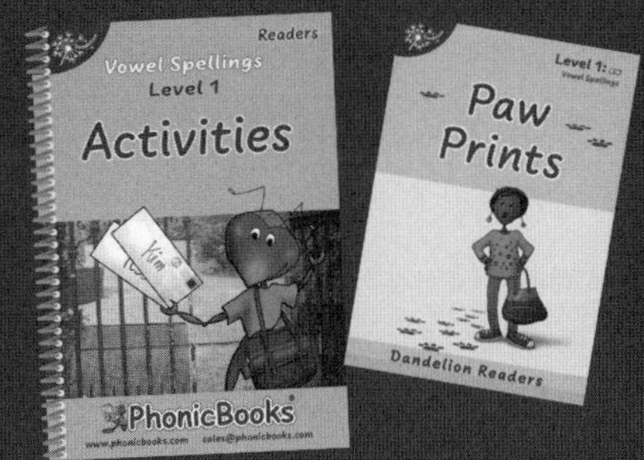

2 Word reading

- Write the words you have created on the whiteboard (if you haven't done so already). Then ask students to segment, blend, and read the words.
- Show how to say each sound individually and then blend them together to read the word. Model blending by using a swishing motion with your finger.
- Encourage students to follow your example with these words: "claw," "saw," and "draw."

3 Segmenting and spelling

- Say a word out loud (e.g. "yawn") and ask students to count the sounds in the word (4). Write the number of lines you need for all the sounds. Now ask students to listen to the sounds in the word and write a letter for every sound in the word as you spell the word.

4 Word chain

- Using sound cards or magnetic letters, demonstrate how to build the word "saw." This word chain would need the sound cards: 's,' 'aw,' 'n,' 'f,' 'l,' 'j,' and 'p.' Explain to the students that you will be making one change to the word. They must be "sound detectives" and notice if you have added a sound, taken away a sound, or swapped a sound.
- Say that you are going to change the word "saw" (moving your finger under the word) to "sawn." Ask the students to listen carefully to where the change has occurred. Move your finger under the words as you say it slowly. Once the change has been identified, invite a student to swap the sound card or letter. Ask all the students to sound out the word and read the new word. e.g. /s/ /aw/ n/ → "sawn."
- Direct students through the following word-chain sequence: saw—sawn—fawn—lawn—law—jaw—paw—saw

STEP 2
Application for reading
15 mins

Before reading (3 mins)

- Revisit the vocabulary taught in Step 1 (e.g. "jaw"). Clearly say the word: /j/ /aw/.
- Provide a simple definition: "The jaw is the bony structure around the mouth that contains the teeth."
- Ask questions such as, "What animals have big jaws?"
- Then write the word on the whiteboard and refer back to it throughout the week for reinforcement.

High-frequency words (2 mins)

- Pre-teach or reiterate these high-frequency words: "home," "she," "the," "ripped," "sofa," "gnawed," "controls," "is," "I," "to," "crawled," "drawer," "said," and "tickled."
- Write the words on the board, showing the separate graphemes in each word. As students learn more of the Alphabetic Code, they will be able to decode those graphemes.

Application (10 mins)

- Read Book 10: Paw Prints.
- Encourage students to sound out each word and then blend to read.

Extension activities

- Complete the **Fluency** activity (Activities, page 176) to develop students' fluency and prosody skills.

STEP 3
Application for spelling
15 mins

Segmenting and spelling (15 mins)

- Ask students to complete the following activity to practice writing whole words: **Segmenting and spelling** (Activities, page 169).
- Dictate the words to the students. In the activity each word is associated with a picture as a visual clue.
- Task students with filling in the squares with the appropriate spelling for each sound.
- Read out the **Dictation** sentences (Activities, page 178): "Mom saw paw prints on the rug. Big claws had ripped the sofa."

STEP 4
Comprehension and consolidation
20 mins

Book reading (5 mins)

- Reread Book 10: Paw Prints.

Comprehension (5 mins)

- Ask students to complete **What happens next?** (Activities, page 173).
- Check students have understood the story by completing **Find the untruths** (Activities, page 174).

Consolidation (10 mins)

- Divide the class into pairs and give each pair a copy of the **4-in-a-row game** (Activities, page 182).
- Have students find and point to these words in Book 10: Paw Prints: "paw," "claws," and "jaws."

STEP 5
Tracking progress
15 mins

- Assign the **Timed word reading** (Activities, page 175). Students can repeat this activity to improve their reading speed.
- Complete the **Spelling assessment** (Activities, page 183) to make a quick, formative assessment of students' progress. A second list of words is provided for additional practice for more advanced students.
- Hide the words and ask students to write them out as you read them, encouraging them to segment each sound.
- Depending on your findings, either revisit some of the activities to reinforce any specific skill gaps, or invite students to complete an extension activity.

Extension activities

- Ask students to complete the **Make a book** activity (Activities, page 172).
- Play the **4-in-a-row game** (Activities, page 182).
- Ask students to complete the **Write the story in your own words** activity (Activities, page 179).

LESSON PLANS

/oi/

STEP 1
Preparation

20 mins

Reviewing sounds (3 mins)

- Using sound cards or a whiteboard, review some previously learned words containing the 'aw' spelling for the /aw/ sound.

Learning goal (2 mins)

- Explain to the students that you will be teaching them to read and spell new words using the spelling 'oi' for the sound /oi/.
- Introduce the book Dandelion Readers, Level 1 Book 11: Oil.
- You will be completing some activities from Dandelion Readers Level 1 Activities.

Preparation (15 mins)

- Introduce the spelling 'oi' for the sound /oi/.
- Show the students a sound card with the letters 'oi.' Model the sound correctly and ask students to copy.

1 Word building and blending

- Tell the students that you are going to build the word "oil." Use only the sound cards for the word "oil."
- Draw two lines on the board and ask the students to listen to the sound in the word "oil." Move your finger under the word as you pronounce it.
- Ask the students to tell you which is the first sound in the word (move your finger again under the word as you say it). Students respond: /oi/.
- Ask a student to show you the spelling for the sound /l/ and to place it on the first line.
- Now ask the students to listen to the next sound in the word "oil": /l/. Ask a student to find the spelling for the sound /l/.
- Ask the students to sound out all the sounds and blend them into a word. /oi/ /l/ → "oil."

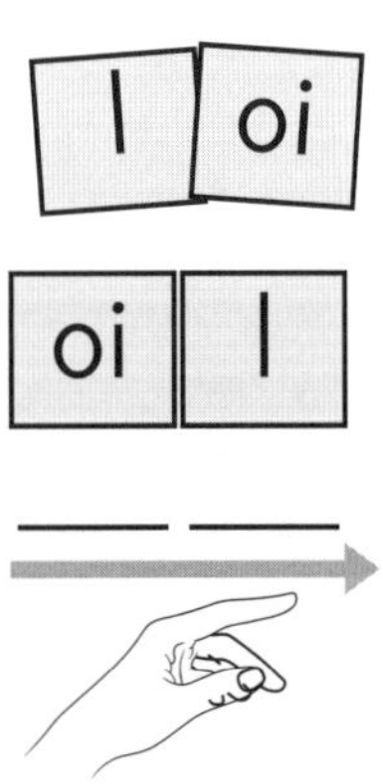

LESSON RESOURCES

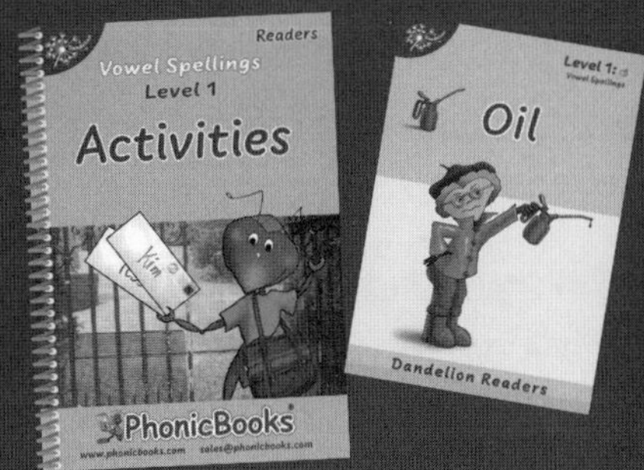

2 Word reading

- Write the words you have created on the board (if you haven't done so already). Then ask students to segment, blend, and read the words.
- Show how to say each sound individually and then blend them together to read the word. Model blending by using a swishing motion with your finger.
- Encourage students to follow your example with these words: "coin," "boil," and "point."

3 Oral segmenting

- Say a word aloud (e.g. "joint") and ask students to listen to the sounds in the word (4). Write the number of lines you need for all the sounds. Now ask students to listen to the sounds in the word and write a letter for every sound in the word as you spell the word.

4 Word chain

- Using sound cards or magnetic letters, demonstrate how to build the word "soil." This word chain would need the sound cards: 's,' 'oi,' 'l,' 'c,' 'f,' and 'b.' Explain to the students that you will be making one change to the word. They must be "sound detectives" and notice if you have added a sound, taken away a sound, or swapped a sound.
- Say that you are going to change the word "soil." (moving your finger under the word) to "coil." Ask the students to listen carefully to where the change has occurred. Move your finger under the word as you say it slowly. Once the change has been identified, invite a student to swap the sound card or letter. Ask all the students to sound out the word and read the new word. e.g. /c/ /oi/ /l/ → "coil."
- Direct students through the following word-chain sequence: soil—coil—foil—boil—oil—soil

STEP 2
Application for reading

15 mins

Before reading (3 mins)

- Revisit the vocabulary taught in Step 1 (e.g. "soil"). Clearly say the word: /s/ /oi/ /l/.
- Provide a simple definition: "Soil is the dark, brown earth in which plants grow."
- Ask questions such as, "What types of things can you find in soil?"
- Then write the word on the whiteboard and refer back to it throughout the week for reinforcement.

High-frequency words (2 mins)

- Pre-teach or reiterate these high-frequency words: "picked," "I'm," "puffed," "noise," "came," "the," "was," "we," "have," "no," "said," "is," "spoiled," "little," "joined," "he," "his," "my," "voice," "I," "gave," and "some."
- Explain that these are high-frequency words that have tricky spellings the students will learn later.
- Write the words on the board, showing the separate graphemes in each word. As students learn more of the Alphabetic Code, they will be able to decode those graphemes.

Application (10 mins)

- Read Book 11: Oil.
- Encourage students to sound out each word and then blend to read.

Extension activities

- Complete the **Fluency** activity (Activities, page 194) to develop students' fluency and prosody skills.

STEP 3
Application for spelling

15 mins

Segmenting and spelling (15 mins)

- Ask students to complete the following activity to practice writing whole words: **Segmenting and spelling** (Activities, page 187).
- Dictate the words to the students. In the activity each word is associated with a picture as a visual clue.
- Task students with filling in the squares with the appropriate spelling for each sound.
- Read out the **Sentence dictation** sentences (Activities, page 195): "The cab had no oil. It was boiling! The trip was spoiled."

STEP 4
Comprehension and consolidation

20 mins

Book reading (5 mins)

- Reread Book 11: Oil.

Comprehension (5 mins)

- Ask students to complete **What happens next?** (Activities, page 191).
- Check students have understood the story by completing **Find the untruths** (Activities, page 192).

Consolidation (10 mins)

- Divide the class into pairs and give each pair a copy of the **4-in-a-row game** (Activities, page 200).
- Have students find and point to these words in Book 11: Oil: "oil," "joined," "noise," "soil," and "spoiled."

STEP 5
Tracking progress

15 mins

- Assign the **Timed word reading** (Activities, page 193). Students can repeat this activity to improve their reading speed.
- Complete the **Spelling assessment** (Activities, page 201) to make a quick, formative assessment of students' progress. A second list of words is provided for additional practice for more advanced students.
- Hide the words and ask students to write them out as you read them, encouraging them to segment each sound.
- Depending on your findings, either revisit some of the activities to reinforce any specific skill gaps, or invite students to complete an extension activity.

Extension activities

- Ask students to complete the **Make a book** activity (Activities, page 190).
- Play the **Reading game** (Activities, page 199).
- Ask students to complete the **Write the story in your own words** activity (Activities, page 197).

LESSON PLANS

/ar/

LESSON RESOURCES

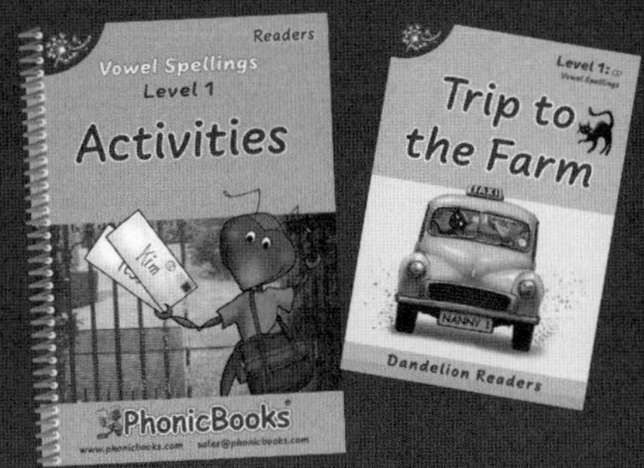

STEP 1
Preparation

20 mins

Reviewing sounds (3 mins)

- Using sound cards or a whiteboard, review some previously learned words containing the 'oi' spelling for the /oi/ sound.

Learning goal (2 mins)

- Explain to the students that you will be teaching them to read and spell new words using the spelling 'ar' for the sound /ar/.
- Introduce the book Dandelion Readers Level 1 Book 12: Trip to the Farm.
- You will be completing some activities from Dandelion Readers Level 1 Activities.

Preparation (15 mins)

- Introduce the spelling 'ar' for the sound /ar/.
- Show the students a sound card with the letters 'ar.' Model the sound correctly and ask students to copy.

1 Word building and blending

- Tell the students that you are going to build the word "jar." Use only the sound cards for the word "jar."
- Draw two lines on the board and ask the students to listen to the sound in the word "jar." Move your finger under the word as you pronounce it.
- Ask the students to tell you which is the first sound in the word (move your finger again under the word as you say it). Students respond: /j/.
- Ask a student to show you the spelling for the sound /j/ and to place it on the first line. Now ask the students to listen to the next sound in the word "jar": /ar/. Ask a student to find the spelling for the sound /ar/.
- Ask the students to sound out all the sounds and blend them into a word. /j/ /ar/ → "jar."

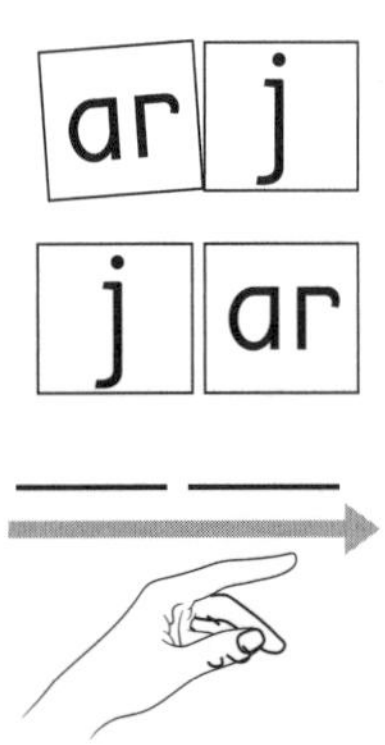

2 Word reading

- Write the words you have created on the board (if you haven't done so already). Then ask students to blend and read the words.
- Show how to say each sound individually and then blend them together to read the word. Model blending by using a swishing motion with your finger.
- Encourage students to follow your example with these words: "car," "star," and "cart."

3 Oral segmenting

- Say a word out loud (e.g. "start") and ask students to count the sounds in the word (4). Write the number of lines you need for all the sounds. Now ask students to listen to the sounds in the word and write a letter for every sound in the word as you spell the word.

4 Word chain

- Using sound cards or magnetic letters, demonstrate how to build the word "art." This word chain would need the sound cards: 'ar,' 'c,' 't,' and 's.' Explain to the students that you will be making one change to the word. They must be "sound detectives" and notice if you have added a sound, taken away a sound, or swapped a sound.
- Say that you are going to change the word "art" (moving your finger under the word) to "cart." Ask the students to listen carefully to where the change has occurred. Move your finger under the words as you say it slowly. Once the change has been identified, invite a student to swap the sound card or letter. Ask all the students to sound out the word and read the new word. e.g. /c/ /ar/ t/ → "cart."
- Direct students through the following word-chain sequence: art—cart—car—scar—star—start—tart—art.

STEP 2
Application for reading
15 mins

Before reading (3 mins)

- Revisit the vocabulary taught in Step 1 (e.g. "farm"). Clearly say the word: /f/ /ar/ /m/.
- Provide a simple definition, for example, "A farm is land used to grow crops and raise animals."
- Ask questions such as, "Can you name some animals that are commonly kept on farms?"
- Then write the word on the whiteboard and refer back to it throughout the week for reinforcement.

High-frequency words (2 mins)

- Pre-teach or reiterate these high-frequency words: "we're," "to," "the," "said," "parked," "gasped," "marched," "into," "pecked," "large," "began," "arched," "his," and "purred."
- Write the words on the board, showing the separate graphemes in each word. As students learn more of the Alphabetic Code, they will be able to decode those graphemes.

Application (10 mins)

- Read Book 12: Trip to the Farm.
- Encourage students to sound out each word and then blend to read.

Extension activities

- Complete the **Fluency** activity (Activities, page 212) to develop students' fluency and prosody skills.

STEP 3
Application for spelling
15 mins

Whole-word writing (15 mins)

- Ask students to complete the following activity to practice writing whole words: **Segmenting and spelling** (Activities, page 205).
- Dictate the words to the students. In the activity each word is associated with a picture as a visual clue.
- Task students with filling in the squares with the appropriate spelling for each sound.
- Read out the **Sentence dictation** sentences (Activities, page 213): "A large farmyard dog began to bark. Arthur arched his back."

Extension activities

- Assign the **Splitting two-syllable words** activity (Activities, page 216) to practice syllable division, and decoding and writing longer words.

STEP 4
Comprehension and consolidation
20 mins

Book reading (5 mins)

- Reread Book 12: Trip to the Farm.

Comprehension (5 mins)

- Ask students to complete **What happens next?** (Activities, page 209).
- Check students have understood the story by completing **Find the untruths** (Activities, page 210).

Consolidation (10 mins)

- Divide the class into pairs and give each pair a copy of the **Reading game** (Activities, page 217).
- Have students find and point to these words in Book 12: Trip to the Farm: "car," "farm," "bark," and "far."

STEP 5
Tracking progress
15 mins

- Assign the **Timed word reading** (Activities, page 211). Students can repeat this activity to improve their reading speed.
- Complete the **Spelling assessment** (Activities, page 219) to make a quick, formative assessment of students' progress. A second list of words is provided for additional practice for more advanced students.
- Hide the words and ask students to write them out as you read them, encouraging them to segment each sound.
- Depending on your findings, either revisit some of the activities to reinforce any specific skill gaps, or invite students to complete an extension activity.
- For a summative assessment of each student's progress for vowel spellings (Level 1), assign the **Reading assessment** (page 95).

Extension activities

- Play the **4-in-a-row game** (Activities, page 218).
- Ask students to complete the **Write the story in your own words** activity (Activities, page 215).
- Use the **Blank reading game** or **Blank 4-in-a-row-game** (pages 220–221) to create your own activities.

LESSON PLANS

a–e

STEP 1
Preparation

20 mins

LESSON RESOURCES

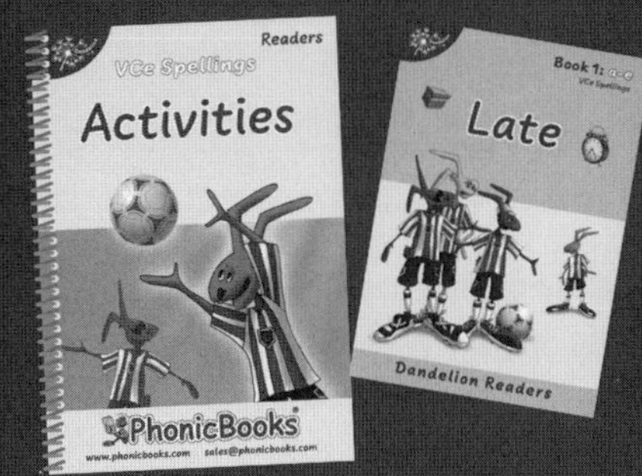

Learning goal (2 mins)

- Explain to the students that you will be teaching them to read and spell new words using the spelling 'a–e' for the sound /ae/.
- Introduce the book Dandelion Readers VCe Spellings Book 1: Late.
- You will be completing some activities from Dandelion Readers VCe Spellings Activities.

Preparation (18 mins)

- Introduce the spelling 'a–e' for the sound /ae/.
- Model the sound correctly and ask students to copy.
- For example, say, "This letter stands for the sound /ae/ as in 'late.' Watch my mouth as I say the sound."
- Read this list of words: "late," "cake," and "plate." For each, point to the letters as you slowly pronounce them, demonstrating how the 'a' and 'e' work together to form the /ae/ sound. Use your thumb and third finger to visually link these letters.

1 Word building and blending

- Assign the **Word-building and blending** activity (Activities, page 6).
- Ask the students to cut out the letters along the dotted lines, which split the 'a' and 'e.'
- For example, demonstrate with the word "gate" how to separate 'a' from 'e' and then rearrange them by placing 'e' at the end after the 't.' Use your fingers to reinforce the connection between letters. Draw a link between the 'a' and the 'e' to remind students that 'a-e' is one spelling that has been split.

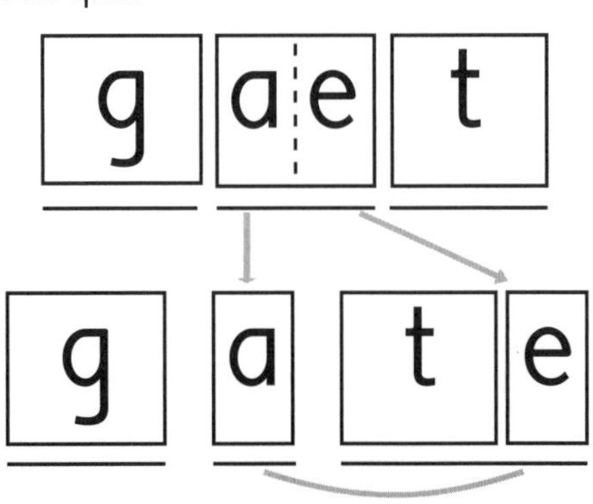

- For the remaining words, direct students through the process of assembling the cut-out letters, always emphasizing how the 'a' and 'e' are connected.
- Explain the spelling rule: in words like "gate," even though a consonant ('t') separates the vowels, the 'a' and 'e' still work together to form the /ae/ sound.

2 Word reading

- Write the words you have created on the whiteboard (if you haven't done so already). Then ask students to blend and read the words.
- Show how to say each sound individually and then blend them together to read the word. Model blending by using a swishing motion with your finger.
- Encourage students to follow your example with these words: "name" and "tale."

3 Oral segmenting

- Say a word aloud (e.g. "cake") and count the sounds in the word (3). Write the number of lines you need for all the sounds. Now ask students to listen to the sounds in the word and write a letter for every sound in the word as you spell the word.

4 Word chain

- Using sound cards or magnetic letters, demonstrate how to build the word "gate." Explain to the students that you will be making one change to the word. They must be "sound detectives" and notice if you have added a sound, taken away a sound, or swapped a sound.
- Say that you are going to change the word "gate" (moving your finger under the word) to "grate." Ask the students to listen carefully to where the change has occurred. Move your finger under the words as you say it slowly. Once the change has been identified, invite a student to swap the sound card or letter. Ask all the students to sound out the word and read the new word. e.g. /g/ /r/ /ae/ /t/ → "grate."
- Direct students through the following word-chain sequence: gate—grate—rate—ate—mate—mane—bane—pane—plane—lane—late—gate

STEP 2
Application for reading
15 mins

Before reading (3 mins)

- Revisit the vocabulary taught in Step 1 (e.g. "wake"). Clearly say the word: /w/ /ae/ /k/. Then explore different meanings for the word "wake," such as waking from sleep, or a trail of disturbed water created by a boat.
- Ask questions such as, "When do you wake up?"
- Then write the word on the whiteboard and refer back to it throughout the week for reinforcement.

High-frequency words (2 mins)

- Pre-teach or reiterate these high-frequency words: "a," "was," "he," "for," "school," "birthday," "no," "said," "the," "his," "they," "she," "goal," and "day."
- Read each high-frequency word, pointing to the graphemes in the word.

Application (10 mins)

- Read Book 1: Late.
- Encourage students to sound out each word and then blend to read.

Extension activities

- Complete the **Fluency** activity (Activities, page 18) to develop students' fluency and prosody skills.

STEP 3
Application for spelling
15 mins

Segmenting and spelling (15 mins)

- Ask students to complete the following activity to practice writing whole words: **Segmenting and spelling** (Activities, page 7).
- In the activity each word is associated with a picture as a visual clue.
- Task students with filling in the squares with the appropriate spelling for each sound.
- Read out the **Sentence dictation** sentences (Activities, page 19): "The box had a clock in it! Frank was not late for the next game." Encourage the students to sound out the words as they spell them. Repeat the sentence if necessary or read it out in phrases to allow students who may need additional time to process the information.

STEP 4
Comprehension and consolidation
20 mins

Book reading (5 mins)

- Reread Book 1: Late.

Comprehension (5 mins)

- Ask students to complete **What happens next?** (Activities, page 16).
- Check students have understood the story by completing **Find the untruths** (Activities, page 17).

Consolidation (10 mins)

- Divide the class into pairs and give each pair a copy of the **Stepping stones game** (Activities, page 22).
- Have students find and point to this word in Book 1: Late: "shame."

STEP 5
Tracking progress
15 mins

- Assign the **Timed word reading** (Activities, page 12). Students can repeat this activity to improve their reading speed.
- To ensure students are confident with the new sounds, blending, and segmenting, complete the **Spelling assessment and bookmarks** (Activities, page 24) to make a quick, formative assessment of their progress.
- Ask students to read and then blend each of the words.
- Hide the words and ask students to write them out as you read them, encouraging them to segment each sound.
- Depending on your findings, either revisit some of the activities to reinforce any specific skill gaps, or invite students to complete an additional activity from the Activities book.

Extension activities

- Print off the **Reading certificate** (Activities, page 130) for students to take home.
- Ask students to check Book 1 on their **Bookmark** (Activities, page 128)
- Check Book 1 on the **Check sheet** (Activities, page 129).
- Play the **4-in-a-row game** (Activities, page 23).

e–e

LESSON RESOURCES

STEP 1
Preparation

20 mins

Learning goal (2 mins)

- Explain to the students that you will be teaching them to read and spell new words using the spelling 'e–e' for the sound /ee/.
- Introduce the book Dandelion Readers VCe Spellings Book 2: Pete.
- You will be completing some activities from Dandelion Readers VCe Spellings Activities.

Preparation (18 mins)

- Introduce the spelling 'e–e' for the sound /ee/.
- Model the sound correctly and ask students to copy.
- For example, say, "This letter stands for the sound /ee/ as in 'Pete.' Watch my mouth as I say the sound."
- Read this list of names: "Pete," "Eve," and "Steve." For each, point to the letters as you slowly pronounce them, demonstrating how the 'e' and 'e' work together to form the /ee/ sound. Use your thumb and third finger to visually link these letters.

1 Word building and blending

- Assign the **Word-building and blending** activity (Activities, page 26).
- Ask the students to cut out the letters along the dotted lines, which split the first 'e' and the second 'e.'
- For example, demonstrate with the word "Pete" how to separate 'e' from 'e' and then rearrange them by placing 'e' at the end after the 't.' Use your fingers to reinforce the connection between letters.

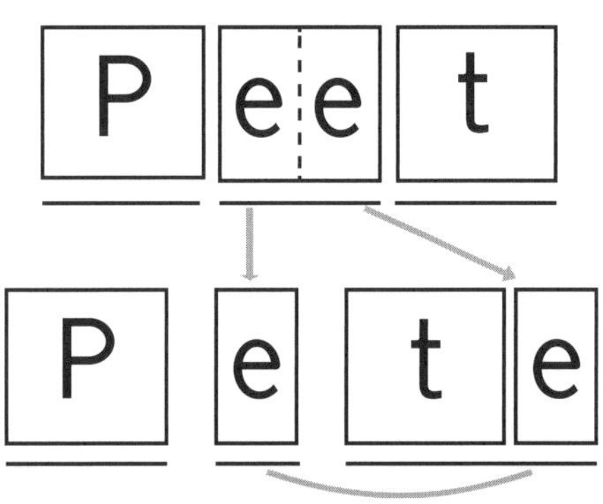

- For the remaining words, direct students through the process of assembling the cut-out letters, always emphasizing how the two 'e' letters are connected.

- Explain the spelling rule: in words like "Pete," even though a consonant ('t') separates the vowels, the two 'e' letters still work together to form the /ee/ sound, which occurs right before the consonant.

2 Word reading

- Write the words you have created on the whiteboard (if you haven't done so already). Then ask students to blend and read the words.
- Show how to say each sound individually and then blend them together to read the word. Model blending by using a swishing motion with your finger.
- Encourage students to follow your example with these words: "Pete," "Eve," and "theme."

3 Oral segmenting

- Say a word aloud (e.g. "delete") count the sounds in the word (5). Write the number of lines you need for all the sounds. Now ask students to listen to the sounds in the word and write a letter for every sound in the word as you spell the word.

4 Word chain

- Using sound cards or magnetic letters, demonstrate how to build the word "these." Explain to the students that you will be making one change to the word. They must be "sound detectives" and notice if you have added a sound, taken away a sound, or swapped a sound.
- Say that you are going to change the word "these" (moving your finger under the word) to "theme." Ask the students to listen carefully to where the change has occurred. Move your finger under the words as you say it slowly. Once the change has been identified, invite a student to swap the sound card or letter. Ask all the students to sound out the word and read the new word. e.g. /th/ /ee/ /m/ → "theme."
- Direct students through the following word-chain sequence: these—theme—meme—deme—theme—these

STEP 2
Application for reading
15 mins

Before reading (3 mins)

- Revisit the vocabulary taught in Step 1 (e.g. "delete"). Clearly say the word: /d/ /e/ /l/ /ee/ /t/. Then provide a simple definition: "To delete something is to remove it."
- Ask questions such as, "When have you deleted something?"
- Then write the word on the whiteboard and refer back to it throughout the week for reinforcement.

High-frequency words (2 mins)

- Pre-teach or reiterate these high-frequency words: "is," "I'll," "make," "to," "said," "his," "he," "the," "began," "boots," "no," and "do."
- Explain that these are high-frequency words that have tricky spellings the students will learn later.
- Read each high-frequency word, pointing to the graphemes in the word.

Application (10 mins)

- Read Book 2: Pete.
- Encourage students to sound out each word and then blend to read.

Extension activities

- Complete the **Fluency** activity (Activities, page 38) to develop students' fluency and prosody skills.

STEP 3
Application for spelling
15 mins

Segmenting and spelling (15 mins)

- Read out the **Sentence dictation** sentences (Activities, page 39): "Pete began to help, but the dishes cracked. Dad had to press 'delete' to stop him!"
- Encourage the students to sound out the words as they spell them.
- Repeat the sentence if necessary or read it out in phrases to allow students who may need additional time to process the information.
- Assign students the **Write the story in your own words** activity (page 41). Ask each student to retell the story orally before writing it.

STEP 4
Comprehension and consolidation
20 mins

Book reading (5 mins)

- Reread Book 2: Pete.

Comprehension (5 mins)

- Ask students to complete **What happens next?** (Activities, page 36).
- Check students have understood the story by completing **Find the untruths** (Activities, page 37).

Consolidation (10 mins)

- Divide the class into pairs and give each pair a copy of the **4-in-a-row game** (Activities, page 43).
- Have students find and point to this word in Book 2: Pete: "delete."

STEP 5
Tracking progress
15 mins

- Assign the **Timed word reading** (Activities, page 32). Students can repeat this activity to improve their reading speed.
- To ensure students are confident with the new sounds, blending, and segmenting, complete the **Spelling assessment and bookmarks** (Activities, page 44) to make a quick, formative assessment of their progress.
- Ask students to read and then blend each of the words.
- Hide the words and ask students to write them out as you read them, encouraging them to segment each sound.
- Depending on your findings, either revisit some of the activities to reinforce any specific skill gaps, or invite students to complete an additional activity from the Activities book.

Extension activities

- Print off the **Reading certificate** (Activities, page 131) for students to take home.
- Ask students to check Book 2 on their **Bookmark** (Activities, page 128)
- Check Book 2 on the **Check sheet** (Activities, page 129).
- Play the **Stepping stones game** (Activities, page 42).

LESSON PLANS

i–e

LESSON RESOURCES

STEP 1
Preparation
20 mins

Learning goal (2 mins)

- Explain to the students that you will be teaching them to read and spell new words using the spelling 'i–e' for the sound /ie/.
- Introduce the book Dandelion Readers VCe Spellings Book 3: A Fine Life.
- You will be completing some activities from Dandelion Readers VCe Spellings Activities.

Preparation (18 mins)

- Introduce the spelling 'i–e' for the sound /ie/.
- Model the sound correctly and ask students to copy.
- For example, say, "This letter stands for the sound /ie/ as in 'life.'"
- Read this list of words: "life," "time," and "shine." For each, point to the letters as you slowly pronounce them, demonstrating how the 'i' and 'e' work together to form the /ie/ sound. Use your thumb and third finger to visually link these letters.

1 Word building and blending

- Assign the **Word-building and blending** activity (Activities, page 46).
- Ask the students to cut out the letters along the dotted lines, which split the 'i' and 'e.'
- For example, demonstrate with the word "dive" how to separate 'i' from 'e' and then rearrange them by placing 'e' at the end after the 'v.' Use your fingers to reinforce the connection between letters.

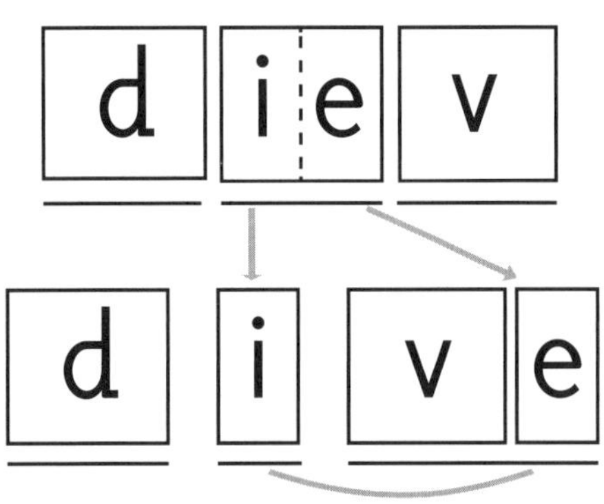

- For the remaining words, direct students through the process of assembling the cut-out letters, always emphasizing how the 'i' and 'e' are connected.
- Explain the spelling rule: in words like "dive," even though a consonant ('v') separates the vowels, the 'i' and 'e' still work together to form the /ie/ sound, which occurs right before the consonant.

2 Word reading

- Write the words you have created on the whiteboard. Then ask students to segment, blend, and read the words.
- Show how to say each sound individually and then blend them together to read the word. Model blending by using a swishing motion with your finger.
- Encourage students to follow your example with these words: "wife" and "glide."

3 Oral segmenting

- Say a word aloud (e.g. "kite") and count the sounds in the word (3). Write the number of lines you need for all the sounds. Now ask students to listen to the sounds in the word and write a letter for every sound in the word as you spell the word.

4 Word chain

- Using sound cards or magnetic letters, demonstrate how to build the word "spine." Explain to the students that you will be making one change to the word. They must be "sound detectives" and notice if you have added a sound, taken away a sound, or swapped a sound.
- Say that you are going to change the word "spine" (moving your finger under the word) to "pine." Ask the students to listen carefully to where the change has occurred. Move your finger under the word as you say it slowly. Once the change has been identified, invite a student to swap the sound card or letter. Ask all the students to sound out the word and read the new word. e.g. /p/ /ie/ /n/ → "pine."
- Direct students through the following word-chain sequence of words: spine—pine—fine—mine—mite—site—spite—spine

STEP 2
Application for reading
15 mins

Before reading (3 mins)

- Revisit the vocabulary taught in Step 1 (e.g. "pipe"). Clearly say the word: /p/ /ie/ /p/. Explore different definitions for pipe, such as a musical instrument or a tube used for carrying substances.
- Ask questions such as, "What are pipes used for?"
- Then write the word on the whiteboard and refer back to it throughout the week for reinforcement.

High-frequency words (2 mins)

- Pre-teach or reiterate these high-frequency words: "his," "were," "little," "they," "lived," "of," "leaves," "he," "to," "the," "we," "my," "said," "politely," "be," and "baby."
- Read each high-frequency word, pointing to the graphemes in the word.

Application (10 mins)

- Read Book 3: A Fine Life.
- Encourage students to sound out each word and then blend to read.

Extension activities

- Complete the **Fluency** activity (Activities, page 58) to develop students' fluency and prosody skills.

STEP 3
Application for spelling
15 mins

Segmenting and spelling (15 mins)

- Ask students to complete the following activity to practice writing whole words: **Segmenting and spelling** (Activities, page 47).
- In the activity each word is associated with a picture as a visual clue.
- Task students with filling in the squares with the appropriate spelling for each sound.
- Read out the **Sentence dictation** sentences (Activities, page 59): "Mike and his wife, Sunshine, were fine little mice. They lived in a nest in a pile of leaves." Encourage the students to sound out the words as they spell them. Repeat the sentence if necessary or read it out in phrases to allow students who may need additional time to process the information.

STEP 4
Comprehension and consolidation
20 mins

Book reading (5 mins)

- Reread Book 3: A Fine Life.

Comprehension (5 mins)

- Ask students to complete **What happens next?** (Activities, page 56).
- Check students have understood the story by completing **Find the untruths** (Activities, page 57).

Consolidation (10 mins)

- Divide the class into pairs and give each pair a copy of the **Stepping stones game** (Activities, page 62).
- Have students find and point to these words in Book 3: A Fine Life: "pipes" and "time."

STEP 5
Tracking progress
15 mins

- Assign the **Timed word reading** (Activities, page 52). Students can repeat this activity to improve their reading speed.
- To ensure students are confident with the new sounds, blending, and segmenting, complete the **Spelling assessment and bookmarks** (Activities, page 64) to make a quick, formative assessment of their progress.
- Ask students to read and then blend each of the words.
- Hide the words and ask students to write them out as you read them, encouraging them to segment each sound.
- Depending on your findings, either revisit some of the activities to reinforce any specific skill gaps, or invite students to complete an additional activity from the Activities book.

Extension activities

- Print off the **Reading certificate** (Activities, page 132) for students to take home.
- Ask students to check Book 3 on their **Bookmark** (Activities, page 128)
- Check Book 3 on the **Check sheet** (Activities, page 129).
- Play the **4-in-a-row game** (Activities, page 63).

o–e

STEP 1
Preparation

20 mins

LESSON RESOURCES

Learning goal (2 mins)

- Explain to the students that you will be teaching them to read and spell new words using the spelling 'o–e' for the sound /oe/.
- Introduce the book Dandelion Readers VCe Spellings Book 4: The Note.
- You will be completing some activities from Dandelion Readers VCe Spellings Activities.

Preparation (18 mins)

- Introduce the spelling 'o–e' for the sound /oe/.
- Model the sound correctly and ask students to copy.
- For example, say, "This letter stands for the sound /oe/ as in 'note.'"
- Read this list of words: "note," "home," and "bone." For each, point to the letters as you slowly pronounce them, demonstrating how the 'o' and 'e' work together to form the /oe/ sound. Use your thumb and third finger to visually link these letters.

1 Word building and blending

- Assign the **Word-building and blending** activity (Activities, page 66).
- Ask the students to cut out the letters along the dotted lines, which split the 'o' and 'e.'
- For example, demonstrate with the word "mole" how to separate 'o' from 'e' and then rearrange them by placing 'o' at the end after the 'l.' Use your fingers to reinforce the connection between letters.

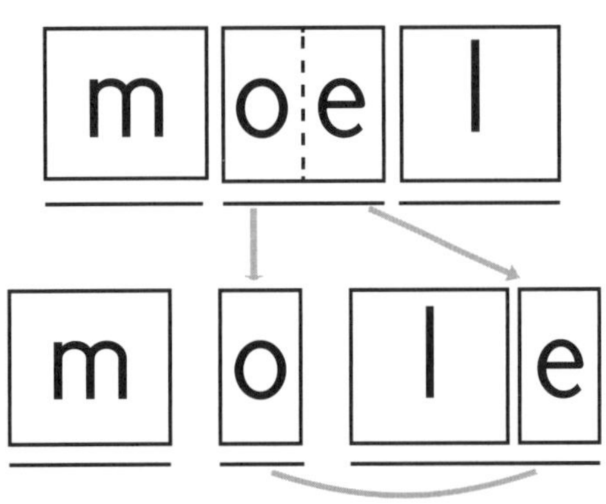

- For the remaining words, direct students through the process of assembling the cut-out letters, always emphasizing how the 'o' and 'e' are connected.
- Explain the spelling rule: in words like "mole," even though a consonant ('l') separates the vowels, the 'o' and 'e' still work together to form the /oe/ sound, which occurs right before the consonant.

2 Word reading

- Write the words you have created on the whiteboard. Then ask students to blend and read the words.
- Show how to say each sound individually and then blend them together to read the word. Model blending by using a swishing motion with your finger.
- Encourage students to follow your example with these words: "cone" and "slope."

3 Oral segmenting

- Say a word aloud (e.g. "home") and count the sounds in the word (3). Write the number of lines you need for all the sounds. Now ask students to listen to the sounds in the word and write a letter for every sound in the word as you spell the word.

4 Word chain

- Using sound cards or magnetic letters, demonstrate how to build the word "cone." Explain to the students that you will be making one change to the word. They must be "sound detectives" and notice if you have added a sound, taken away a sound, or swapped a sound.
- Say that you are going to change the word "cone" (moving your finger under the word) to "clone." Ask the students to listen carefully to where the change has occurred. Move your finger under the word as you say it slowly. Once the change has been identified, invite a student to swap the sound card or letter. Ask all the students to sound out the word and read the new word. e.g. /c/ /l/ /oe/ /n/ → "clone."
- Direct students through the following word-chain sequence of words: cone—clone—lone—bone—tone—hone—hope—home—hone—cone

STEP 2
Application for reading
15 mins

Before reading (3 mins)

- Revisit the vocabulary taught in Step 1 (e.g. "note"). Clearly say the word: /n/ /oe/ /t/. Explore different definitions for note, such as a written record of ideas or paying attention to something.
- Ask questions such as, "What do you write notes for?"
- Then write the word on the whiteboard and refer back to it throughout the week for reinforcement.

High-frequency words (2 mins)

- Pre-teach or reiterate these high-frequency words: "the," "Toad," "he," "saw," "said," "follow," "to," "onto," "was," "into," "my," "hello," "you," "have," and "me."
- Read each high-frequency word, pointing to the graphemes in the word.

Application (10 mins)

- Read Book 4: The Note.
- Encourage students to sound out each word and then blend to read.

Extension activities

- Complete the **Fluency** activity (Activities, page 78) to develop students' fluency and prosody skills.

STEP 3
Application for spelling
15 mins

Segmenting and spelling (15 mins)

- Ask students to complete the following activity to practice writing whole words: **Segmenting and spelling** (Activities, page 67).
- In the activity each word is associated with a picture as a visual clue.
- Task students with filling in the squares with the appropriate spelling for each sound.
- Read out the **Sentence dictation** sentences (Activities, page 79): "When Toad woke up, he saw a note and a rope. The note said, 'Follow the rope.' 'I hope this is not a joke!' said Toad." Encourage the students to sound out the words as they spell them. Repeat the sentence if necessary or read it out in phrases to allow students who may need additional time to process the information.

STEP 4
Comprehension and consolidation
20 mins

Book reading (5 mins)

- Reread Book 4: The Note.

Comprehension (5 mins)

- Ask students to complete **What happens next?** (Activities, page 76).
- Check students have understood the story by completing **Find the untruths** (Activities, page 77).

Consolidation (10 mins)

- Divide the class into pairs and give each pair a copy of the **4-in-a-row game** (Activities, page 83).
- Have students find and point to these words in Book 4: The Note: "rope," "joke," and "slope."

STEP 5
Tracking progress
15 mins

- Assign the **Timed word reading** (Activities, page 72). Students can repeat this activity to improve their reading speed.
- To ensure students are confident with the new sounds, blending, and segmenting, complete the **Spelling assessment and bookmarks** (Activities, page 84) to make a quick, formative assessment of their progress.
- Ask students to read and then blend each of the words.
- Hide the words and ask students to write them out as you read them, encouraging them to segment each sound.
- Depending on your findings, either revisit some of the activities to reinforce any specific skill gaps, or invite students to complete an additional activity from the Activities book.

Extension activities

- Print off the **Reading certificate** (Activities, page 133) for students to take home.
- Ask students to check Book 4 on their **Bookmark** (Activities, page 128)
- Check Book 4 on the **Check sheet** (Activities, page 129).
- Play the **Stepping stones game** (Activities, page 82).

LESSON PLANS

u–e

STEP 1
Preparation

20 mins

Learning goal (2 mins)

- Explain to the students that you will be teaching them to read and spell new words using the spelling 'u–e' for the sound /ue/.
- Introduce the book Dandelion Readers VCe Spellings Book 5: Club Rules.
- You will be completing some activities from Dandelion Readers VCe Spellings Activities.

Preparation (18 mins)

- Explain that the spelling 'u–e' can make two different sounds: /oo/ ("flute") and /ue/ ("cute.")
- Clearly model the /oo/ sound and the /ue/ sound and ask students to copy.
- To demonstrate the /oo/ sound: position your lips as if you are going to whistle, then produce the /oo/ sound.
- To demonstrate the /ue/ sound: position the tip of your tongue just behind your lower front teeth. Keep your lips rounded and slightly protruded. Push air out of your mouth while engaging your vocal cords to produce the /ue/ sound.
- Read the following words: "flute," "rude," "rule," and "cube."
- For each word, point to the letters as you slowly pronounce them, demonstrating how the 'u' and 'e' work together to form the sounds /oo/ or /ue/.
- Use your thumb and third finger to visually link these letters.

1 Word building and blending

- Assign the **Word-building and blending** activity (Activities, page 86).
- Ask the students to cut out the letters along the dotted lines, which split the 'u' and 'e.'
- For example, demonstrate with the word "cube" how to rearrange the letters.

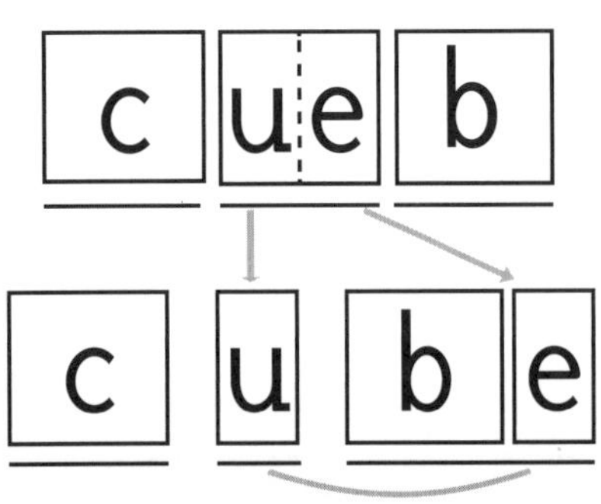

- For the remaining words, direct students through the process of assembling the cut-out letters, always emphasizing how the 'u' and 'e' are connected.

LESSON RESOURCES

- Explain the spelling rule: in words like "cube," even though a consonant ('b') separates the vowels, the 'u' and 'e' still work together to form the /ue/ sound, which occurs right before the consonant.

2 Word reading

- Write the words you have created on the whiteboard . Then ask students to blend and read the words.
- Show how to say each sound individually and then blend them together to read the word. Model blending by using a swishing motion with your finger.
- Encourage students to follow your example with these words: "mute" and "flute."

3 Oral segmenting

- Say a word aloud (e.g. "cute") and count the sounds in the word (3). Write the number of lines you need for all the sounds. Now ask students to listen to the sounds in the word and write a letter for every sound in the word as you spell the word.

4 Word chain

- Using sound cards or magnetic letters, demonstrate how to build the word "mute." Explain to the students that you will be making one change to the word. They must be "sound detectives" and notice if you have added a sound, taken away a sound, or swapped a sound.
- Say that you are going to change the word "flute" (moving your finger under the word) to "lute". Ask the students to listen carefully to where the change has occurred. Move your finger under the words as you say it slowly. Once the change has been identified, invite a student to swap the sound card or letter. Ask all the students to sound out the word and read the new word. e.g. /l/ /ue/ /t/ → "lute."
- Direct students through the following word-chain sequence of words: flute—lute—mute—cute—lute—flute
- Explain that the words in this word chain include both the /oo/ and /ue/ sounds.

STEP 2
Application for reading
15 mins

Before reading (3 mins)

- Revisit the vocabulary taught in Step 1 (e.g. "rule"). Clearly say the word: /r/ /ue/ /l/. Explore different meanings for "rule," such as an instruction for how to behave or a ruler used for measuring objects.
- Ask questions such as, "What rules do you follow in class?"
- Then write the word on the whiteboard and refer back to it throughout the week for reinforcement.

High-frequency words (2 mins)

- Pre-teach or reiterate these high-frequency words: "play," "said," "we," "the," "they," "to," "began," "cheat," "you," "are," "by," "I," and "again."
- Read each high-frequency word, pointing to the graphemes in the word.

Application (10 mins)

- Read Book 5: Club Rules.
- Encourage students to sound out each word and then blend to read.

Extension activities

- Complete the **Fluency** activity (Activities, page 98) to develop students' fluency and prosody skills.

STEP 3
Application for spelling
15 mins

Segmenting and spelling (15 mins)

- Ask students to complete the following activity to practice writing whole words: **Segmenting and spelling** (Activities, page 87).
- In the activity each word is associated with a picture as a visual clue.
- Task students with filling in the squares with the appropriate spelling for each sound.
- Read out the **Sentence dictation** sentences (Activities, page 99): "'Rex is rude!' Jill said to Zig and Zog. 'Let's set up a club. Let's not include Rex.' Rex got upset." Encourage the students to sound out the words as they spell them.
- Repeat the sentence if necessary or read it out in phrases to allow students who may need additional time to process the information.

STEP 4
Comprehension and consolidation
20 mins

Book reading (5 mins)

- Reread Book 5: Club Rules.

Comprehension (5 mins)

- Ask students to complete **What happens next?** (Activities, page 96).
- Check students have understood the story by completing **Find the untruths** (Activities, page 97).

Consolidation (10 mins)

- Divide the class into pairs and give each pair a copy of the **Stepping stones game** (Activities, page 102).
- Have students find and point to these words in Book 5: Club Rules: "rules," "cubes," and "brute."

STEP 5
Tracking progress
15 mins

- Assign the **Timed word reading** (Activities, page 92). Students can repeat this activity to improve their reading speed.
- To ensure students are confident with the new sounds, blending, and segmenting, complete the **Spelling assessment and bookmarks** (Activities, page 104) to make a quick, formative assessment of their progress.
- Ask students to read and then blend each of the words.
- Hide the words and ask students to write them out as you read them, encouraging them to segment each sound.
- Depending on your findings, either revisit some of the activities to reinforce any specific skill gaps, or invite students to complete an additional activity from the Activities book.

Extension activities

- Print off the **Reading certificate** (Activities, page 134) for students to take home.
- Ask students to check Book 5 on their **Bookmark** (Activities, page 128)
- Check Book 5 on the **Check sheet** (Activities, page 129).
- Play the **4-in-a-row game** (Activities, page 103).

LESSON PLANS

a–e, e–e, i–e, o–e, and u–e

LESSON RESOURCES

STEP 1
Preparation

20 mins

Learning goal (2 mins)

- Explain to the students that you will be teaching them to read and spell new words using all VCe spellings: a–e, e–e, i–e, o–e, and u–e.
- Introduce the book that the lessons are based around: Dandelion Readers VCe Spellings Book 6: Show Time.
- You will be completing some activities from Dandelion Readers VCe Spellings Activities.

Preparation (18 mins)

1 Word building and blending

- Create words with VCe spellings (e.g. “cake” or “hope”) by drawing lines on the whiteboard for each sound in a word.
- Demonstrate how to identify each sound in the word by saying the word slowly and pointing to the letters at the same time. Highlight the split spellings for the sounds /ae/, /ee/, /ie/, /oe/, /oo/, and /ue/. Then sound out all the sounds in the word and move your finger under the word as the sounds are blended, reinforcing the concept of the VCe spelling and how it indicates a long vowel sound.
- Assign the **Word-building and blending** activity (Activities, page 106). Ask the student to cut along the dotted lines and insert the split spellings a–e, e–e, i–e, o–e, u–e into the words.

2 Word reading

- Write the words you have created on the whiteboard (if you haven’t done so already). Then ask students to segment, blend, and read the words.
- Show how to say each sound individually and then blend them together to read the word. Model blending by using a swishing motion with your finger.
- Encourage students to follow your example with these words: “wife” and “theme.”

3 Oral segmenting

- Say a word out loud (e.g. “tube”) and to listen to the sounds in the word. Students then spell the word sound by sound. This is important as it links reading and spelling.

4 Reading and sorting

- Complete the **Reading and sorting: VCe spellings** activity for students to practice differentiating a–e, e–e, i–e, o–e, and u–e words (Activities, page 110).
- Cut the words into reading cards.
- Read each word aloud to the class, emphasizing the correct pronunciation and demonstrating the VCe sound it makes.
- Ask students to sort the words into categories based on the VCe sound they make.
- Students can discuss and compare their choices with their peers to reinforce learning through collaboration.
- For students who need extra practice or finish early, create additional lists of VCe words.
- These additional lists can be used for extra sorting activities to ensure all students are engaged and supported at their individual levels.
- Additionally, the reading cards can be used to play a simple bingo game. For example: draw a card and read the word aloud. Students look for the word on their bingo cards and mark it if they have it. The first student to get three words in a row (horizontally, vertically, or diagonally) shouts “Bingo!” and wins the game.

Extension activities

- Practice blending the list of words on the **Reading practice** page in Book 6: Show Time.
- Play the **Jumping Jack** or **Reading** games in Book 6: Show Time to familiarize students with the vocabulary in the book.
- Use the **Reading practice** cards (Activities, pages 108–109) to play a bingo game.
- Complete the **Splitting two-syllable words** activity (Activities, page 114) to practice syllable division as a strategy for decoding longer words.

STEP 2
Application for reading
15 mins

Before reading (3 mins)

- Revisit the vocabulary taught in Step 1 (e.g. "plane"). Clearly say the word: /p/ /l /ae/ /n/. Explore different meanings for "plane," such as an airplane or a flat surface.
- Ask questions such as, "What are planes used for?" Then write the word on the whiteboard and refer back to it throughout the week for reinforcement.
- Explore homophones. Is there another word that sounds the same? Write the word "plain" on the board next to the word "plane". Ask the students, "What is the meaning of the other word 'plain'?" Discuss the difference between the meanings and spellings for the two words.

High-frequency words (2 mins)

- Pre-teach or reiterate these high-frequency words: "show," "said," "the," "robot," "say," "who," "of," "began," "play," "he," "put," "his," "I," "they," "as," "was," "to," "all," "were," and "give."
- Read each high-frequency word, pointing to the graphemes in the word.

Application (10 mins)

- Read Book 6: Show Time.
- Encourage students to sound out each word and then blend to read.

Extension activities

- Complete the **Fluency** activity (Activities, page 118).

STEP 3
Application for spelling
15 mins

Segmenting and spelling (15 mins)

- Ask students to complete the following activity to practice writing whole words: **Segmenting and spelling** (Activities, page 107).
- In the activity each word is associated with a picture as a visual clue.
- Task students with filling in the squares with the appropriate spelling for each sound.
- Read out the **Dictation** sentences (Activities, page 119): "Pete sat on a throne made of cubes. Jill began to play the flute. "That's a fine tune!" said Pete." Encourage the students to sound out the words as they spell them.
- Repeat the sentence if necessary or read it out in phrases to allow students who may need additional time to process the information.

STEP 4
Comprehension and consolidation
20 mins

Book reading (5 mins)

- Reread Book 6: Show Time.

Comprehension (5 mins)

- Ask students to complete **What happens next?** (Activities, page 116).
- Check students have understood the story by completing **Find the untruths** (Activities, page 117).

Consolidation (10 mins)

- Have students find and point to these words in Book 6: Show Time: "cubes," "flute," and "spoke."

STEP 5
Tracking progress
15 mins

- Assign the **Timed word reading** (Activities, page 112). Students can repeat this activity to improve their reading speed.
- To ensure students are confident with the new sounds, blending, and segmenting, complete the **Spelling assessment and bookmarks** (Activities, page 124) to make a quick, formative assessment of their progress.
- Ask students to read and then blend each of the words.
- Hide the words and ask students to write them out as you read them, encouraging them to segment each sound.
- Depending on your findings, either revisit some of the activities to reinforce any specific skill gaps, or invite students to complete an additional activity from the Activities book.
- For a summative assessment of each student's progress for VCe spellings, assign the **Reading Assessment** (page 113).

Extension activities

- Print off the **Reading certificate** (Activities, page 135) for students to take home.
- Ask students to check Book 6 on their **Bookmark** (Activities, page 128)
- Check Book 6 on the **Check sheet** (Activities, page 129).
- Play the **4-in-a-row game** (Activities, page 123).
- Divide the class into pairs and give each pair a copy of the **Stepping stones game** (Activities, page 122).

GLOSSARY

Alphabetic Code The framework that shows how the 44 sounds of English are represented by letters and letter combinations.

Alphabetic Principle A fundamental concept in phonics instruction where written letters or graphemes correspond to specific sounds (phonemes) of a spoken language. These sounds come together to form words, which is crucial for learning to read as it allows students to decode written text into spoken language.

Analytic phonics A method of teaching reading that focuses on breaking the word into parts. This begins with an analysis of the whole word, which is broken into onset and rime, e.g. 'fr' + 'og' for "frog."

Blending The process where students learning to read with explicit systematic phonics are encouraged to sound out letters in words and push the sounds together into words. Each letter is sounded out separately and blended from left to right throughout the word. This is the most reliable strategy to read a new word.

Consonant blend Also called a consonant cluster, these are two or more adjacent consonants in a word that spell two or more separate sounds. For example, in the word "stop," the letters 's' and 't' spell the sounds /s/ and /t/.

Consonant digraph When two letters represent a consonant sound. For example, the letters 's' and 'h' spell the sound /sh/ in the word "ship."

Decodable text Text that students can sound out using phonics they have been taught. Decodable texts encourage students to use blending sounds into words as the first strategy when reading.

Decoding Involves translating symbols or letters into sounds and words.

Encoding The process of translating words and sounds into symbols or letters.

Fluency The ability to read text accurately and quickly, including proper expression, known as prosody.

Grapheme A written representation or spelling of a sound (phoneme) in a word.

High-frequency words Common words with "tricky spellings" that students have not yet learned. Students are encouraged to use their phonic knowledge while the teacher provides the "tricky spelling" until the students can decode these words independently.

Letter A character used for representing sounds in speech.

Morpheme A unit of meaning in a word.

Phoneme The smallest unit of sound in a word. For example, the word "cat" has three phonemes: /k/ /a/ /t/.

Phonemic awareness The ability to identify and manipulate individual sounds in words, which includes blending, segmenting, and manipulating sounds.

Phonics A method of teaching reading and writing that focuses on the relationship between sounds (phonemes) and their spellings (graphemes).

Phonological awareness The ability to break down words into smaller parts, such as syllables (e.g. mag-net), alliteration (e.g. Bobby beetle bounced), onset and rime (e.g. m-at), and phonemic awareness (e.g. m-a-t).

Phonology An area of linguistics that deals with speech sound systems and sound patterns of spoken language.

Schwa A weak vowel sound in an unstressed syllable, e.g. the word "chicken" becoming "chickin" or "chick'n."

Science of Reading An evidence-based approach to teaching reading that emphasizes phonemic awareness, phonics, fluency, vocabulary, and comprehension.

Segmenting The ability to separate sounds in words. When spelling, students learn to isolate each sound in the word and represent it with a spelling.

Simple View of Reading A model that demonstrates reading as having two basic components: word recognition and language comprehension. This model offers a clear and effective framework for reading instruction.

Sounds-Write® Reading and Spelling Program A structured literacy program focusing on teaching reading and spelling using a systematic and explicit phonics approach.

Syllables Mouthfuls of words, typically containing a vowel sound.

Synthetic Phonics A method of teaching reading where the reader is taught to sound out individual sounds in a word and blend these sounds together to form the word. This method emphasizes the synthesis (blending) of individual sounds into a word. For example, the word "frog" is learned by sounding out each phoneme, /f/ /r/ /o/ /g/, and then blending these sounds to say "frog."

Systematic Synthetic Phonics (SSP) A method that focuses on the systematic instruction of phonics. In this approach, students are taught to sound out graphemes and blend (synthesize) them into words.

Vowel-Consonant-e (VCe) Spelling When the spelling for the vowel sounds /ae/, /ee/, /ie/, /oe/, /oo/, and /ue/ is split by a consonant. For example, /ae/ is represented as a–e in the word "gate."

Vowel team Two or more letters that represent a vowel sound. For example, the letters 'a' and 'i' spell the sound /ae/ in the word "rain."

Word chain A list of words used to develop phonemic awareness skills such as blending, segmenting, and phoneme manipulation. For example: nip—nap—tap—top—mop—map—sap—sip—tip—nip.

Word A distinct meaningful unit of speech or writing.

3-Cueing vs. Decoding Strategies While the 3-cueing approach focuses on using context and visual cues to identify words, the decoding approach emphasizes systematically breaking down words into their phonetic components. The 3-cueing approach is considered a guessing strategy that can lead the reader away from the text, whereas the decoding approach focuses on letter–sound correspondences in words.